Certification Study Companion Series

The Apress Certification Study Companion Series offers guidance and hands-on practice to support technical and business professionals who are studying for an exam in the pursuit of an industry certification. Professionals worldwide seek to achieve certifications in order to advance in a career role, reinforce knowledge in a specific discipline, or to apply for or change jobs. This series focuses on the most widely taken certification exams in a given field. It is designed to be user friendly, tracking to topics as they appear in a given exam and work alongside other certification material as professionals prepare for their exam.

More information about this series at `https://link.springer.com/bookseries/17100`.

Red Hat RHCSA 10 Study Companion

Getting Ready for the EX200 Exam

Andrey Markelov

Apress®

Red Hat RHCSA 10 Study Companion: Getting Ready for the EX200 Exam

Andrey Markelov
Täby, Sweden

ISBN-13 (pbk): 979-8-8688-2225-4 ISBN-13 (electronic): 979-8-8688-2226-1
https://doi.org/10.1007/979-8-8688-2226-1

Managing Director, Apress Media LLC: Welmoed Spahr
Acquisitions Editor: James Robinson-Prior
Editorial Assistant: Gryffin Winkler

Cover designed by eStudioCalamar

Distributed to the book trade worldwide by Springer Science+Business Media New York, 1 New York Plaza, New York, NY 10004. Phone 1-800-SPRINGER, fax (201) 348-4505, e-mail orders-ny@springer-sbm.com, or visit www.springeronline.com. Apress Media, LLC is a Delaware LLC and the sole member (owner) is Springer Science + Business Media Finance Inc (SSBM Finance Inc). SSBM Finance Inc is a **Delaware** corporation.

For information on translations, please e-mail booktranslations@springernature.com; for reprint, paperback, or audio rights, please e-mail bookpermissions@springernature.com.

Apress titles may be purchased in bulk for academic, corporate, or promotional use. eBook versions and licenses are also available for most titles. For more information, reference our Print and eBook Bulk Sales web page at http://www.apress.com/bulk-sales.

Any source code or other supplementary material referenced by the author in this book is available to readers on GitHub. For more detailed information, please visit https://www.apress.com/gp/services/source-code.

If disposing of this product, please recycle the paper

To my wife, Elena, for her love and support, and to my feline companion, Barsic IV.

Table of Contents

About the Author

Andrey Markelov is an experienced Linux and cloud architect who has worked for large international companies (Red Hat, Wind River, and Ericsson, currently). He has written and published more than 50 articles about Linux and Unix systems services, virtual systems, and open source (Linux Format RE, Computerra, PCWeek/RE, and others). Andrey is the author of several OpenStack and Kubernetes books. He has been teaching Microsoft and Red Hat authorized courses for over 15 years. Andrey is a Red Hat Certified Architect since 2009 and is also a Microsoft Certified System Engineer, Cisco Certified Network Associate, Novell Certified Linux Professional, and VMware Certified Professional. Although Andrey has been working with cloud computing for a decade, he avoids clouds in real life by enjoying private piloting as a hobby.

About the Technical Reviewers

Aleksey Usov is a principal architect at Li9 Technology Solutions, specializing in containerization, virtualization, DevOps, CI/CD, infrastructure-as-a-code (IaC), and automation. He works daily with Linux, OpenShift, Ansible, Terraform, GitLab, and many other technologies, including most Red Hat products. In his role as an architect, Aleksey is deeply involved in every stage of customer engagement, including gathering requirements, designing solutions, performing hands-on implementation, and presenting results to stakeholders. Some of his largest customers include Anthem, Sutter Health, Wells Fargo, and Shambaugh & Son. A strong proponent of continuous learning, he became a Red Hat Certified Architect Level XXV (world record) in 2023 and earned the Kubestronaut status in 2025. Aleksey is also a book author himself, having published *Learn OpenShift, 2nd edition* with Packt Publishing in 2026.

Iuliia Kozlova is a lead QA expert with experience in Linux, software testing, and Kubernetes. She has provided her expertise to a number of businesses of national significance, automating the QA process and helping build business-focused teams. Iulia was also a technical proofreader for the books *Acing the Certified Kubernetes Administrator Exam, 2nd Edition* published by Manning in 2025 and *Learn OpenShift, 2nd edition* published by Packt in 2026. Having passed all Kubernetes-related certifications from the Linux Foundation, she also earned the title of Kubestronaut in 2025. Iuliia has also made numerous other contributions to the industry in the form of scientific articles on the topics of software testing, cloud technologies, and Kubernetes. In her work, she uses Linux and Kubernetes to build isolated and disposable test environments as part of software integration and delivery pipelines.

CHAPTER 1

Exam Overview

In this chapter, we will discuss how to prepare for the exam and provide some tips on how to work efficiently during the exam itself.

What Is the RHCSA Certification?

The best definition can be taken from the landing page of the exam at Red Hat's site: "An IT professional who has earned the Red Hat Certified System Administrator (RHCSA®) is able to perform the core system administration skills required in Red Hat Enterprise Linux environments." The link to the page is `https://www.redhat.com/en/services/certification/rhcsa`. This page should be the main source of truth for you while you are studying topics. From the exam link, you can get the objectives and study points. Objectives at the time of writing and mapping to the chapters can be found in Table 1-1.

If you look at the study points for the exam, you will find that many of them are generic and applicable to other GNU/Linux distributions. And if, for example, you are mainly working with Ubuntu Linux, studying and preparing for the RHCSA exam will be helpful anyway. Plus, certification in your CV will differentiate you from other candidates for your next position. Red Hat Certified System Administrator certification can be the first step toward Red Hat Certified Engineer (RHCE) or Red Hat Certified Architect (RHCA).

A. Markelov, *Red Hat RHCSA 10 Study Companion*, Certification Study Companion Series,
https://doi.org/10.1007/979-8-8688-2226-1_1

Table 1-1. *Study points for the exam*

Chapter	Objectives
2	Understand and use essential tools • Access a shell prompt and issue commands with correct syntax • Use input/output redirection (>, >>, |, 2>, etc.) • Use grep and regular expressions to analyze text • Access remote systems using SSH • Log in and switch users in multiuser targets • Archive, compress, unpack, and uncompress files using tar, gzip, and bzip2 • Create and edit text files • Create, delete, copy, and move files and directories • Create hard and soft links • List, set, and change standard ugo/rwx permissions • Locate, read, and use system documentation including man, info, and files in /usr/share/doc
9	Manage software • Configure access to RPM repositories • Install and remove RPM software packages • Configure access to Flatpak repositories • Install and remove Flatpak software packages
3	Create simple shell scripts • Conditionally execute code (use of: if, test, [], etc.) • Use Looping constructs (for, etc.) to process file, command-line input • Process script inputs ($1, $2, etc.) • Processing output of shell commands within a script

(continued)

Table 1-1. (*continued*)

<table>
<tr><th>Chapter</th><th>Objectives</th></tr>
<tr><td>7</td><td>Operate running systems<ul><li>Boot, reboot, and shut down a system normally</li><li>Boot systems into different targets manually</li><li>Interrupt the boot process in order to gain access to a system</li><li>Identify CPU/memory-intensive processes and kill processes</li><li>Adjust process scheduling</li><li>Manage tuning profiles</li><li>Locate and interpret system log files and journals</li><li>Preserve system journals</li><li>Start, stop, and check the status of network services</li><li>Securely transfer files between systems</li></ul></td></tr>
<tr><td>5, 6</td><td>Configure local storage<ul><li>List, create, and delete partitions on GPT disks</li><li>Create and remove physical volumes</li><li>Assign physical volumes to volume groups</li><li>Create and delete logical volumes</li><li>Configure systems to mount file systems at boot by universally unique ID (UUID) or label</li><li>Add new partitions and logical volumes, and swap to a system non-destructively</li></ul></td></tr>
<tr><td>6</td><td>Create and configure file systems<ul><li>Create, mount, unmount, and use VFAT, ext4, and xfs file systems</li><li>Mount and unmount network file systems using NFS</li><li>Configure autofs</li><li>Extend existing logical volumes</li><li>Diagnose and correct file permission problems</li></ul></td></tr>
</table>

(*continued*)

Table 1-1. (*continued*)

Chapter	Objectives
8	Deploy, configure, and maintain systems • Schedule tasks using cron and systemd timer units • Start and stop services and configure services to start automatically at boot • Configure systems to boot into a specific target automatically • Configure time service clients • Install and update software packages from Red Hat Content Delivery Network, a remote repository, or from the local file system • Modify the system bootloader
10	Manage basic networking • Configure IPv4 and IPv6 addresses • Configure hostname resolution • Configure network services to start automatically at boot • Restrict network access using firewalld and firewall-cmd
4	Manage users and groups • Create, delete, and modify local user accounts • Change passwords and adjust password aging for local user accounts • Create, delete, and modify local groups and group memberships • Configure privileged access

(*continued*)

Table 1-1. (*continued*)

Chapter	Objectives
8, 10, 11	Manage security • Configure firewall settings using firewall-cmd/firewalld • Manage default file permissions • Configure key-based authentication for SSH • Set enforcing and permissive modes for SELinux • List and identify SELinux file and process context • Restore default file contexts • Manage SELinux port labels • Use boolean settings to modify system SELinux settings

One essential aspect of certification is that it is practical; you cannot just remember or guess answers in the test. You should do tasks practically in a real system. This can be harder than a multiple-choice test on one hand, but on the other hand, it is easy. You can achieve tasks in your preferred way, using any tools: graphical, command line, or by editing configuration files.

Below are the key facts about the exam at the time of writing the book. Again, please check the RHCSA certification and exam pages for the latest updates. It is not typical that a vendor will introduce changes before a new major version of the Red Hat Enterprise Linux distribution, but it can happen. Here are key facts:

- The exam is performance-based. It means you have to solve tasks on a real system.
- No Internet access is available, but most RHEL documentation is accessible during the exam.
- Exam duration is three hours.

- Score on the exam will usually be reported by email within three US business days, regardless of your local time zone.
- You will get only the total score. In the past, you were provided with a score for each exam objective, but this is no longer the case.
- You are eligible for one exam retake if you fail on your first attempt. This represents a significant improvement in Red Hat policy, as the exam cost is $500 for the United States and can be slightly below or above 500 EUR in Europe. The cost varies by country.
- Certification will be valid for three years; however, RHCE or another eligible credential can extend the RHCSA certification for an additional three years. This means you can pass the exam once and maintain currency by passing other Red Hat exams.

Ordering an Exam

Order the exam and pay for it online with a credit card. You can do so directly from the exam page by selecting your country of residence and following the instructions on the next screen. I will not describe this process since it can be changed. Before starting, you need to know that you can take the exam at the training facility or, more conveniently, remotely with your own laptop.

You will also need your Red Hat login to schedule and start the exam. Make sure you have it. The same login you will use for downloading the RHEL image, as described in Appendix A of this book.

Red Hat has an FAQ available about remote exams if you choose this option: `https://www.redhat.com/en/resources/certification-remote-exams-FAQ`. It has a link to the technical requirements for your hardware and the room where you will take the exam.

Generally, you will need a computer capable of running a special, live USB Fedora-based distribution preconfigured for the exam. Do not worry, it will not destroy your data on the disk; it will work in RAM. ARM processors, such as those found in all modern MacBooks, will not work. You also need an external Webcam for remote proctor, allowing you to be observed during the exam. For sure, you need a reliable Internet connection.

I recommend testing your hardware before purchasing the exam. You can follow the instructions in the PDF available for download from the FAQ page to test your hardware. It is also essential to test the connection from the exam live USB environment in the same facility where you will take the exam. For example, you don't want to be surprised in case you did test at home, but during the real exam, which you're taking from the meeting room at work, you will find that the corporate firewall prevents communications.

Consider that you can reschedule your exam after payment up to 24 hours before the exam. Also, be aware that not every day and hour can be accessible for booking. It may depend, for example, on the proctor's team availability, but in general, it is not difficult to find a slot, especially if you book upfront for a week or so.

Exam Preparation

You don't need to take an official preparation class from Red Hat to be allowed to take an exam. However, I highly recommend this if you have the opportunity. Official courses are the best way to prepare for the exam. It is true for almost all IT certifications. However, this book will be helpful in cases where you took the class as a complementary source of information. This book is designed to sit alongside official documentation and study guides. It will be especially helpful if you are preparing for an exam through self-study.

To pass the exam, you should also be familiar with documentation. There are several types of documentation that you can use during the exam:

- Official documentation from `https://docs.redhat.com/en`
- `man` and `info` pages, embedded help into tools (-h and --help)
- Documentation from `/usr/share/doc` in the form of text files

The first two sources are the most important. You will not have time to read the documentation during the exam. Instead, you need to be able to quickly find the necessary commands or configuration file information in the documentation.

Check man pages for all tools mentioned in the exam. And read at least the most essential books from the documentation. They contain more information than needed for the exam, but you will have an understanding of where to find information.

Here are books relevant to the RHCSA exam:

- Administering RHEL by using the GNOME desktop environment
- Managing software with the DNF tool
- Managing systems in the RHEL web console
- Monitoring and managing system status and performance (chapter about TuneD)

- Managing, monitoring, and updating the kernel (chapters about GRUB2)
- Configuring time synchronization
- Configuring secured networks and network communication (chapters about OpenSSH)
- Using SELinux
- Configuring firewalls and packet filters (chapters about firewalld)
- Configuring and managing networking (chapter about configuring an Ethernet connection)
- Managing file systems (chapters about local file systems and mounting NFS)
- Managing storage devices (chapters about disk partitions)

It may look extensive, but this book is your road map. Try to find in the documentation what is mentioned in this book. Again, you cannot take this book or any other material to the exam, but documentation will be available at the workplace during the exam.

And the most important thing is practice. Repeat all examples in the book and do all exercises. Try to reproduce all examples and exercises from this book from your memory. The better option is to use CLI tools, because if you know them, you can be faster. However, GUI tools or Cockpit are also fine, as long as you are familiar with the interface and remember where and what to click to complete tasks.

During an Exam

The night before the exam, try to get a good night's sleep and be well-rested the next day. For some people, it is more efficient to take the exam in the first half of the day; for others, it is the second part. You know your performance peak better than anyone.

Be in the training center upfront. If you are using a remote exam, start the environment promptly as well. The instruction will tell you if it is 20 or 15 minutes before the scheduled time.

When the exam starts, read the tasks carefully. Do not skip any parts of the instructions.

Since all changes should be preserved after reboot, the best approach is to check if everything is correct, reboot, and then verify again. Indeed, if you add a user or change the password, these settings will not be lost after a reboot. However, you will find that some systems, such as firewalls, service status, or SELinux, can have both runtime and permanent configurations. Your task is to make all changes permanent.

Be extra careful with things that can prevent booting, such as manipulation with file systems and the bootloader. It is better to spend an additional 30 seconds to double-check for mistakes than five minutes to recover.

For a sensitive thing that you can misspell, it is better to use copy/paste to make sure you will type all symbols correctly.

Do backups in case you need to revert changes. For example, before changing a configuration file, `config`, run the command `cp config config.bak`.

Summary

In this chapter, we introduced the Red Hat Certified System Administrator (RHCSA) certification and discussed how to prepare for it.

The RHCSA confirms proficiency in core system administration skills necessary for Red Hat Enterprise Linux (RHEL) environments. The exam is performance-based, meaning test-takers must solve tasks practically on a live system within a three-hour time limit.

The objectives cover a wide range of essential topics, including the use of command-line tools, managing local storage and networking, system operation, and security (such as SELinux and firewalld). Preparation should focus on extensive hands-on practice and the efficient use of available documentation (man and info pages), as no Internet access is provided. Crucially, all configurations must be made permanent and verified to survive a system reboot.

CHAPTER 2

Basic Command-Line Tools

This is the first chapter in the book where you will start working with basic GNU/Linux commands. It covers essential topics like working with command-line tools, managing files, text processing, and file archives.

Accessing the Command Line

This chapter contains quite a basic thing and many tools and concepts we will touch on, which you are probably already familiar with. But before we go into details, it is worth talking about some principles followed by Unix-like systems, particularly Linux.

1. Each program does one thing but does it well. This means developers prefer to create ten different small programs that can do one thing instead of one Swiss knife-like tool.

2. For solving complex tasks, Linux will allow you to use "piping" to connect tools into chains for results processing. We will cover this later in the chapter.

A. Markelov, *Red Hat RHCSA 10 Study Companion*, Certification Study Companion Series,
https://doi.org/10.1007/979-8-8688-2226-1_2

3. Everything is a file. This statement is not one hundred percent true, but most interfaces, including interfaces to the hardware of the server, will somehow be represented in the file system.
4. Avoiding interactive commands that require user input. Most command-line tools will expect options and arguments provided right after the name of the command before you press the Enter key.
5. Configuration information is stored in flat text files. You usually need only a simple text editor to change the system or service configuration.

But let's start with some hands-on, finally. Installation of the operating system is not part of the exam requirements. So, the procedure on how to build a lab for exercises is covered in Appendix A. We assume you already have one virtual or physical machine with an installed RHEL 10 or CentOS Stream 10.

SSH connection is the most common way you will use during your career to connect to the Linux server. It is also a convenient way to access the test virtual machine during exam time. Using base syntax, you need to provide a username; then you have to put the symbol "@" and then the hostname or IP address of the server:

```
$ ssh user@host1.test.local
user@host1.test.local's password: ********
Web console: https://host1.test.local:9090/ or
https://192.168.122.111:9090/

Last login: Thu May 17 19:38:56 2025 from 192.168.122.1
[user@host1 ~]$
```

If you connect to this particular server for the first time, you will be provided with an SSH key fingerprint, and the ssh command will ask you for confirmation to continue the connection.

If you have "physical" access to the server, you can log in via text virtual console or, if the server has a GUI installed, by using graphical login. To access the command line after logging in via a graphical console, simply open the Terminal application from the application menu, as shown in Figure 2-1. RHEL uses a desktop environment named GNOME to work with a graphical user interface. Terminal Emulator is one of its basic tools.

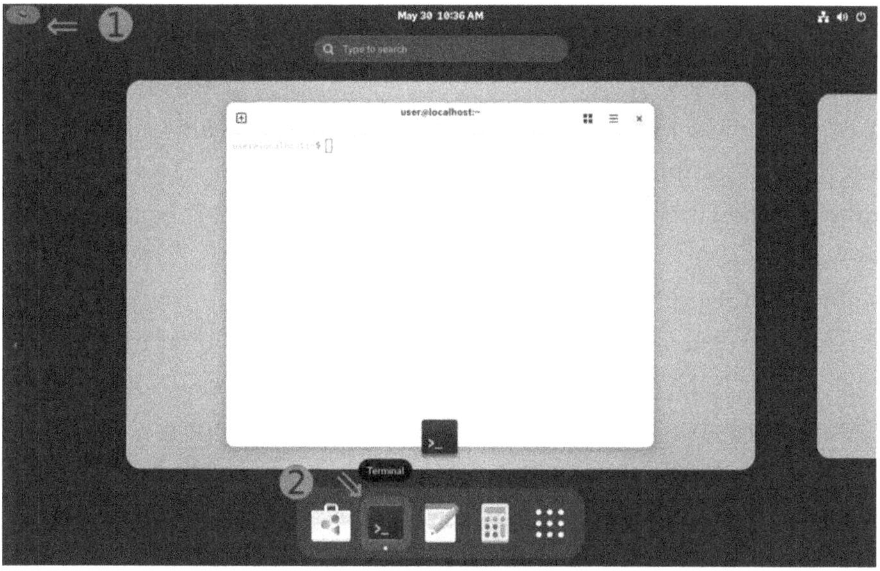

***Figure 2-1.** Opening the Terminal application in graphical mode*

Tip Compared to previous versions of RHEL, the last one switched from the old one, GNOME Terminal, to Ptyxis: a container-oriented terminal for GNOME with additional features: `https://gitlab.gnome.org/chergert/ptyxis`.

At the same time, you have several running text virtual consoles and can switch between them by typing `Ctrl-Alt-F2...F6`. To return to the graphical console, press `Ctrl-Alt-F2`. Here, you can see what a virtual text console looks like:

```
Red Hat Enterprise Linux 10.0 (Coughlan)
Kernel 6.12.0-55.9.1.el10_0.x86_64 on X86_64

Web console: https://localhost:9090/ or https://192.168.122.
111:9090/

localhost login: _
```

You may notice the message about the web console, which is available by using a browser at the server's IP address or at the localhost at port 9090. This is another way to interact with the system. You can use it for some common administration and exam tasks. Instead of logging in as a system administrator to the web console, log in as a regular user, and then enable administrative access.

The web console is based on Project Cockpit (`https://cockpit-project.org/`). If you point your browser to the IP address shown in the login message, you will be asked to provide your username and password. The user interface of the Cockpit console is shown in Figure 2-2. You may notice the message on the banner that the tool runs in limited access mode. To unblock administrative functions, click the blue button in the Overview tab, and enter your password again. Also, you can click the Limited access button and any other tab.

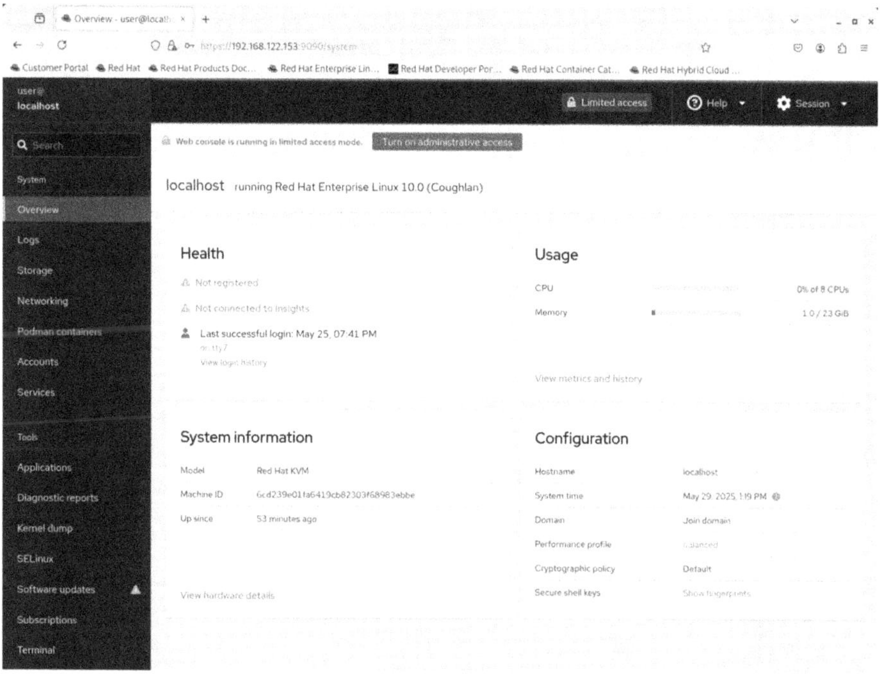

***Figure 2-2.** Web console Overview page in the limited access mode*

You don't have to use the web console, but it can make some tasks easy, especially for people new to GNU/Linux system administration. So, I would advise you to familiarize yourself with the console. It is better to do this after you learn how to do things in the command line. At the documentation portal, we will later discuss a separate book named "Managing systems in the RHEL web console" that is available.

Tip By default, not all Cockpit's add-ons are installed in the system. You can get additional functionality in the web console by installing add-ons at the Applications tab at the left part of the user interface. You can check the corresponding part of the Cockpit user interface in Figure 2-3. Also, you can search for packages with "cockpit" in the name by using the CLI tool `dnf`. Installation of packages will be covered later in the book.

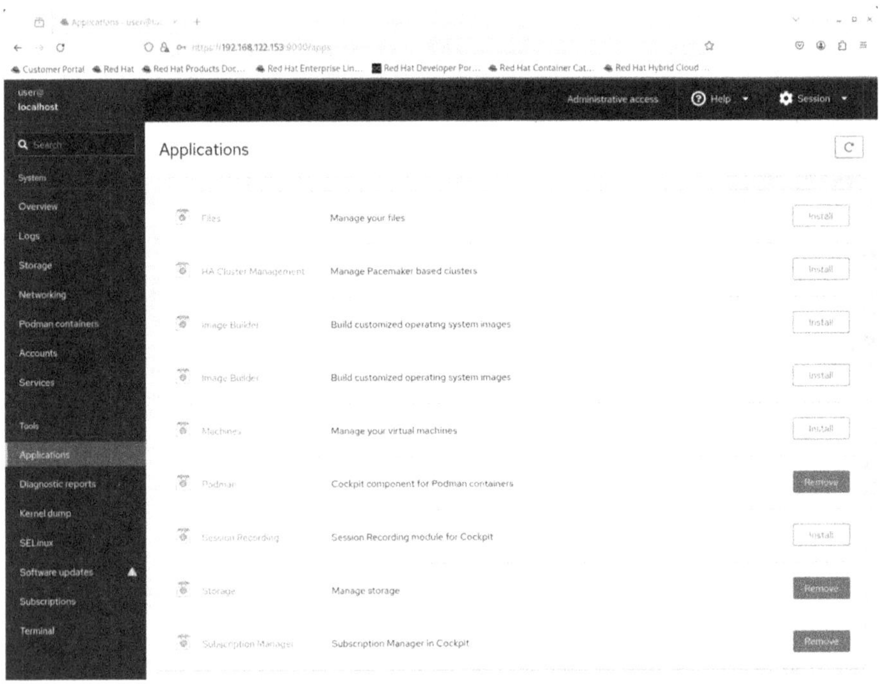

Figure 2-3. *Installation of additional add-ons in the web console*

Running Commands in Bash Shell

If you logged in using a graphical console, you need to choose the Terminal application in the application menu to start using the command line. In web console, you have to choose Terminal on the left side of the screen. By using a text console or SSH connection, you get a command-line shell prompt by default. Shell is the program that allows you to interact with the operating system. Unix-like systems have many different shells, and you can switch the default shell if you want. For example, MacOS uses `zsh`, which can also be used in RHEL. But by default, most of the GNU/Linux distributions use the Bash shell. Bash is short for "*Bourne Again Shell*," and `sh` was the original Unix shell.

The default prompt will consist of several parts and looks like this example:

```
user@localhost:/usr/share/doc$
```

Components of the default prompt:

- `user` - The username of the current user.
- `@` - Delimiter.
- `localhost` - The hostname, up to the first symbol dot.
- `:` - Delimiter.
- `/usr/share/doc` - Current working directory (CWD) of the shell. In Unix-like systems, every process has this attribute.
- `$` - By agreement, a dollar symbol is used for regular users' prompts, and a hashtag sign (#) is used for administrative user root.

Tip If you have ever worked with other distributions or previous versions of RHEL, you may notice that the default prompt has changed in RHEL 10. Thanks to the script provided by the package bash-color-prompt. However, you may prefer not to see the full path of CWD in the prompt. To trim path, you can uncomment PROMPT_DIRTRIM variable in /etc/profile.d/bash-color-prompt.sh. You can check other settings here. To revert to old-school bash prompt default settings, you can simply remove the package bash-color-prompt.

Let's talk a bit more about the root, or superuser administrative account. It is so important that it has a special indication in the prompt. Root has near complete control over the GNU/Linux operating system. It is such a powerful account that it can destroy the whole system and its data. You do not want to break your system, but you can do this by mistake, such as mistyping. It is the essential rule you do not log in as root unless necessary.

There are two basic ways to change user identities for administrative purposes: the su and the sudo commands. Let's look at the example you can repeat in your terminal:

```
user@localhost:~$ id
uid=1000(user) gid=1000(user) groups=1000(user),10(wheel) conte
xt=unconfined_u:unconfined_r:unconfined_t:s0-s0:c0.c1023
user@localhost:~$ su -
Password:
Last login: Thu May 29 17:00:35 CEST 2025 on pts/2
root@localhost:~# id
uid=0(root) gid=0(root) groups=0(root) context=unconfined_u:unc
onfined_r:unconfined_t:s0-s0:c0.c1023
root@localhost:~# Ctrl+d)
logout
user@localhost:~$ sudo whoami
[sudo] password for user:
root
user@localhost:~$
```

I used five commands in this example, and you can see five prompts. Let's review them.

As you can see from the first prompt, I am logged in as a regular user with the name user. Command `id` shows information about the current user. As you can see, uid (user identifier) is 1000, and the name is user. Then, you can see information about groups and the SELinux context. This is not important for now and will be discussed later.

The following command is `su -`. You can add a username, but if you skipped it, the command assumes you want to become root. The symbol "`-`" I added to the command line as an argument means I want to start a login shell, and without it, a non-login shell will be started. The difference between login and non-login shells is that specific configuration files will be read and executed. The login shell usually starts when you log in to the system locally or using ssh. A non-login shell example is opening a new terminal window within a graphical environment. We will touch on differences at the end of the chapter in the exercise section.

The third command in the listing, as you can see, is `id` again. But now, the output shows you logged in as a root user. The fourth command is to exit the terminate bash session. Instead of `exit`, you can use the `Ctrl+d` shortcut. Some other shortcuts that can significantly boost your productivity can be found in Table 2-1.

Table 2-1. *Useful Bash shell shortcuts*

Shortcut	Shortcut description
Ctrl+r	Search through the history of commands in reverse order. Type characters to find matching commands. To see the next match, press Ctrl+r again.
Ctrl+l	Clear the screen. It works as a `clear` command.
Alt+. (dot)	Inserts the last argument of the previous command.
Ctrl+s	Stops output to the terminal.
Ctrl+q	Resumes output after Ctrl+s.
Ctrl+d	Signals end-of-file (EOF) to the shell, which typically logs you out of the current shell session. It works as an `exit` command.
Ctrl+c	Kill the foreground process (sends `SIGINT` signal).
Ctrl+z	Pause running command (sends `SIGTSTP` signal). The paused command can be resumed with the `fg` command in the foreground or `bg` in the background. This is part of jobs control in the Bash shell.
Tab	Autocompletion of command or argument.
!!	Execute the most recent command again.

The last example, "`sudo whoami`", introduces two commands simultaneously. The `sudo` command allows a user to execute a command as the superuser or another user. I will describe how to configure permissions to use sudo in the chapter about user management. But if you configured your system as described in Appendix B, then you will be able to use `sudo`. The command `whoami` shows an effective username. It is basically a subset of the information command `id` provided.

In general, a command consists of the command name itself, followed by options and arguments. Arguments are things that the command works on, such as a username or file name. Options modify the command behavior. Usually, if an option consists of one letter, it is preceded by one dash symbol. Several one-letter options can be joined without separation. If the option is a word, it is preceded by two dash symbols. The "Short" and "long" options can be combined, and quite often, the same option can have two versions – "short" and "long". Here are some examples:

```
$ command1 -a -b -c argument1 argument2
$ command1 -abc argument1 argument2
$ command2 --option1 --option2 argument
$ command3 --long-option -s argument
```

Tip Due to the historical and diverse development of tools, there are exceptions to the use of double and single dashes. For example, the command `find` uses a single dash with "long" options, and the command `tar` can use one letter, "short" options without a dash at all.

You can also run several commands in the same command line with the symbol ";" (semicolon). The following command will be started after the previous one is finished.

It is good to know that commands are divided into internal (built-in), external, and aliases. Internal commands are embedded in the shell, external are stored as executable files, and aliases are user-defined shortcuts. We will dive into aliases later in the book and will learn how to know where to search for external commands.

How to Get Help for Command-Line Tools

If you work regularly with GNU/Linux, you will know the most common syntaxes and options for common tools. But what if you need some specific command behavior or do a particular task once per year? First of all, you can run the command with standard options -h or --help. Usually, one of them or both will be implemented in the command-line tools. For example:

```
user@localhost:~$ sha256sum --help
Usage: sha256sum [OPTION]... [FILE]...
Print or check SHA256 (256-bit) checksums.
With no FILE, or when FILE is -, read standard input.
  -b, --binary          read in binary mode
...
user@localhost:~$ cal -h
Usage:
 cal [options] [[[day] month] year]
 cal [options] <timestamp|monthname>
Display a calendar, or some part of it.
Without any arguments, display the current month.
Options:
 -1, --one              show only a single month (default)
 -3, --three            show three months spanning the date
```

As you can see, the help option shows a one- or two-line description of the command and syntax, using a common format and list of options. You can refer to the command syntax description conventions in Table 2-2.

Table 2-2. *Command syntax description conventions in GNU/Linux documentation*

<table>
<tr><th>Syntax</th><th>Example</th><th>Description</th></tr>
<tr><td>[ ]</td><td>touch – Change file timestamps
touch [OPTION]... FILE...
uniq – Report or omit repeated lines
uniq [OPTION]... [INPUT [OUTPUT]]</td><td>Anything in braces is optional. If no braces are used, then an argument or option will be mandatory. In the first example, FILE is mandatory, but options can be skipped. Braces can be nested as in the second example. You can use INPUT with no OUTPUT but cannot use OUTPUT without INPUT.</td></tr>
<tr><td>CAPS or < ></td><td>Cal – Display a calendar, or some part of it
cal [options] <timestamp|monthname></td><td>Variable data.</td></tr>
<tr><td>...</td><td>wc – Print newline, word, and byte counts for each file
wc [OPTION]... [FILE]...</td><td>Anything followed by ... can be a list of this argument or option. In the example with the wc command, you can pass zero or many OPTION and FILE.</td></tr>
<tr><td>A|B|C</td><td>tar – An archiving utility
tar {A|c|d|r|t|u|x} [GnSkUWOmpsMBiajJzZhPIRvwo] [ARG...]</td><td>Mutual exclusive arguments or options. With the tar command, you cannot use at the same time operation modes A, c, d, r, t, u, or x.</td></tr>
</table>

The --help/-h option usually includes only a short command description or a link to other sources. The most used type of comprehensive help source in Unix-like operations systems, including GNU/Linux, is man pages. Almost all commands and many configuration files have their own man pages. To read about man pages itself, you should call `man man`. This will open the page shown in Figure 2-4.

Figure 2-4. *GNU/Linux manual pages*

As you can see, the man page consists of several parts divided by standard man page headings:

`NAME` – One-line description of the tool.

`SYNOPSIS` – Syntax of the command.

`DESCRIPTION` – Long description.

`EXAMPLES` – Usable examples. It can contain ready-to-use recipes for your exam tasks.

`OPTIONS` – Options description.

`FILES` – Files related to this tool. It can be configuration files, for example.

`SEE ALSO` – Related tools and documentation.

Every man page belongs to one of the sections. Section descriptions can be found in Table 2-3. The system can have man pages with the same name in different sections. In the documentation, to define which section we are talking about, it is referred to as a number within round squares after the name of the man page. For example, `write(1)` or `write(2)`. The man page in section one referred to the command "write" that sends a message to another user and in section two referred to the system call write.

Table 2-3. Section numbers of the manual

Shortcut	Shortcut description
1	Executable programs or shell commands
2	System calls (functions provided by the kernel)
3	Library calls (functions within program libraries)
4	Special files (usually found in /dev)
5	File formats and conventions, e.g., /etc/passwd
6	Games and funny little programs available on the system
7	Miscellaneous (including macro packages and standards)
8	System administration commands (usually only for root)
9	Kernel internal routines

By default, when you call man, it will show you a page with a minimal section number. To see the page about write system call, you must add the section number:

```
user@localhost:~$ man 2 write
```

You can search on the content of NAME sections of man pages by using the `man -k` option:

```
user@localhost:~$ man -k passwd
chgpasswd (8)        - update group passwords in batch mode
chpasswd (8)         - update passwords in batch mode
fgetpwent_r (3)      - get passwd file entry reentrantly
getpwent_r (3)       - get passwd file entry reentrantly
gpasswd (1)          - administer /etc/group and /etc/gshadow
...
```

Tip In the just-installed system, the command man -k may not work since it requires manual page index caches built by the mandb tool. The index is updated by the cron scheduler once per day. Check that the package man-db-cron is installed on the system. You can run mandb directly on the command line as the root user if needed.

By default, man pages use the `less` tool as a pager (viewer). This means for man page navigation, you need to use `less` utility hotkeys. The `less`'s goal is to display the contents of a file in a terminal. As the tool's man page states, "`less` is a program similar to `more(1)`, but it has many more features." This definition leads us to question what is `more`. `more` is a filter for paging through text one screenful at a time. Now you can forget what is `more` and use only `less`.

You can scroll through text using the arrow keys and the PgUp and PgDn keys. `/text` will search `text` forward. If you press `n`, it will show the next part where `text` is present. Capital `N` will perform a backward search of the `text`. Key `h` will show you a help page where you can find other key combinations.

Another embedded in Linux help commands is `info`. `info` is primarily used by the GNU project. Compared to `man`, it provides a more rich hypertext help system. Not all commands have an info page. You will work with `info` as part of the exercises at the end of this chapter. Please keep in mind `info` is not installed in the system by default because it is not considered an essential utility. You need to install the `info` package.

When you install the majority of packages in RHEL, you will get a new subdirectory within `/usr/share/doc/` with a name similar to the package's name. This subdirectory usually contains license information, configuration file examples, and other non-standardized additional content.

Last but not least, the source of information is official Red Hat documentation, which will be available during the exam. You should familiarize yourself with the documentation related to RHEL at the link `https://docs.redhat.com/`.

File System Hierarchy

We will start by looking into the Linux file system hierarchy. The man pages `man file-hierarchy` and `man hier` provide detailed descriptions of standard directories in GNU/Linux. The most notable directories you should know are listed in Table 2-4.

Table 2-4. *The most notable directories in RHEL 10*

Directory	Short description
/	The top of the file system hierarchy is "/" or root directory. Do not confuse with root user.
/boot/	This directory is a separate disk partition and stores the Linux kernel and bootloader. RHEL 10 disk images, like those used with AWS or KVM, don't have a separate /boot partition.
/bin/	Binaries files for regular users' commands and programs, which are part of the operating system. This is a symbolic link to `usr/bin`. What is the symbolic link? We will study it shortly.
/dev/	`/dev` is a pseudo file system for device nodes. The Linux kernel manages it.
/etc/	System-specific configuration. You may find here many subdirectories for different subsystems of your server and lots of default configuration files created during system installation.
/home/	/home/ directory is the location of non-administrative users' home directories. Usually, the subdirectory's name is the same as the user's name. This directory is quite often mounted from a separate partition. It can also be network-attached.
/lib/ and /lib64/	Libraries that provide shared code to applications. This is a symbolic link to `corresponding directories within usr/`.

(continued)

Table 2-4. (*continued*)

Directory	Short description
/media/ and /mnt/	Directories used for mounting devices. /media is targeted to removable, and /mnt is targeted to temporary.
/opt/	The directory for optional is probably "Third-Party Packages". There is no standard for how this data should be organized. In RHEL, by default, it is usually empty.
/proc/, /sys/	It is a virtual file system representing structures in the server's memory that are not stored anywhere on disk. The Linux kernel manages it. It can be considered as part of Kernel API.
/root/	This is the root user's home directory. It is separate from regular users' home directories because it can be a situation when /home/ is not mounted due to an issue. However, this situation should not affect the system administrator.
/run/	This is "runtime" data that will not survive a reboot. One example is removable file systems like USB drives and CD disks mounted by default in the `/run/media/<username>/`.
/sbin/	Binaries files for system administrators' commands and programs, which are part of the operating system. This is a symbolic link to `usr/sbin`.
/srv/	Server-related data. There is no standard for how this data should be organized. It sometimes has a "legacy" perception. In RHEL, by default, it is usually empty.
/tmp/	Temporary files are stored here. This directory is flushed every reboot.
/usr/	Binaries, libraries, and documentation files for commands and programs are not part of the operating system itself.
/var/	Dynamic system information that needs to survive during the reboot of the system. Examples of such data are system log files (/var/log/), web server content (/var/www/), virtual machines images (/var/lib/libvirt/), and temporary files that need to be stored for a relatively long time (/var/tmp/).

These are several basic things you need to know about the GNU/Linux file system:

- Names of directories and files are case-sensitive.
- The file system represents a tree-like inverted structure with a "root" directory- "/". For GNU/Linux, `File` and `file` would be two different names.
- Sub-directories are divided by the "/" symbol. For example, `/usr/share/doc/`. It's important to differentiate it from the Windows backslash "\".
- You can use a dot symbol and two dots to refer to files and directories by using a relative path. The dot symbol "`.`" represents the current directory, and the two dots "`..`" represent the parent directory. Every process, including the shell, has a current working directory (CWD). In the root directory, "`..`" points to itself.
- You can point to a directory with absolute and relative paths. The absolute path always starts from the root directory, and relative can begin from CWD.
- If you are using remotely attached or removable file systems like NFS or USB-attached flash drives, they anyway will be included in the only tree. To make the file system accessible, you (or the operating system itself) need to attach or "mount" separate file systems into the only tree. Mounting would be performed into the existing local empty directory. If the directory is not empty, then the "local" files inside would not be visible until unmounting the remote file system. We will touch on this later.

- File and directory names can start with a dot symbol. Such files and directories are named "hidden." This is not truly correct since it is not a special attribute of a file. This is not any kind of security feature. Graphical and command-line tools do not show such files by default. Hidden files and directories are usually used for configuration data, and you simply don't want to see them during a "normal" work pattern with your data.

You can use several essential graphical tools to learn about directories and browse the file system without knowledge of the command line. Files GUI tool and Mozilla browser are examples. They are shown in Figure 2-5. In Files, you can press Ctrl+h to see hidden files. However, this book aims to teach you system administration skills, and we will learn how to perform operations with directories and files in the command line.

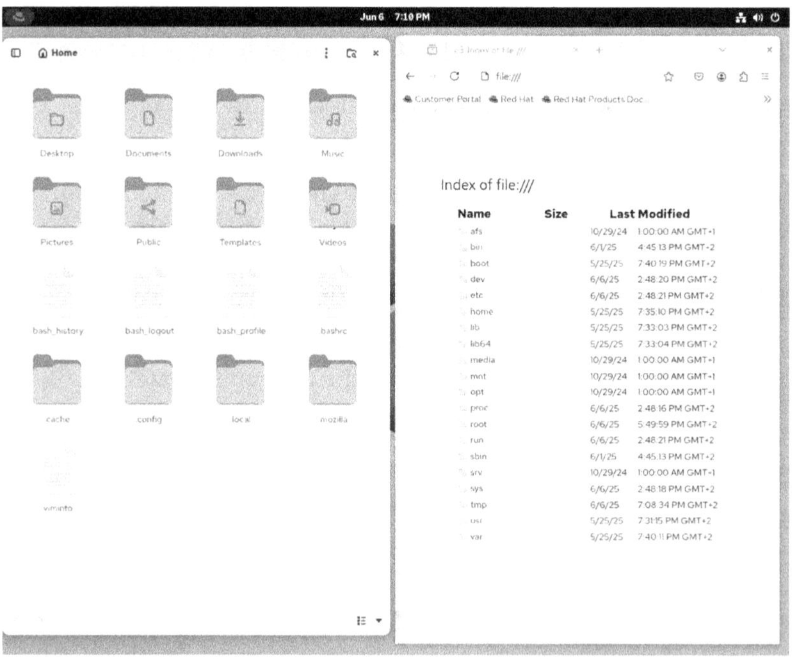

***Figure 2-5.** Browsing the file system with the Files GUI tool (Nautilus) and Mozilla Firefox*

Managing Files and Directories in the Command Line

When you log into the system, your current working directory (CWD) will be your home directory. It is easy to check with the command `pwd`:

```
user@localhost:~$ pwd
/home/user
```

To change CWD, you can use the Bash shell embedded command `cd`:

```
user@localhost:~$ cd /usr/share/doc/bash
user@localhost:/usr/share/doc/bash$ cd ../bash-completion/
user@localhost:/usr/share/doc/bash-completion$ cd -
/usr/share/doc/bash
user@localhost:/usr/share/doc/bash$ cd ~
```

In the example above, you can see four cd commands demonstrating different syntaxes. With the first command, `cd /usr/share/doc/bash`, you change CWD by using the absolute path, starting from the root directory.

The second command shows relative path syntax. You virtually go "up" one level with two dots to the directory `/usr/share/doc/` and then "down" to `bash-completion/` at the same level as `bash/`. The third command `cd -` is a shortcut to returning to your previous CWD. It was `/usr/share/doc/bash`, as the output shows us. The last is the user symbol ~, representing your home directory. You can also use ~ in the relative path. For example:

```
user@localhost:~$ cd ~/../../etc/rc.d/
user@localhost:/etc/rc.d$ pwd
/etc/rc.d
```

Your home directory is a second-level directory counting from the root. By typing `~/../../`, you return to the root and then go to `/etc/rc.d/`.

If you use cd without any arguments, you will also set your CWD to home directory. The syntax ~<user name> will refer to the home directory of <user name>, for example, ~andrey.

The following command we will look at is ls. The purpose of the command is to list directory content. ls without options will show you a "short" listing. You can add the path to the command. Without a path, it will list CWD:

```
user@localhost:~$ ls
Desktop  Documents  Downloads  Music  Pictures  Public
Templates  Videos
```

By adding option -a, you can see hidden files and directories. Compare this output with the one shown before:

```
user@localhost:~$ ls -a
.   .bash_history  .bash_profile  .cache   Desktop    Downloads
.mozilla  Pictures  Templates  .viminfo
..  .bash_logout   .bashrc        .config  Documents  .local
Music     Public    Videos

user@localhost:~$ ls -la
total 32
drwx------. 14 user user 4096 May 30 09:40 .
drwxr-xr-x.  3 root root   18 May 25 19:35 ..
-rw-------.  1 user user 2304 Jun  7 18:08 .bash_history
-rw-r--r--.  1 user user   18 Oct 29  2024 .bash_logout
-rw-r--r--.  1 user user  144 Oct 29  2024 .bash_profile
-rw-r--r--.  1 user user  522 Oct 29  2024 .bashrc
drwx------. 14 user user 4096 Jun  1 18:47 .cache
drwx------. 11 user user 4096 Jun  6 19:08 .config
drwxr-xr-x.  2 user user    6 Jun  7 17:50 Desktop
...
```

Another very often used option of ls is `-l`. It shows a "long" listing of the specified directory with seven columns in a line. Tables 2-5 describe each column.

Table 2-5. *Explanation of the "long" output of the ls -l command*

Column	Example	Description
1	drwxr-xr-x.	Eleven symbols line. The first symbol describes the type of the file. Some of them are d – Directory - – Regular file l – Symbolic link c – Character device file (like `/dev/tty0` or `/dev/urandom`) b – Block device file (like `/dev/vda`) Then, nine symbols represent permissions. Permissions will be described later in this chapter. The last one is the security context indicator. It will be touched on later in another chapter.
2	2	For files – Number of hard links. For directories, there are a number of subdirectories and hard links to files. For an empty directory, this number will be two because dot (`.`) and two dots (`..`) entries exist in any directory.
3	user	Username of the owner.
4	user	Group owning a file or directory.
5	6	Size in bytes for files and size of metadata for directories. You can add the option `-h` to get "human-readable" output in sizes like 5K, 10M, or 15G.
6	Jun 7 17:50	Date and time of last modification. You can reset it manually to current with the command `touch <name of the file>`.
7	Desktop	Name of the file or directory.

The last useful option we need to mention is -d. Compare the output of two ls commands with the same argument:

```
user@localhost:~$ ls -l Desktop/
total 0
user@localhost:~$ ls -ld Desktop/
drwxr-xr-x. 2 user user 6 Jun  7 17:50 Desktop/
```

The command without the -d option shows you the content of the directory, but if you want information about the directory itself, you need the -d option.

Another tool that can be used in addition to ls is a tree. It shows a pseudographical representation of the directories and files as an inverted tree. Option -L defines the maximum display depth of the directory tree:

```
user@localhost:~$ tree /etc -L 2
/etc
├── adjtime
├── aliases
├── alsa
│   ├── alsactl.conf
│   ├── conf.d
│   └── state-daemon.conf
├── alternatives
│   ├── apropos -> /usr/bin/apropos.man-db
...
```

Before we start modifying files, let's introduce Bash pathname globbing. I recommend reading man glob(7) to examine the topic deeply. In the book, I will cover the minimal information needed. The symbol "?" matches any single character. In the place where you will put "?", there should be exactly one symbol. The place cannot be empty. The symbol "*" matches any string, including the empty string. The expression

[ABCD] means one character from the list provided, i.e., A, B, C, or D. The expression [^ABCD] means one character with an exception from the list provided.

Let's use some examples of globbing while learning new commands. First, we will create several files and directories to work on.

```
user@localhost:~$ mkdir myfiles; cd myfiles
user@localhost:~/myfiles$ mkdir -p backup/daily
user@localhost:~/myfiles$ touch file{A,B,C,D,Dd}.txt
user@localhost:~/myfiles$ touch file{0..2}.txt
user@localhost:~/myfiles$ tree
.
├── backup
│   └── daily
├── file0.txt
├── file1.txt
├── file2.txt
├── fileA.txt
├── fileB.txt
├── fileC.txt
├── fileDd.txt
└── fileD.txt

3 directories, 8 files
```

The command mkdir is used to create directories. We created the directory myfiles and changed CWD to it. The second mkdir command has the option -p which creates a directory daily, and it is a parent backup.

Command touch is used to manually reset the date and time of the last file modification. However, if the file does not exist, it will create it. I used a method named curly brace expansion with this command. In the first example, Bash shell expands part in braces into a list of strings:

A, B, C, D, Dd. It then combines each string with the file at the beginning and .txt at the end. As a result, we have five arguments for the command touch. The second touch has brace expansion with a sequence. When Bash sees A..Z inside curly braces, it expands to a sequence from A to Z. A and Z can be numbers or letters.

There are two very similar commands, cp and mv. First, it is used for copying files and directories, and second, it is used for moving. The main difference is that the source will disappear in the case of mv, and in the case of cp, you will get two copies. Command mv is also commonly used for renaming files.

```
user@localhost:~/myfiles$ cp file1.txt file2.txt backup/daily
user@localhost:~/myfiles$ mv file0.txt backup/daily
user@localhost:~/myfiles$ tree
.
├── backup
│   └── daily
│       ├── file0.txt # Only one copy. Original not
exist anymore
│       ├── file1.txt # File has two copies
│       └── file2.txt # File has two copies
├── file1.txt
├── file2.txt
├── fileA.txt
├── fileB.txt
├── fileC.txt
├── fileDd.txt
└── fileD.txt
```

Take into account that if the destination is a file, then the original will overwrite the destination. Also, it is not possible to copy or move several files into one:

```
user@localhost:~/myfiles$ cp file1.txt fileD.txt fileC.txt
cp: target 'fileC.txt': Not a directory
```

It is possible to copy the content of several files into one. We will learn this later in the chapter.

One of the most useful options for cp is -r. This option gives the ability to copy the directory recursively with all subdirectories and files. When moving a directory, mv implicitly moves its entire contents. Therefore, mv doesn't need the -r option.

```
user@localhost:~/myfiles$ cp backup/daily/ .
cp: -r not specified; omitting directory 'backup/daily/'
user@localhost:~/myfiles$ cp -r backup/daily/ .
user@localhost:~/myfiles$ tree
.
├── backup
│   └── daily
│       ├── file0.txt
│       ├── file1.txt
│       └── file2.txt
├── daily
│   ├── file0.txt
│   ├── file1.txt
│   └── file2.txt
├── file1.txt
...
```

There are some similar options for `cp` and `mv`:

- `-i` – Interactive mode. Prompts you for confirmation before overwriting an existing destination file.
- `-f` – Do not prompt before overwriting.

Now we can play with directory and file removal:

```
user@localhost:~/myfiles$ rm daily/
rm: cannot remove 'daily/': Is a directory
user@localhost:~/myfiles$ rm -r daily/
user@localhost:~/myfiles$ rm -i *[Dd]*
rm: remove regular empty file 'fileDd.txt'? y
rm: remove regular empty file 'fileD.txt'? n
user@localhost:~/myfiles$ rmdir backup/daily/
rmdir: failed to remove 'backup/daily/': Directory not empty
user@localhost:~/myfiles$ rm backup/daily/*
user@localhost:~/myfiles$ rmdir backup/daily/
user@localhost:~/myfiles$ tree
.
├── backup
├── file1.txt
├── file2.txt
├── fileA.txt
├── fileB.txt
├── fileC.txt
└── fileD.txt

2 directories, 6 files
```

As you can see, neither `rm` nor `rmdir` can delete a non-empty directory. However, `rm` can override this by using the "recursive" option `-r`. Command `rm` has options `-i` and `-f` that have the same meaning as the corresponding options of the cp command.

As you remember, the second column in the "long" file listing by ln -l is a number of hard links. Let's try to figure out what this means. But first, we will remove all files with the exception of one. Also, we will keep a directory backup:

```
user@localhost:~/myfiles$ rm file[^1]*
user@localhost:~/myfiles$ ls
```

```
backup  file1.txt
user@localhost:~/myfiles$ tree
.
├── backup
└── file1.txt

2 directories, 1 file
```

I strongly recommend that you use command-line tools for exams and in daily work as well, since it is faster. However, you can definitely use the Files graphical tool, also known as Nautilus in GNOME, which is similar to File Explorer in Windows or Finder in macOS.

You have another option as well. You can install the Cockpit file browser plug-in from the Applications tab. The interface of the File browser is shown in Figure 2-6.

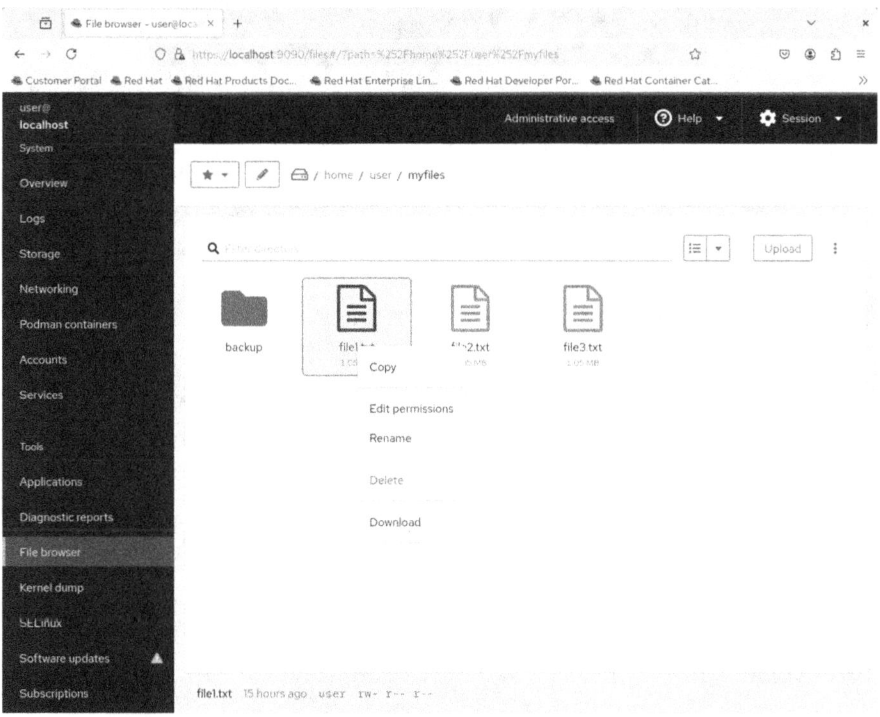

Figure 2-6. Cockpit file browser plug-in

As part of RHEL 10 applications, you can install Midnight Commander (package mc), a text-based file manager, in the virtual terminal or via SSH remote session. It uses characters and colors to create a dual-pane visual interface similar to the old MS DOS-based file manager Norton Commander. You can run it using command mc. The interface of mc is shown in Figure 2-7. Documentation for Midnight Commander is available on the site `https://midnight-commander.org/`.

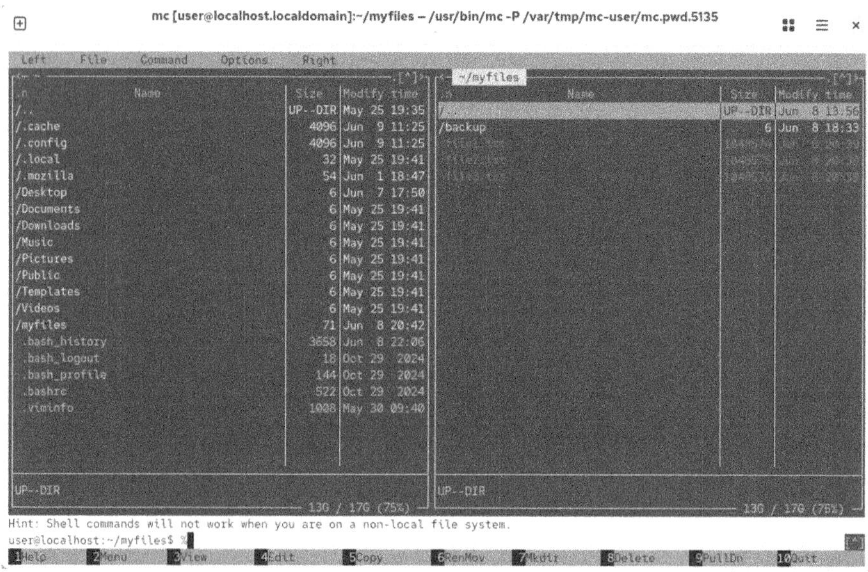

Figure 2-7. *Interface of Midnight Commander*

The next topic we must cover is soft (symbolic) links and hard links. For the demonstration's clarity, we will fill our only file, `file1.txt`, in the directory `myfiles` with random data:

```
user@localhost:~/myfiles$ dd if=/dev/urandom of=file1.txt
bs=1M count=1
1+0 records in
1+0 records out
```

```
1048576 bytes (1.0 MB, 1.0 MiB) copied, 0.00532608 s, 197 MB/s
user@localhost:~/myfiles$ du -h
0     ./backup
1.0M  .
```

The dd utility is a "data duplicator" often used to copy raw data. In our case, it copies one block of data with size 1M from /dev/urandom to the file file1.txt. /dev/urandom is a character device file that provides an interface to the Linux kernel's random number generator. The second utility in the example is du. It estimates file space usage recursively for directories. The option -h means "human-readable" output in K, M, or G. Du shows 1M, which is exactly the same number as the size of the only file. All as expected.

Next, we will copy file1.txt to file2.txt and confirm du shows 2M:

```
user@localhost:~/myfiles$ cp file1.txt file2.txt
user@localhost:~/myfiles$ du -h
0     ./backup
2.0M  .
```

In the default file system in RHEL, xfs, and the previous default file system, ext4, every file or directory has an inode (or index descriptor) with a unique number. The inode contains essential metadata about the file, such as permissions, ownership, timestamps, and information about where to find the file's data on the disk. To see the index descriptor number, we can use ls with the -i option:

```
user@localhost:~/myfiles$ ls -li
total 2048
 2757322 drwxr-xr-x. 2 user user       6 Jun  8 18:33 backup
51381036 -rw-r--r--. 1 user user 1048576 Jun  8 20:39 file1.txt
51381010 -rw-r--r--. 1 user user 1048576 Jun  8 20:39 file2.txt
```

As we can see, the two files have different inodes. Now, let's create a hard link named file3.txt from file1.txt:

```
user@localhost:~/myfiles$ ln file1.txt file3.txt
user@localhost:~/myfiles$ ls -li
total 3072
 2757322 drwxr-xr-x. 2 user user       6 Jun  8 18:33 backup
51381036 -rw-r--r--. 2 user user 1048576 Jun  8 20:39 file1.txt
51381010 -rw-r--r--. 1 user user 1048576 Jun  8 20:39 file2.txt
51381036 -rw-r--r--. 2 user user 1048576 Jun  8 20:39 file3.txt
user@localhost:~/myfiles$ du -h
0    ./backup
2.0M .
```

The example shows three things: the index descriptor is the same for the new file as for the source file, the count of hard links for `file1.txt` and `file3.txt` is two, and the directory's file space usage did not change from 2M to 3M.

What does this mean? It means the file's data and metadata (inode) are stored only once, but two different pointers exist in the directory. At this point, no difference between the source and destination files exists. If I change `file1.txt` or its metadata, `file3.txt` will be changed as well. Again, data is stored only once. What if I will delete `file1.txt`? The counter of hard links in metadata will be changed from two to one, and only `file3.txt` remains. Deletion only happens when the counter of hard links in metadata is zero, i.e., if I delete `file3.txt`.

If I know the index descriptor to the file, I can find all hard links, or I can just refer to the file by the `-samefile` option of the command `find`:

```
user@localhost:~/myfiles$ find /home -inum 51381036
/home/user/myfiles/file1.txt
/home/user/myfiles/file3.txt
user@localhost:~/myfiles$ find /home -samefile file1.txt
/home/user/myfiles/file1.txt
/home/user/myfiles/file3.txt
```

Disadvantages of hard links: they can be used only within one file system and are only for files. To mitigate this, we can create soft links or symbolic links with the same command `ln` but with the `-s` option:

```
user@localhost:~/myfiles$ ln -s file1.txt file4.txt
user@localhost:~/myfiles$ ln -s backup backup2
user@localhost:~/myfiles$ ln -s /home/user/myfiles/
backup backup3
user@localhost:~/myfiles$ ls -li
total 3072
 2757322 drwxr-xr-x. 2 user user       6 Jun  8 18:33 backup
51381043 lrwxrwxrwx. 1 user user       6 Jun  9 21:54 backup2
-> backup
51381045 lrwxrwxrwx. 1 user user      25 Jun  9 22:00 backup3
-> /home/user/myfiles/backup
51381036 -rw-r--r--. 2 user user 1048576 Jun  8 20:39 file1.txt
51381010 -rw-r--r--. 1 user user 1048576 Jun  8 20:39 file2.txt
51381036 -rw-r--r--. 2 user user 1048576 Jun  8 20:39 file3.txt
51381037 lrwxrwxrwx. 1 user user       9 Jun  9 21:53 file4.txt
-> file1.txt
```

As you can see, symbolic links have different types of files "`l`" instead of "`d`" or "`-`", have their own unique inode, and have sizes equal to the number of characters in the link's name (compare `backup2` and `backup3`).

What if you try to delete the directory to which the soft link was pointed?

```
user@localhost:~/myfiles$ cd backup2
user@localhost:~/myfiles/backup2$ cd ..
user@localhost:~/myfiles$ rmdir backup
user@localhost:~/myfiles$ cd backup2
-bash: cd: backup2: No such file or directory
```

As you can see, it is impossible to change the directory using a symbolic link, but the link still exists. You can expect similar behavior with files:

```
user@localhost:~/myfiles$ rm file1.txt
user@localhost:~/myfiles$ cat file4.txt
cat: file4.txt: No such file or directory
```

As you can see in the "long" listing, broken symbolic links will be highlighted by color:

```
user@localhost:~/myfiles$ ls -l
total 2048
lrwxrwxrwx. 1 user user       6 Jun  9 21:54 backup2 -> backup
lrwxrwxrwx. 1 user user      25 Jun  9 22:00 backup3 -> /home/
user/myfiles/backup
-rw-r--r--. 1 user user 1048576 Jun  8 20:39 file2.txt
-rw-r--r--. 1 user user 1048576 Jun  8 20:39 file3.txt
lrwxrwxrwx. 1 user user       9 Jun  9 21:53 file4.txt ->
file1.txt
```

Standard Files and Directories Permissions

Let's explore columns one, three, and four of the output of the ls -l command. You can refer to Table 2-5.

Every file or directory belongs to a user and group. In column three, you can see the user; in column four, you can see the group owning the file. To be more precise, in the metadata of files, the user ID (UID) and group ID (GID) are stored. The command ls used files `/etc/passwd` and `/etc/group` to map UID and GID to human-readable names. If you ever see a number instead of the user and group names, it means the mapping does not exist for some reason. For example, the user was deleted, or the file system is remote, and you do not have a corresponding local user. Group and user management will be taught in a separate chapter. Now, we are more interested in permissions.

Every process also has a UID and at least one GID. To determine whether a process can get access, the operating system first compares the corresponding IDs of processes and files and then looks at the particular set of permissions. Files and directories have three permissions: for the user, the group, and others.

Here is an algorithm GNU/Linux will follow:

1. If UIDs are matching, then user permissions will apply.

2. If GID of file or directory is matching one of the processes' GID, then group permissions will apply.

3. If nothing is matched, then permissions from other sets will apply.

In the first column of "long" `ls` output symbols, from the second to fourth, is user permission; next, from five to seven, is group, and for others, from eight to ten.

Here is the explanation:

`r` - Read the file or list files within a directory.

`w` - Write to the file or change the content of the directory.

`x` - Execute the file or entries within the directory can be accessed. It means `cd` to the directory and do a "long" listing.

If you see a dash "`-`" in the position of `r`, `w`, or `x`, it means the absence of this permission.

For changing permissions, we can use the command chmod. It has three types of syntax, as you can see from the man page chmod(1):

```
chmod [OPTION]... MODE[,MODE]... FILE...
chmod [OPTION]... OCTAL-MODE FILE...
chmod [OPTION]... --reference=RFILE FILE...
```

The first method is symbolic. Let's see how MODE can be constructed. It consists of three parts: who, operator, and permissions. The first part is optional; the other two are mandatory.

The first part is about which permissions will be affected:

- u - The owner.
- g - The group owning the file or directory.
- o - Others.
- a - All. This is the same as ugo. a is assumed if you will skip the first part.

The second part is defining what you want to do with permissions:

- + - Add permissions on top of the existing.
- - - Remove permissions.
- = - Make permissions the same as you will provide in the third part.

The third part is permissions, which can be a combination of r, w, and x. They can also be s, t, and X, but we will describe what they mean later in the book.

Let's assume the initial permissions were rw-r--r--. There are several examples of chmod usage:

- `chmod uo+x file # permissions will be rwxr--r-x.`
- `chmod a=rw file # permissions will be rw-rw-rw-.`
- `chmod ug+x,o-rw # permissions will be file rwxrwx---.`

Another method for assigning permissions is octal mode or numeric mode. You can not combine it with symbolic mode. You also need to provide a single number that combines all permissions for the user, group, and others. Here's how it works:

Each permission type is assigned a specific numerical value:

- **Read (`r`)** - Two to the power of two = 4
- **Write (`w`)** - Two to the power of one = 2
- **Execute (`x`)** - Two to the power of zero =1

For each of the three categories (owner, group, others), you need to get a sum of the numerical values of the permissions you want to grant. Let's check an example in Figure 2-8.

USER	GROUP	OTHER
4 2 1	4 2 1	4 2 1
r w -	r - x	r - -
4+2 = 6	4 + 1 = 5	4

```
$ touch file
$ ls -l file
-rw-r--r--. 1 user user 0 Jun 20 15:34 file
$ chmod 654 file
$ ls -l file
-rw-r-xr--. 1 user user 0 Jun 20 15:34 file
```

Figure 2-8. *Representation of the octal (numeric) method of changing permissions*

For the user, you want to get `rw-` permissions. That is mean 4(r) + 2(w) = 6. For the group, you want `r-x`, i.e., 4(r)+1(x)=5. And for others, `r--`, i.e., 4(r). The resulting mode we need for the `chmod` command is `654`:

```
user@localhost:~$ chmod 654 file
```

The command chmod has the option -R for a recursive set of permissions.

How does the system define default permissions for files and directories? The base permissions for a directory are 777 and for a file are 666. The value set up by umask will be subtracted from the base.

You may check the current values using the command:

```
user@localhost:~$ umask
0022
```

It is the default setting, as we haven't changed it yet. Usually, the default umask value 0022 is defined in shell configuration files. For the directory, default permissions will be 777-22=755, and for the file, 666-22=644. Let's verify and try to change the umask and see the results:

```
user@localhost:~$ touch newfile
user@localhost:~$ mkdir newdir
user@localhost:~$ ls -l newfile
-rw-r--r--. 1 user user 0 Jun 30 19:25 newfile
user@localhost:~$ ls -ld newdir/
drwxr-xr-x. 2 user user 6 Jun 30 19:25 newdir/
user@localhost:~$ umask 644
user@localhost:~$ touch newfile2
user@localhost:~$ mkdir newdir2
user@localhost:~$ ls -l newfile2
-----w--w-. 1 user user 0 Jun 30 19:26 newfile2
user@localhost:~$ ls -ld newdir2/
d--x-wx-wx. 2 user user 6 Jun 30 19:26 newdir2/
```

The new umask value will be kept until you finish the current bash session.

At the end of this section, we will learn how to change ownership of files and directories with chown. This command requires root permissions:

```
user@localhost:~$ sudo chown ftp:ftp file
user@localhost:~$ touch file1; ls -l file1
-rw-r--r--. 1 user user 0 Jun 20 19:01 file1
user@localhost:~$ sudo chown ftp:ftp file1
user@localhost:~$ ls -l file1
-rw-r--r--. 1 ftp ftp 0 Jun 20 19:01 file1
```

The current owner of a file can only change its group ownership to a group that you are also a member of. For this, chgrp can be used:

```
user@localhost:~$ ls -l file
-rw-r-xr--. 1 user user 0 Jun 20 15:34 file
user@localhost:~$ chgrp wheel file
user@localhost:~$ ls -l file
-rw-r-xr--. 1 user wheel 0 Jun 20 15:34 file
```

Both chown and chgrp have the option -R for a recursive set of ownership.

Keep in mind two things: these are basic permissions, and we will explore more in the book. Second, in RHEL, another mechanism of mandate control applied by SELinux that works on top of standard permissions exists.

Text Processing

In most cases, Linux configuration files are simple text files. As a result, working with and editing text files is an essential skill for GNU/Linux system administrators. As a system administrator, you will often work from the command line, for example, by connecting via SSH. Therefore, it is necessary to know how to edit files from the command line, not just in a graphical environment.

There are powerful and widely used command-line text editors, such as Vim or Emacs, available in RHEL. We will cover Vim in the exercise section as an optional topic. However, for users who are new to the command line or prefer a less complex editor than powerful alternatives, the Nano editor is installed by default in RHEL. You can see its interface in Figure 2-9.

***Figure 2-9.** User interface of Nano command-line text editor*

Nano is designed for ease of use, operating much like a typical graphical text editor. You interact with it through keyboard shortcuts, which are listed in a help bar at the bottom of the screen for reference (^ stands for Ctrl key). To open a file, just type `nano filename` in the command line.

Next, we will examine several text-processing command-line tools. However, before that, we need to understand the concept of standard input, output, and standard error channels in GNU/Linux. In GNU/Linux and other Unix-like operating systems, standard input (`STDIN`), standard output (STDOUT), and standard error (STDERR) are fundamental communication channels that every process has access to by default.

By default, standard input is connected to your keyboard. Standard output and standard error are connected to your terminal screen.

A representation of standard channels is shown in Figure 2-10. You may notice numbers assigned to each of the channels. There is a fixed number of file descriptors for the particular process. A file descriptor is a unique number the operating system gives to a file once it is opened. You can remember one of the Unix-like systems principles from the beginning of the chapter: "Everything is a file." Standard communication channels are no exception.

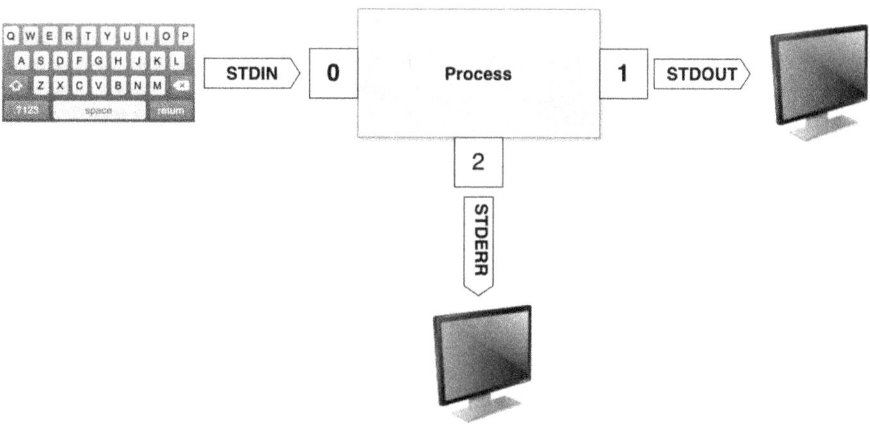

Figure 2-10. *Standard input, output, and standard error channels*

We can illustrate how STDOUT and STDERR work with an example. The following find command will search the /etc/ directory (and all its subdirectories) for a file named passwd:

```
user@localhost:~$ find /etc/ -name passwd
find: '/etc/lvm/devices': Permission denied
...
find: '/etc/pki/rsyslog': Permission denied
```

```
/etc/pam.d/passwd
find: '/etc/nftables': Permission denied
find: '/etc/sos/cleaner': Permission denied
/etc/passwd
find: '/etc/cups/ssl': Permission denied
...
```

As you can see, it found two files, `/etc/pam.d/passwd` and `/etc/passwd`. Also, you can see "`Permission denied`" error messages about directories where you do not have access as a regular user. This output combines standard output and standard error. By using the redirection operator, we can separate them. In Unix-like operating systems, a special file `/dev/null` exists. It is a "null device" file. All data you redirect to the file will be gone. For sure, we can use regular files in this example instead of `/dev/null`.

```
user@localhost:~$ find /etc/ -name passwd 2> /dev/null
/etc/pam.d/passwd
/etc/passwd
```

The operator `2>` will redirect all error messages to the "recycle bin" file, and you can have a "clean" output.

```
user@localhost:~$ find /etc/ -name passwd > /dev/null
find: '/etc/lvm/devices': Permission denied
find: '/etc/lvm/archive': Permission denied
```

The operator `>` or `1>` will redirect all output to the file, and on the terminal, you will see only errors. Some other redirection operators can be found in Table 2-6.

Table 2-6. *The redirection operators*

Operator	Description
>, 1>	Redirects STDOUT to a file. If a file exists, it will be overwritten.
>>, 1>>	Append STDOUT to a file.
2>	Redirects STDERR to a file. If a file exists, it will be overwritten.
2>>	Append STDERR to a file.
<	Redirects STDIN of a command to come from a file instead of the keyboard.
&>	Redirects STDOUT and STDERR to a file. If a file exists, it will be overwritten.
&>>	Append STDOUT and STDERR to a file.

In the same way as you redirect STDOUT from the command to a file, you can redirect STDOUT from the command to the STDIN of another command. This is named piping. Check Figure 2-11 for an example.

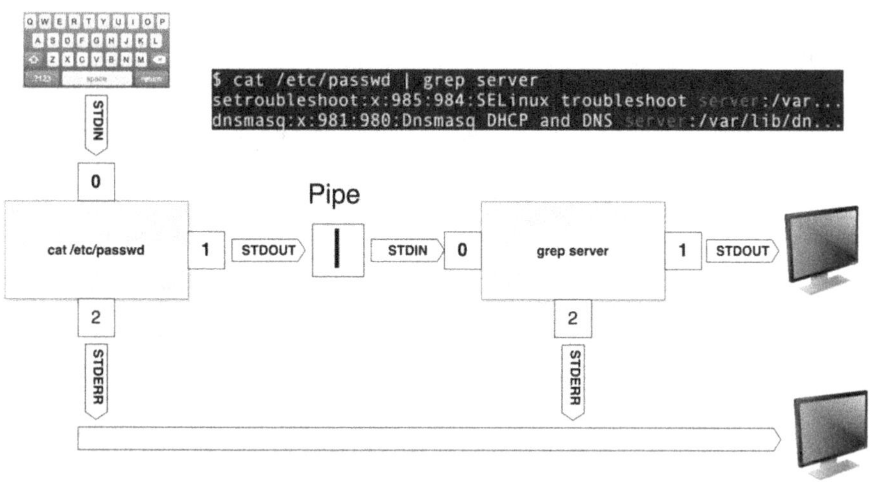

Figure 2-11. *Piping*

You can connect several tools in one pipe by using "|" as in the example. Command `cat` prints file or files to standard output. Then, you connect it by using a pipe to `grep`, which searches lines using a pattern `server` and prints lines to STDOUT.

If you need to store intermediate results in a file before sending them to the following command in the chain, you can use `tee`:

```
user@localhost:~$ cat /etc/passwd | tee results_before_grep.txt
|  grep server
setroubleshoot:x:985:984:SELinux troubleshoot server:/var...
dnsmasq:x:981:980:Dnsmasq DHCP and DNS server:/var/lib/d...
```

Several additional text processing tools can be found in Table 2-7.

Table 2-7. *Text processing tools*

Tool	Example	Description
head	head -n 3 /etc/passwd	Output the first part of the files. By default, ten lines are shown. With the -n option, you can change the number of lines.
tail	tail -n 5 /etc/passwd	Output the last part of the files. By default, ten lines are shown. With the -n option, you can change the number of lines.
cut	cut -d: -f1,3 /etc/passwd	**Extracts** sections from each line of the files. In the example, you cut the first and third columns of the file /etc/passwd and use the delimiter ":".
wc	wc /etc/passwd	Print the number of lines, words, and byte counts for each file or STDIN.
sort	sort /etc/passwd	Sort lines of text files in lexicographical ascending order.

(*continued*)

Table 2-7. (*continued*)

Tool	Example	Description
uniq	sort file I uniq	Report or omit repeated lines. Often used with sort.
diff	diff -u original_file.txt modified_file.txt > patchfile	Compare files line by line. Output can be stored in a file named patchfile.
patch	patch original_file.txt < patchfile	Apply a patchfile to an original.

Regular Expressions for Text Analysis

For more sophisticated text processing, you can use regular expressions (Regex) and the `grep` (Global Regular Expression Print) command. A regular expression is a search pattern that uses "metacharacters" to represent a portion of text.

Let's take examples. I want to search all lines starting from a or A:

```
user@localhost:~$ grep ^[aA] /usr/share/doc/vim-common/docs/
tips.txt
archive file on your closest gnu-ftp-mirror).
Also consider setting 'scrolloff' to a larger value...
```

The symbol ^ is an "anchor" that means the start of the line. And in the square brackets, the enumeration of possible characters in this place. Keep in mind, it should be one character. The symbol $ works as ^, but it means the end of the line. Instead of symbols within a bracket expression, you can put the name of a character class. In that case, you need to add `[[:` and `:]]` on the sides of the class name. In this example, you will print all lines ending with a digit:

```
user@localhost:~$ grep [[:digit:]]$ /usr/share/doc/vim-common/
docs/tips.txt
*tips.txt*      For Vim version 9.1.  Last change: 2023 Aug 10
          exit 0
     :set tw=70
...
```

Here is another example:

```
user@localhost:~$ grep ^[^a-z]y /usr/share/doc/vim-common/docs/
tips.txt
By default, help is displayed in a split window...
```

Symbol ^ before the bracket expression, as we know, means the start of the line. The next ^ symbol within a bracket expression means "not". In another world, the line should start from anything but `a,b,c...z`, and the second symbol should be `y`.

Some other examples can be found in Table 2-8. To learn more about regexp, read `regex(7)`.

Table 2-8. Regular expressions (Regex)

Pattern	Description
.	Any single character.
[abc], [a-c]	One single character from the bracket.
*	Multiplier. Zero or more previous characters. [12]* will mean nothing, or 1, 2, 12, or 1212111.
?	Multiplier. Zero or more previous characters.
+	Multiplier. One or more previous characters.
\{n\}	Multiplier. n previous characters.
\{n,\}	Multiplier. n or more previous characters.
a|b	Alternate – match either a or b.
\b	Word boundary (matches the position between a word character and a non-word character).
\B	Non-word boundary.

Useful options that you can add to grep:

- `-i` - Ignore case.
- `-v` - Display lines that do not contain the Regex provided.
- `-r` - Search recursively in files or directories.

Working with Archive Tools

In the Unix and GNU/Linux world, archiving and compressing are not the same concepts. Archiving is consolidating files and directories, along with their metadata, into a single file. Archiving does not involve size reduction algorithms. Compression is the application of such algorithms.

We can create a test directory with five files to play with. We will use a new construction, for loop:

```
user@localhost:~$ mkdir test1
user@localhost:~$ for i in {1..5}; do head /dev/urandom | head
-c 100 > "test1/file$i"; done
```

In this example, we will iterate over variable i from one to five, and the loop body is between the do and done keywords. The first head will work until ten lines (newline characters) are randomly generated, and the second head will cut the first hundred characters from the sequence. At the end, STDOUT will be written to the file:

```
user@localhost:~$ ls -l test1
total 20
-rw-r--r--. 1 user user 100 Jul  5 11:34 file1
-rw-r--r--. 1 user user 100 Jul  5 11:34 file2
-rw-r--r--. 1 user user 100 Jul  5 11:34 file3
-rw-r--r--. 1 user user 100 Jul  5 11:34 file4
-rw-r--r--. 1 user user 100 Jul  5 11:34 file5
```

Now we can create a tar archive:

```
user@localhost:~$ tar -cvf test.tar test1/
test1/
test1/file1
test1/file2
test1/file3
test1/file4
test1/file5
user@localhost:~$ ls -l test.tar
-rw-r--r--. 1 user user 10240 Jul  5 11:35 test.tar
```

Option c means create, v means verbose, and f means we want to name the archive with the provided name. At the end, we need to point tar to the files or directories we want to add.

We can also compress an archive after creation with the same command by using one of the compression types: gzip, bzip2, or xz:

```
user@localhost:~$ tar -czf test.tar.gz test1/
user@localhost:~$ tar -cjf test.tar.bz2 test1/
user@localhost:~$ tar -cJf test.tar.xz test1/
user@localhost:~$ ls -l test.tar*
-rw-r--r--. 1 user user 10240 Jul  5 11:35 test.tar
-rw-r--r--. 1 user user   931 Jul  5 11:38 test.tar.bz2
-rw-r--r--. 1 user user   775 Jul  5 11:38 test.tar.gz
-rw-r--r--. 1 user user   756 Jul  5 11:38 test.tar.xz
```

As you can see, the size of the archive is different due to the efficiency of algorithms.

To extract data, first you need to uncompress:

```
user@localhost:~$ gunzip test.tar.gz
user@localhost:~$ bunzip2 test.tar.bz2
user@localhost:~$ unxz test.tar.xz
```

Keep in mind that you cannot run all three commands one by one as in the example. If test.tar exists already, the command will fail. Additionally, you will notice that after uncompressing, the compressed file will be deleted. And now you can untar the archive:

```
user@localhost:~$ tar xvf test.tar
test1/
test1/file1
test1/file2
```

```
test1/file3
test1/file4
test1/file5
```

To list the contents of an archive without extracting it, you can use -t:

```
user@localhost:~$ tar -vtf test.tar
```

Summary

This chapter introduces the Linux command line, which is essential for efficient system interaction.

We covered accessing the command line and running commands in the Bash shell, including basic syntax and execution. We explored how to obtain help for command-line tools using man pages and the `--help` option.

Understanding the file system hierarchy (e.g., `/home`, `/etc`) was foundational for managing files and directories with commands like `ls`, `cd`, `mkdir`, `rm`, `cp`, and `mv`. We then delved into standard files and directory permissions, learning to control access with `chmod` and `chown` for security.

Text processing tools were introduced for manipulating and analyzing textual data. This was enhanced by the use of regular expressions for text analysis, enabling robust pattern matching.

Finally, we explored working with archive tools such as `tar` combined with compression utilities.

Exercises

1) Check the man page for the file `passwd` to find the name of the fifth field and why it has this name.
2) Call `info info` and read the tutorial.
3) Find in the `bash` manual page description of aliases and create an alias `lls` for `ls -lah`.
4) By using a pipe and a find tool, make a command that will display the number of files in the `/etc` directory containing "`an`" in the name.
5) Run the command vimtutor, and follow the exercises (it will take about 20 minutes).

CHAPTER 3

Bash and Shell Scripts

In this chapter, we will study how to create very simple shell scripts. The chapter will cover the following topics: conditionally executing code, using looping constructs, and processing script inputs and outputs.

Basics of the Shell Scripts

Every bash script starts with the symbols `#!` and then the path to the interpreter. This combination is often referred to as a "shebang":

```
#!/bin/bash
```

Since `/bin` is a symbolic link to `usr/bin`, you can also use

```
#!/usr/bin/bash
```

Let's create our first simple script by using `nano` or `vim`. After creation, I used the tool `nl`. `nl` prints the file but adds line numbers, which is useful when you want to refer to a particular line. And finally, we can run the script.

```
user@localhost:~$ nl hello.sh
     1	#!/bin/bash
     2	# Get the current username
```


A. Markelov, *Red Hat RHCSA 10 Study Companion*, Certification Study Companion Series,
https://doi.org/10.1007/979-8-8688-2226-1_3

```
     3    USERNAME=$(whoami)
     4    # Get the user's home directory
     5    HOME_DIR=$HOME
     6    # Get the current date and time
     7    CURRENT_DATE=$(date)
     8    echo "Hi, $USERNAME!"
     9    echo "Your home directory is: $HOME_DIR"
    10    echo "Current Date and Time: $CURRENT_DATE"
user@localhost:~$ ./hello.sh
Hi, user!
Your home directory is: /home/user
Current Date and Time: Thu Jul  5 16:15:55 CEST 2025
```

Lines 2, 4, and 6 start from #. In shell scripting, a # indicates a comment. Comments are ignored by the shell when the script is run. Lines 3, 5, and 7 perform variable assignment. Lines 3 and 7 are also examples of command substitution. The `$(command)` syntax tells the shell to execute the command inside the parentheses (`whoami` and `date` in our cases). Line 5, instead of substitution, demonstrated a special built-in shell variable `HOME`. The bash shell automatically sets the `HOME` to the absolute path of the current user's home directory. The $ before `HOME` means "the value of the variable `HOME`". Lines 8–10 print the specified text and values of our three variables using the `echo` command.

Take into account that after creating the file, you need to give `+x` execute permission. As you can see, I added "`./`" before the script name for the invocation. I asked to run the script from the CWD. You may ask why I don't need to provide a path for other commands. First, some of the commands we have already learned are embedded in the bash shell and do not have a separate executable file. Additionally, bash has a `PATH` environment variable. If an executable file is within one of the `PATH` parameters, you don't need to specify the path to it:

```
user@localhost:~$ echo $PATH
/home/user/.local/bin:/home/user/bin:/usr/local/bin:/usr/bin:/
usr/local/sbin:/usr/sbin
```

To find where the executable is stored, you can use the `which` command:

```
user@localhost:~$ which man
/usr/bin/man
user@localhost:~$ which ls
alias ls='ls --color=auto'
    /usr/bin/ls
user@localhost:~$ which hello.sh
/usr/bin/which: no hello.sh in (/home/user/.local/bin:/home/
user/bin:/usr/local/bin:/usr/bin:/usr/local/sbin:/usr/sbin)
```

As you can see from the example, `man` is stored in `/usr/bin`, `ls` is an alias, and `hello.sh` is not in any of the paths from the `PATH` variable.

`PATH` is an environment variable. Environment variables are variables that you can use in your applications or scripts, stored outside your code. Your operating systems or other programs set them, and your application can access them while it's running. To define a variable as an environment variable, you need to use the `export` keyword. `export` makes a variable available to the current shell's subprocesses like scripts.

We can demonstrate environment variables and variable behavior with this example:

```
user@localhost:~$ VAR1="local"
user@localhost:~$ export VAR2="environment"
user@localhost:~$ cat test.sh
#!/bin/bash
echo "Variable =" $VAR1
echo "Environment variable =" $VAR2
```

```
user@localhost:~$ ./test.sh
Variable =
Environment variable = environment
```

As you can see, the script has access to VAR2, but not to VAR1. To list all environment variables, you can use env or printenv:

```
user@localhost:~$ env
SHELL=/bin/bash
HISTCONTROL=ignoredups
HISTSIZE=1000
HOSTNAME=localhost
GPG_TTY=/dev/pts/0
PWD=/home/user
LOGNAME=user
XDG_SESSION_TYPE=tty
...
```

With positional parameters, you can allow your scripts to dynamically accept inputs directly from the command line when they are executed. Bash shell automatically assigns arguments you pass on the command line to special predefined variables inside your script:

```
user@localhost:~$ nl input.sh
     1	#!/bin/bash
     2	echo "Script name: $0"
     3	echo "Number of arguments: $#"
     4	echo "First argument: $1"
     5	echo "Second argument: $2"
     6	echo "All arguments:" $@
user@localhost:~$ ./input.sh one two three four
Script name: ./input.sh
Number of arguments: 4
```

```
First argument: one
Second argument: two
All arguments: one two three four
```

This script is self-explanatory. Apart from the used variables `$1` and `$2`, you can use `$3`, `$4`, and so forth.

Conditional Code Execution

First, we need to become familiar with another embedded shell variable, $?. Let's execute the following commands:

```
user@localhost:~$ cat /etc/passwd > /dev/null; echo $?
0
user@localhost:~$ cat /etc/shadow > /dev/null; echo $?
cat: /etc/shadow: Permission denied
1
```

The first command is trying to read the file `/etc/passwd`. This file contains user-related information, excluding passwords. It is generally readable by all users. Content of file, but not `STDERR`, is forwarded to `/dev/null`. We don't need the content itself for demonstration. The following command will print the exit status (or return code) of the most recently executed command. An exit status of zero conventionally means that the most recently executed command was successful, without any errors.

The second command line has cat trying to read the file `/etc/shadow`. The regular user cannot do this since the file contains password-related information. As you can see, the `cat` prints a message about a lack of permissions to `STDERR`. In this case, the return code is not zero. Any number other than zero means the command failed. There is no general convention on what non-zero return codes mean; however, some commands may have distinctions between them that are usually described in the documentation.

You, as a script developer, can also define exit codes with the `exit` command for your script:

```
user@localhost:~$ mkdir bin; cd bin
cat << EOF > exit42
#!/bin/bash
echo "The answer to life the universe and everything"
exit 42
EOF
user@localhost:~/bin$ chmod +x exit42
user@localhost:~/bin$ cd
user@localhost:~$ exit42; echo $?
The answer to life the universe and everything
42
```

First, we will create a `bin` directory in the user's home directory. The `PATH` variable has this directory by default, so you will be able to call scripts from `/home/user/bin` without adding the path. `cat << EOF` tells the cat command to read input until it encounters the literal string `EOF` on a line by itself. `> exit42` redirects all the input that `cat` reads into a new file named `exit42`. This is called a **heredoc**, and it doesn't necessarily have to be `EOF`.

Shell has a `test` command that generates `$?` value depending on a particular test. For example, we can test if a file exists. If true, `$?` will have a value of zero.

```
user@localhost:~$ test -f /home/user/bin/exit42; echo $?
0
user@localhost:~$ test -f /home/user/bin/exit43; echo $?
1
```

We can use another syntax of the `test` command, the equivalent of the first example:

```
user@localhost:~$ [[ -f /home/user/bin/exit42 ]]; echo $?
0
user@localhost:~$ [[ -f /home/user/bin/exit43 ]]; echo $?
1
```

The man page `test(1)` lists all the checks that you can perform. Here is the script with some tests. Also, this script introduces the `if-then-else` construction:

```
user@localhost:~$ nl example-test.sh
#!/bin/bash
# This script demonstrates the use of various test commands in Bash.
# Test for file non-existence
if [ ! -f /path/to/nonexistent/file ]; then
    echo "File does not exist."
fi
# Test for directory existence
if [ -d /path/to/directory ]; then
    echo "Directory exists."
else
    echo "Directory does not exist."
fi

# Test for file/directory existence and executability
if [ -x /path/to/file ]; then
    echo "File is executable."
else
    echo "File is not executable."
fi
# Test numeric comparison
```

```
if [ 100 -eq 100 ]; then
    echo "100 is equal to 100."
else
    echo "100 is not equal to 100."
fi
# Test string comparison
if [ "apple" = "äpple" ]; then
    echo "Strings are equal."
else
    echo "Strings are not equal."
fi
```

The syntax is straightforward, and no additional comments are needed. If you need to check more than one condition, you can use an `if-then-elif-else` construction:

```
user@localhost:~$ nl example-test2.sh
#!/bin/bash
MYSTRING="ccc"
echo "Checking string variable: '$MYSTRING'"
if test "$MYSTRING" = "aaa"; then
    echo "The string is 'aaa'."
elif [[ "$MYSTRING" = "bbb" ]]; then
    echo "The string is 'bbb'."
else
    echo "The string is neither 'aaa' nor 'bbb'."
fi
echo ""
user@localhost:~$ ./example-test2.sh
Checking string variable: 'ccc'
The string is neither 'aaa' nor 'bbb'.
```

Looping Constructs

Another pervasive and useful pattern in the Bash is the loop. This construct iterates commands a specified number of times or while a particular condition is met.

The most common type of loop is the `for` loop, which iterates over a sequence:

```
user@localhost:~$ cat for1.sh
#!/bin/bash
for i in "one" "two" "three"; do
    echo "  Number A: $i"
done
for i in $(seq 1 3); do
    echo "  Number B: $i"
done
user@localhost:~$ ./for1.sh
  Number A: one
  Number A: two
  Number A: three
  Number B: 1
  Number B: 2
  Number B: 3
```

In the first loop, the sequence was explicitly defined. In the second loop for sequence generation, we used the command `seq`.

Another example of a for loop that iterates over command-line arguments. For checking arguments that are provided, we can use `if-then-else`:

```
user@localhost:~$ cat for2.sh
#!/bin/bash
if [[ "$#" -eq 0 ]]; then
    echo "Provide at least one argument"
```

```
else
    for argument in "$@"; do
        echo "Argument: '$argument'"
    done
fi
user@localhost:~$ ./for2.sh
Provide at least one argument
user@localhost:~$ ./for2.sh a b c d
Argument: 'a'
Argument: 'b'
Argument: 'c'
Argument: 'd'
```

In the last example, we will process files in the current working directory and print out all with a name ending in "`.sh`":

```
user@localhost:~$ cat for3.sh
#!/bin/bash
for file in *.sh; do
    if [[ -f "$file" ]]; then # Ensure it is a regular file
        echo "  Found script file: '$file'"
    fi
done
user@localhost:~$ ./for3.sh
  Found script file: 'example-test2.sh'
  Found script file: 'example-test.sh'
  Found script file: 'for1.sh'
  Found script file: 'for2.sh'
  Found script file: 'for3.sh'
...
```

Another form of the for loop exists. It is typically used for numeric counting. It is similar to for loops in C and Java:

```
user@localhost:~$ cat for4.sh
#!/bin/bash
for (( i=0; i<10; i++ )); do
            echo "$i";
done
user@localhost:~$ ./for4.sh
0
1
...
9
```

Other types of loops exist in Bash, such as `while` or `until`, but they are outside the scope of this book.

Summary

This chapter introduces the fundamentals of creating simple Bash shell scripts. The concept of environment variables is further detailed, showing how `export` makes variables accessible to child processes and how the `env` list contains them. The chapter covers positional parameters, which allow scripts to accept dynamic input from the command line. Conditional code execution is introduced through the special variable, which holds the exit status of the last executed command. The `test` command is used for evaluating conditions (e.g., file existence, numeric/string comparisons), which leads to `if-then-else` and `if-then-elif-else` constructs for controlling script flow based on these conditions. Finally, the chapter explores looping constructs, with a focus on the `for` loop.

Exercises

1) Create a script that takes two numbers as command-line arguments and prints their sum.
2) Write a script that checks if a file provided as a command-line argument exists.
3) Create a script that creates a directory if it doesn't already exist.
4) Create a script that performs a numeric countdown from a given starting number to 1. If no argument is provided or the argument is not a positive integer, print an error message and exit.
5) Write a script that lists all executable regular files in the current directory.

CHAPTER 4

Manage Users and Groups

In this chapter, we will explore the management of local user accounts and groups. You will gain an understanding of how to create, delete, and modify user accounts, ensuring proper access control on your system. We will also cover the essential security practices of changing passwords and adjusting password aging policies. Furthermore, you'll learn to effectively create, delete, and modify local groups and manage user memberships. Finally, we'll explore methods for configuring superuser access, empowering you to perform administrative tasks safely and effectively while adhering to best security practices. Please note that we will only cover local users. We do not cover NIS, LDAP, or any other systems.

Local Authentication Information Files

Local authentication information is stored in three files, which we will explore:

```
root@localhost:~# ls -l /etc/passwd /etc/shadow /etc/group
-rw-r--r--. 1 root root  905 Jul  6 16:55 /etc/group
-rw-r--r--. 1 root root 2395 Jul  6 16:55 /etc/passwd
----------. 1 root root 1123 Jul  6 16:55 /etc/shadow
```


A. Markelov, *Red Hat RHCSA 10 Study Companion*, Certification Study Companion Series,
https://doi.org/10.1007/979-8-8688-2226-1_4

Why do we want to look at those files? We will not change them directly, but it is beneficial to understand what is behind the tools we use to update users' information.

We are already familiar with the file `/etc/passwd`. It is a text file that describes user local accounts for the system. Let's look at its content in detail:

```
user@localhost:~$ head -1 /etc/passwd
root:x:0:0:Super User:/root:/bin/bash
```

A separate line represents every local user in the system. The line consists of seven fields divided by a colon:

- `root` - User's login name.
- `x` - This is where encrypted user passwords were stored in old Unix-like operating systems. In modern systems, a placeholder is used here. Usually, it is `x`. The actual hash of the password is stored in another file, `/etc/shadow`.
- `0` - UID, unique identifier for the user. Zero is always the root user, and UIDs from 1 to 999 in RHEL are reserved for system users used by system services and daemons.
- `0` - GID, primary group ID for this user. Additional groups for the user are defined in the `/etc/group` file. As you are already aware, when a user creates a new file or directory, its group ownership is typically set to the user's primary group.
- `Super User` - "comment field". If you completed the exercise for Chapter 2, you should be aware of why it is called the GECOS field.

- `/root` – The home directory of the user. It will be assigned to the `HOME` environment variable. Also, this would be CWD right after login.
- `/bin/bash` – Default shell. This is the program to run at login. You can find `/usr/sbin/nologin` as the default login shell for system users who should not perform an interactive login session.

The second file we will review is `/etc/shadow`:

```
root@localhost:~#tail -3 /etc/shadow
dnsmasq:!:20233::::::
tcpdump:!:20233::::::
user:$y$j9T$...dk09::0:99999:7:::
```

As you see, many of the columns are empty by default, so it would be more convenient to describe them in the Table 4-1.

Table 4-1. *Description of /etc/shadow columns*

#	Example	Description
1	root	Username.
2	:yj9T$... dk09	Hashed password. If this field starts with "*" or "!", it means this account is locked. The hash includes information about the hashing algorithm. The default password hashing algorithm in RHEL 10 is yescrypt. It is indicated by y at the start of the hash. Before yescrypt in previous versions of RHEL, SHA-512 was used (6).
3	20280	Days since January 1, 1970, the password was last changed.

(continued)

Table 4-1. *(continued)*

#	Example	Description
4	0	Minimum password age, i.e., the number of days before which a password may not be changed. The number 0 means no minimum age.
5	99999	Maximum password age. A value of 99999 indicates no maximum age.
6	7	Days before the password is to expire, that user is warned during login of pending password expiration.
7		If a user doesn't log in for this number of days after their password expires, the account becomes locked. Before that, the user has the opportunity to change their password and continue using the account.
8		Days since January 1, 1970, when the account will be disabled.
9		Reserved for future use.

The third file, `/etc/group`, contains a database of groups. Groups can be used for sharing access to files and directories. As you know, the primary group of the user is stored in the `/etc/passwd`. When a user creates a new file or directory, its group ownership is set to the user's primary group with some exceptions. One of the main exceptions is the `setgid` bit. We will learn about it in another chapter.

You can also temporarily change your primary group to one of your secondary groups with the command `newgrp groupname`. The `groupname` will be your primary group until you use the `exit` command or `Ctrl-d`.

Secondary groups are stored in the /etc/group. Let's check the file itself:

```
user@localhost:~$ tail -3 /etc/group
tcpdump:x:72:
plocate:x:979:
user:x:1000:
```

The first field is the group name. The second always has the symbol `x`. In past Unix-like operating systems, passwords were stored in a group. This is not the case anymore. The third field is the `GID` number of the group. The last, fourth field is empty in the example. It can have a comma-separated list of the users. For example:

```
devops:x:1020:alice,bob,charlie
```

RHEL uses the user private group schema by default when creating a user. For a new user, a *new group* is created that has the same name as the user. This group becomes the primary group for the new user. No other users will be added to this group. This means that, by default, no one will have access to user files via group permissions.

Managing Local Users and Groups with GUI

During the exam, you can achieve the requested goals by using any tooling - graphical or command line. Graphical user interface (GUI) tools are usually less flexible and do not provide all functionalities of the command line. However, for simple, non-repetitive tasks, a GUI may be more suitable, especially if you are new to GNU/Linux.

The first tool you may look for is the GNOME Settings application. You need to find "Settings" in the application menu and then click "System" on the left-side menu. In the central part of the window, choose Users as shown in Figure 4-1. The capabilities of this utility are limited, but for creating a user and changing the password, they are sufficient.

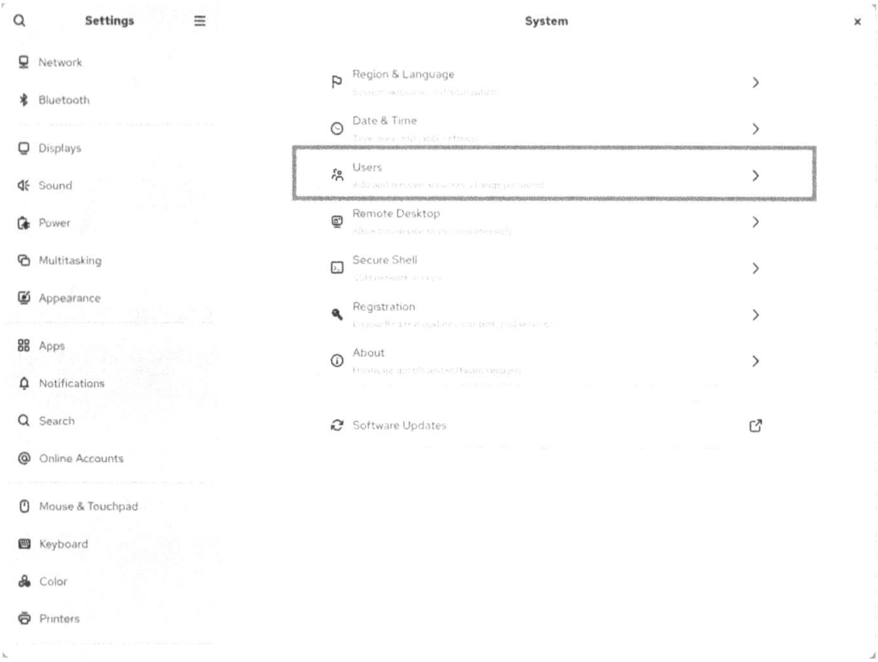

***Figure 4-1.** Users management in the GNOME Settings application*

The second graphical tool is Cockpit, a browser-based administration tool with which you're already familiar. It is more advanced than the Gnome Settings tool.

Connect to the console and select "Accounts" from the menu. You will see the interface as in Figure 4-2. By clicking the three dots at the user's line, you can edit the user, kick them out of the system if they are logged in, and lock or delete the account.

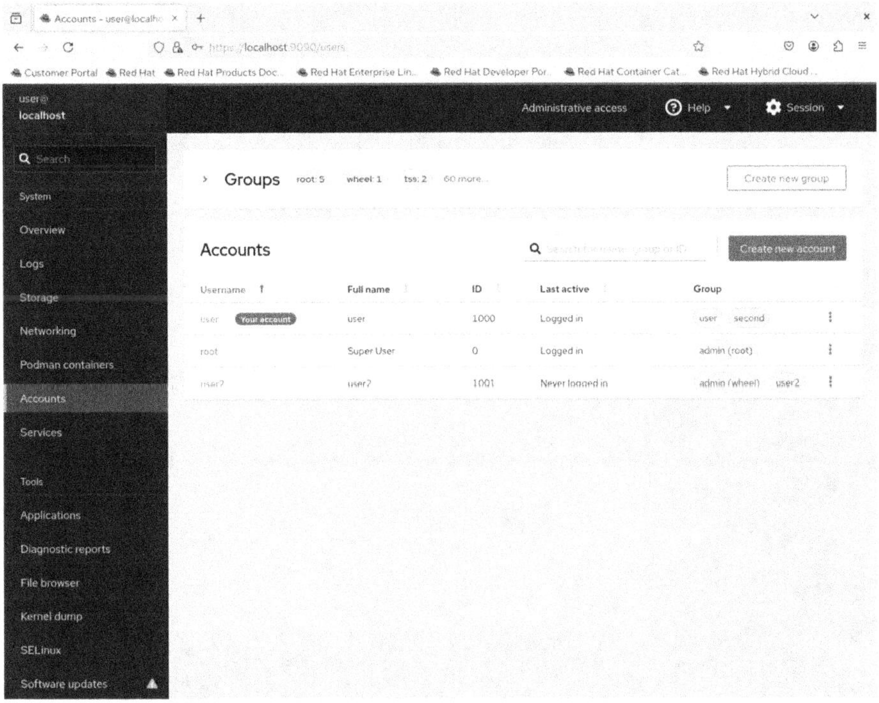

***Figure 4-2.** Users' view in the Cockpit tool*

By clicking the "Create new account" button, you will see a dialog window, as represented in Figure 4-3. As you can see, you can enter the main properties of the user, such as name, GECOS field (full name), UID, home directory, and default shell.

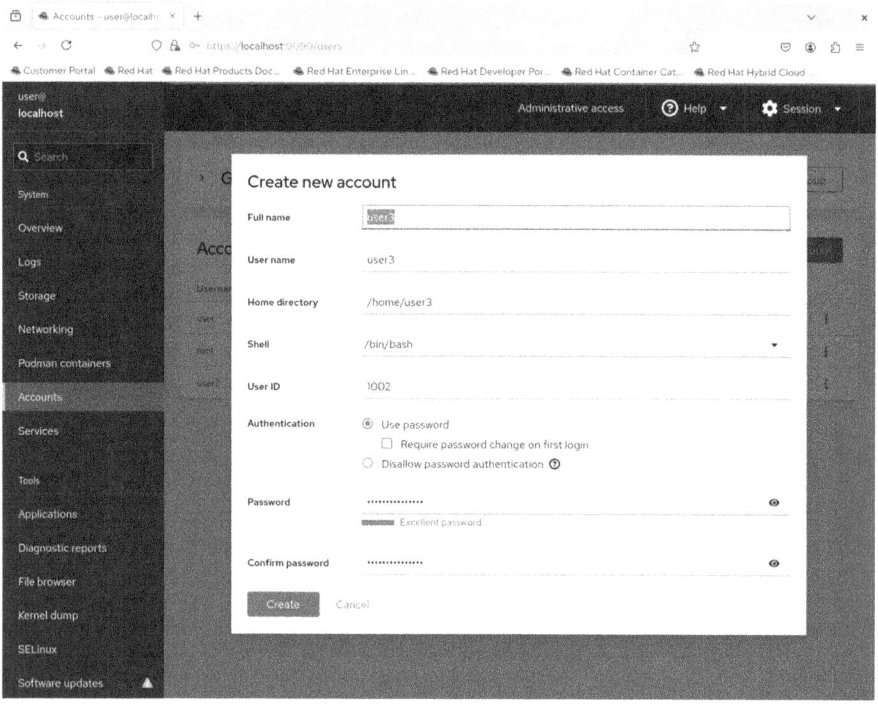

Figure 4-3. *New user creation*

If you click "Groups", you will get a list similar to accounts but related to groups. You can create a new group and rename or delete an existing non-system group with a GUID >= 1000. You cannot add new members to the group here. Instead, you need to edit particular user properties and add a group in the user's settings.

The group's view in the Cockpit tool is shown in Figure 4-4.

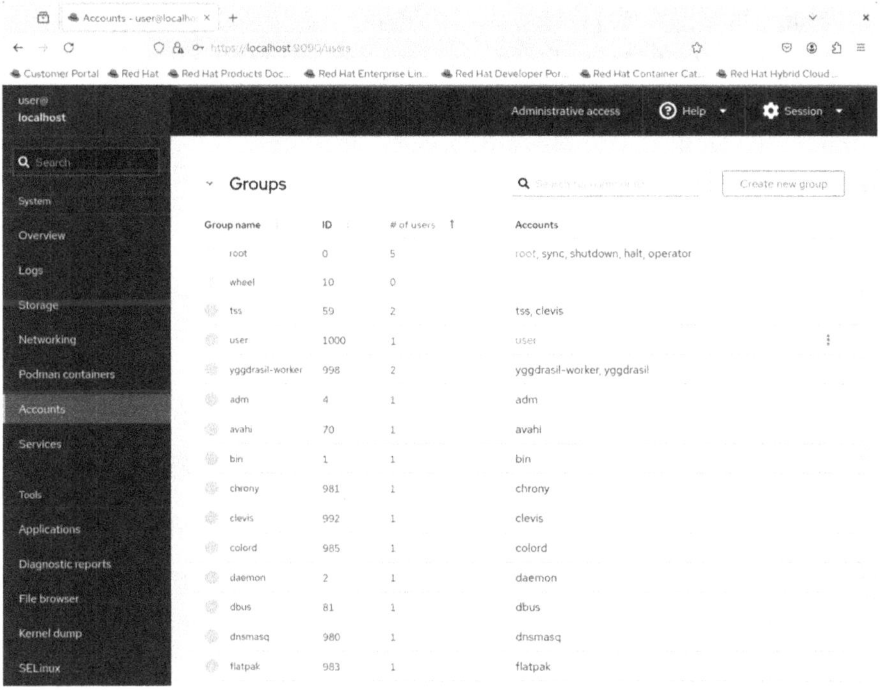

Figure 4-4. The group's view in the Cockpit tool

Managing Local Users and Groups with CLI

We will now continue to work with the command line. The `useradd` command allows you to create a new user. Modifying users and groups requires administrative privileges, so we must use the `su` or `sudo` commands familiar from Chapter 2.

By using the next command, I will create a user named `alice` with a comment field `Alice`, `UID` 2000, with a group with the same name and `GID`, home directory `/home/alicehome`, an expiration date of the account of Jan 31, 2027, secondary groups `ftp` and `user`, and a default shell `/bin/zsh`.

```
root@localhost:~# useradd -c Alice -u 2000 -U -d /home/
alicehome -e 2027-01-31 -G ftp,user -m -s /bin/zsh alice
```

```
root@localhost:~# tail -1 /etc/passwd
alice:x:2000:2000:Alice:/home/alicehome:/bin/zsh
root@localhost:~# tail -1 /etc/shadow
alice:!:20282:0:99999:7::20848:
root@localhost:~# grep alice /etc/group
ftp:x:50:alice
user:x:1000:alice
alice:x:2000:
root@localhost:~# ls -ld /home/alicehome/
drwx------. 3 alice alice 109 Jul 13 17:20 /home/alicehome/
```

Tip The previous command will warn an error if `zsh` is not installed. You may replace the shell with `/bin/bash` or install the `zsh` package.

To see all `useradd` options, check `useradd(8)`.

You can run a command with default options like this:

```
root@localhost:~# useradd bob
```

If you check the content of the freshly created home directory, you can find that it has some files already:

```
root@localhost:~# ls -la /home/bob
total 20
drwx------. 3 bob  bob  109 Jul 13 17:53 .
drwxr-xr-x. 7 root root  72 Jul 13 17:53 ..
-rw-r--r--. 1 bob  bob   18 Oct 29  2024 .bash_logout
-rw-r--r--. 1 bob  bob  144 Oct 29  2024 .bash_profile
-rw-r--r--. 1 bob  bob  522 Oct 29  2024 .bashrc
...
```

The command useradd copies files and directories from /etc/skel/ after creating a home directory.

As the root user, you can set up a password for any user with the passwd command and the username. As a regular user, you can change only your password:

```
root@localhost:~# passwd alice
New password: 123
BAD PASSWORD: The password is shorter than 8 characters
Retype new password: 123
passwd: password updated successfully
```

As a superuser, you can bypass password complexity rules, but this is not recommended. You should not do this in a production environment.

For changing an existing user, we have the usermod command. It is similar to useradd from the options perspective:

```
root@localhost:~# usermod -c 'Alice in Wonderland' -g user -aG
sshd -d /tmp -s /bin/bash alice
```

The only new option here is -a together with -G. This means adding a new secondary group to the existing list. Without option -a, secondary groups will be replaced. You can find selected usermod options in Table 4-2.

Table 4-2. *Command usermod options*

Option	Shortcut description
-a	Add the user to the supplementary groups when used with the -G option.
-G	Change secondary groups.
-c	Update the comment.
-d	Update the home directory.
-e	Expire date in the format YYYY-MM-DD.
-f	Grace period before the account becomes inactive. Value -1 will clear it.
-g	GID of primary group.
-L	Lock an account (add "!" in front of the encrypted password).
-U	Unlock an account.
-l	New login name.
-s	Change shell to provided.
-m	Move the home directory to the new location. Must be used with the -d option.

To delete a user, use the `userdel` command. In this example, Bob will be removed, but the home directory will be preserved. User Alice will be deleted with his home directory:

```
root@localhost:~# userdel -r alice
root@localhost:~# userdel bob
```

If you check the directory of the deleted user, you will see UID and GID instead of names:

```
root@localhost:~# ls -ld /home/bob
drwx------. 3 1003 1003 109 Jul 14 13:52 /home/bob
```

By default, the useradd command assigns new users the first free UID greater than or equal to 1000. If, in our case, 1000, 1001, and 1002 are busy, then the following useradd command will create a new user, let's say Victor, with a UID of 1003. And "old" Bob's files will belong to Victor. Be aware of this potential security issue.

Two more commands we need to learn before the end of this section: groupadd and groupdel. The first command can create a new group. With option -g, you can also specify a GUID:

```
root@localhost:~# groupadd -g 30000 grpa
root@localhost:~# tail -1 /etc/group
grpa:x:30000:
```

The command groupdel will delete the group:

```
root@localhost:~# groupdel grpa
```

Password Aging for Local User Accounts

Another command we need to know for an exam is chage. It can be used to change password aging parameters, which are stored in /etc/shadow. If you want to list current settings for a user, you can use the -l option as shown:

```
root@localhost:~# chage -l user
Last password change                                    : never
Password expires                                        : never
Password inactive                                       : never
Account expires                                         : never
Minimum number of days between password change          : 0
Maximum number of days between password change          : 99999
Number of days of warning before password expires: 7
```

A regular user can also see parameters, but only their own. We can, for example, change the maximum and minimum number of days between password changes:

```
root@localhost:~# chage -M 30 -m 2 user
root@localhost:~# chage -l user
Last password change                               : never
Password expires                                   : never
Password inactive                                  : never
Account expires                                    : never
Minimum number of days between password change     : 2
Maximum number of days between password change     : 30
Number of days of warning before password expires: 7
```

Other useful options are shown in Table 4-3.

Table 4-3. *Command chage options*

Option	Shortcut description
-m <num>	Minimum number of days between password changes.
-M <num>	Maximum number of days between password changes. Can be -1 to remove.
-d YYYY-MM-DD	Sets the last change date for a password. You can set it to 0 to force the user to change the password on the next login.
-E YYYY-MM-DD	Sets the expiration date for an account. On this day, the account will no longer be accessible.
-I <num> (uppercase i)	Set the number of days of inactivity after a password has expired before the account is locked. -1 will remove the inactivity restriction.
-W <num>	Set the number of days of warning before a password change is required.
-l	List current settings for a user.

Configure Superuser Access

From Chapter 2, we are already familiar with the commands `id` and `whoami`, which display your identity information, and the commands `sudo` and `su`, which can be used to obtain root permissions.

If you follow the installation instructions in Appendix A, your first created user will have settings that permit the use of `sudo`. The corresponding screen of the installer is shown in Figure 4-5.

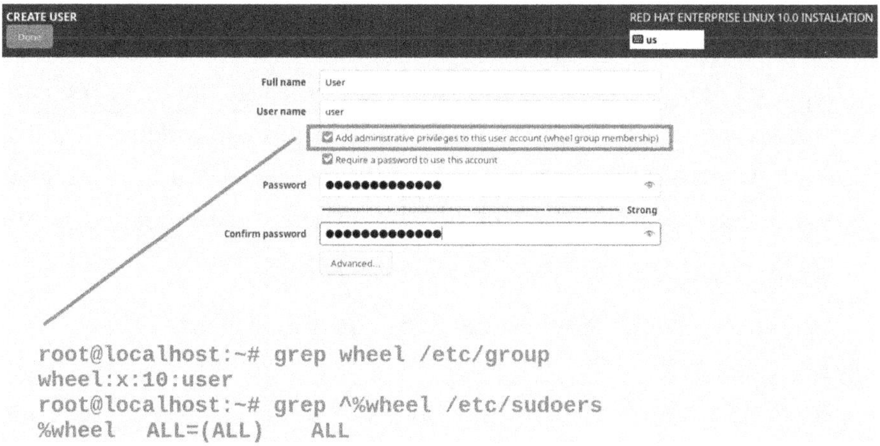

Figure 4-5. *The group's view in the Cockpit tool*

But how to tweak these settings and add more users or groups? It can be done by editing the `/etc/sudoers` file. The recommended way is by using the `visudo` command. This command prevents multiple administrators from editing the file simultaneously. Another `visudo's` value is automatic parsing of the `sudoers` file after editing and checking for syntax errors.

The `/etc/sudoers` file contains numerous examples in the comments, and you will likely not need any additional documentation during the exam beyond the file itself. Let's open the default file and look at the examples together.

Lines from 9 to 13 have examples of host aliases. They are needed only if one file is used for several servers. This is not the case for the exam. We have to solve tasks for one or many single servers without central management.

```
 9  ## Host Aliases
10  ## Groups of machines. You may prefer to use hostnames
(perhaps using
11  ## wildcards for entire domains) or IP addresses instead.
12  # Host_Alias     FILESERVERS = fs1, fs2
13  # Host_Alias     MAILSERVERS = smtp, smtp2
```

Users' aliases (lines 14–18) also have debatable functionality. You can group users with aliases at the sudoers file level, but you will likely use operating system groups. By syntax, you will use usernames as is, i.e., alice, bob, etc. Names of groups you will distinguish with the symbol of percent.

```
14  ## User Aliases
15  ## These aren't often necessary, as you can use
regular groups
16  ## (ie, from files, LDAP, NIS, etc) in this file - just use
%groupname
17  ## rather than USERALIAS
18  # User_Alias ADMINS = jsmith, mikem
```

Command aliases, as you can imagine, can group several tools into one word:

```
19  ## Command Aliases
20  ## These are groups of related commands...
21  ## Networking
22  # Cmnd_Alias NETWORKING = /sbin/route, /sbin/ifconfig...
23  ## Installation and management of software
24  # Cmnd_Alias SOFTWARE = /bin/rpm, /usr/bin/up2date, /usr/
bin/yum...
```

Starting from line 70, you will get several examples of granting superuser access:

```
70  ## Next comes the main part: which users can run what software on
71  ## which machines (the sudoers file can be shared between multiple
72  ## systems).
73  ## Syntax:
74  ##
75  ##      user    MACHINE=COMMANDS
76  ##
77  ## The COMMANDS section may have other options added to it.
78  ##
79  ## Allow root to run any commands anywhere
80  root    ALL=(ALL)       ALL
```

The syntax for granting privileges is one line that consists of three parts: who will get access, on what machine, and what commands. Line 80 is a very common entry that can be found in the /etc/sudoers file in many Unix-like operating systems:

- `root` – This is the user field. It specifies that this rule applies to the root user. If the field starts with %, it means group instead of user.
- `ALL` – This is the machine field. This means the rule applies to all hosts. In our case, it applies only to the server where we are looking into this file.

- `(ALL)` – This is the "run as user" and "run as group field". The first ALL inside the parentheses specifies that the root user can run commands as all possible users. If a "run as group" were stated, it would be separated by a colon, e.g., `(ALL:ALL)`.
- `ALL` – This is the command field. It means the root user can run ALL commands.

Another good example you can find on line 87:

```
87  # %wheel          ALL=(ALL)         NOPASSWD: ALL
```

The `NOPASSWD` option means that members of the `wheel` group will not be prompted for a password when executing commands. By the way, do not confuse what password is required in the `sudo` command. It is your password, not the root password or any others. In contrast, the `su` command is asked to enter the password of the target user.

The last line of the default file informed us that the sudo command includes the contents of the `/etc/sudoers.d/` directory. Rules in `/etc/sudoers.d/` follow the same syntax as `in /etc/sudoers` file.

Summary

This chapter focuses on local user and group management within a GNU/Linux system. We have learned three critical local authentication files:

- `/etc/passwd` – Stores user account information
- `/etc/shadow` – Stores the hashed passwords and password aging parameters
- `/etc/group` – Manages local groups

We have covered the methods for managing users and groups with GUI and CLI.

Also, we have learned how to manage password aging policies using the `chage` command.

The chapter concludes by mentioning the configuration of superuser access for regular users and `/etc/sudoers` file syntax.

Exercises

1) Create a new `devusers` group. Create new users named `devuser1`, `devuser2`, and `devuser3`, and add them to the `devusers` group. Add `devuser1` to the `wheel` group.

2) Modify the `devuser3` account. Change the comment field to "`Senior Developer - devuser3`", add him to an existing secondary group named `sshd`, and change their default shell to `/usr/sbin/nologin`. Ensure that existing secondary groups are preserved.

3) Lock the `devuser2` account. Verify the change by checking the entry in `/etc/shadow`.

4) Delete the `devuser2` account, ensuring the home directory is also deleted. Verify that the entry is no longer in `/etc/passwd`.

5) For `devuser1`, set the minimum number of days between password changes to 8 and the maximum number of days to 40. Set the warning period before devuser1's password expires to 14 days. Force devuser1 to change their password on the next login. Set the devuser1's account to expire on December 31, 2028.

6) Add `devuser2` back. Create a new file `/etc/sudoers.d/devs` using `visudo` with option `-f`. In this new file, add a rule that allows the user `devuser2` to run all commands as `root` without needing a password. Add a rule that allows the group `devusers` to run all commands defined by alias `SERVICES` from `/etc/sudoers` as root that require a password. Will `devuser2` be required to use a password for `/usr/bin/systemctl start`?

CHAPTER 5

Local Storage Configuration

To effectively use storage devices in an operating system, you must first create partitions. Partitions serve as logical divisions on a physical disk, allowing you to organize data, use different file systems, and meet specific security or performance needs. Understanding the difference between MBR and GPT is crucial for a system administrator, as is knowing how to manage them. This chapter will guide you through the essentials of disk partitioning, block device naming conventions, and the command-line tools used in RHEL to manage these layouts. We will also explore the powerful capabilities of Logical Volume Management (LVM), an abstraction layer that provides enhanced flexibility and control over your storage.

Working with Partitions on MBR and GPT Disks

To use hard drives (HDDs), solid-state disks (SSDs), or other block devices, most operating systems and applications require partitions on these devices. In general, it is possible to have only one partition, but using several can be beneficial for various reasons, such as distinguishing between different types of data, file systems, or meeting different security or performance requirements.

A. Markelov, *Red Hat RHCSA 10 Study Companion*, Certification Study Companion Series,
https://doi.org/10.1007/979-8-8688-2226-1_5

RHEL can use two partition schemes for devices:

- The MBR (Master Boot Record) was first introduced in 1983 with IBM PC DOS 2.0. Initially, it was able to support only four primary partitions. With DOS 3.0, it is possible to have one extended partition instead of one primary partition, which serves as a container for logical partitions. Currently, you can have up to 56 logical partitions. Each partition has its type. If you see types of MBR partitions in tools like `fdisk`, you can find many types related to discontinued operating systems, such as CP/M, OS/2, or Novell NetWare.
- GPT (GUID Partition Table) is a modern partition layout scheme. It is part of the Unified Extensible Firmware Interface (UEFI) standard. GPT offers several benefits compared to MBR, including a larger partition size, more partitions, and a backup copy of the partition table. For modern computers with UEFI instead of BIOS, in many cases, GPT is the only viable method for installing and booting an operating system.

To learn how to name partitions, we must first understand the naming conventions for block devices. In Table 5-1, you can find some of the kernel names for commonly used devices. In Figure 5-1, you can find examples of how MBR partitions and GPT partitions can look on the second (sdb) disk that uses the SCSI driver.

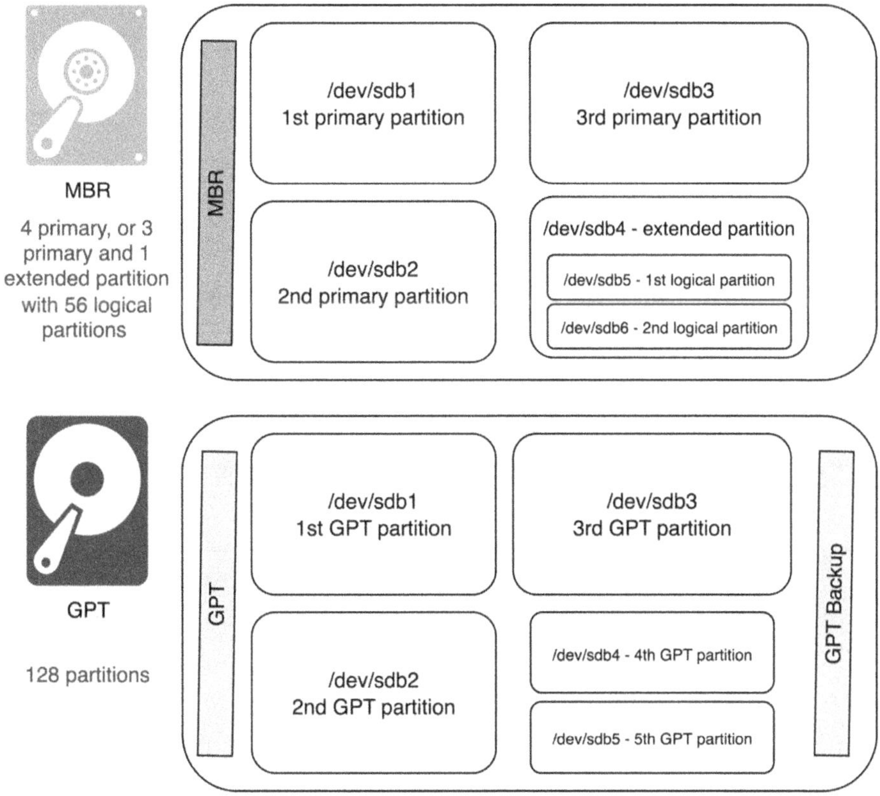

Figure 5-1. *Comparison of MBR and GPT*

Table 5-1. Disk device types

Device	Description
/dev/nvme*	Non-Volatile Memory Express physical disks.
/dev/hd*	The hard disk used ATA (Advanced Technology Attachment)/IDE. It is a legacy nowadays.
/dev/sd*	The hard disk used SCSI. However, over time, it became the generic naming scheme for almost all block devices that are not legacy ATA (IDE) drives. It can be a SCSI or SATA drive, a USB stick, an SD card, a RAID array, or a disk on the virtual machine as well.
/dev/vd*	VirtIO (Virtual Input Output). Virtual disks presented to a Linux guest using Virtio drivers.

In Figure 5-1, you can see two examples of a partition layout of a SCSI-attached disk: MBR and GPT. The disk is named `/dev/sdb`, so it is the second disk. The first disk is `sda`, the second is `sdb`, the third is `sdc`, and so on. MBR has three primary and one extended partition. An extended partition cannot be used for data storage directly – it is a container for logical partitions. As a result, you have five usable partitions where you can create, for example, one of the supported file systems: `/dev/sdb{1,2,3}` and `/dev/sdb{5,6}`. GPT partition has no concept of logical partitions, so you can create partitions as shown partitions `/dev/sdb{1,2,3,4,5}`.

You can certainly list, create, and delete partitions, as well as create file systems and logical volumes, using the Cockpit GUI. File systems and logical volumes will be studied later, but for now, you can refer to Figures 5-2 and 5-3, which include interface screenshots.

Figure 5-2 shows the storage tab of the Cockpit web user interface on a BIOS virtual machine with the default layout. And Figure 5-2 shows the storage tab on the UEFI virtual machine. We will cover the difference between BIOS and UEFI when discussing the boot process. Still, you can see that even the default layout can vary depending on hardware or other circumstances.

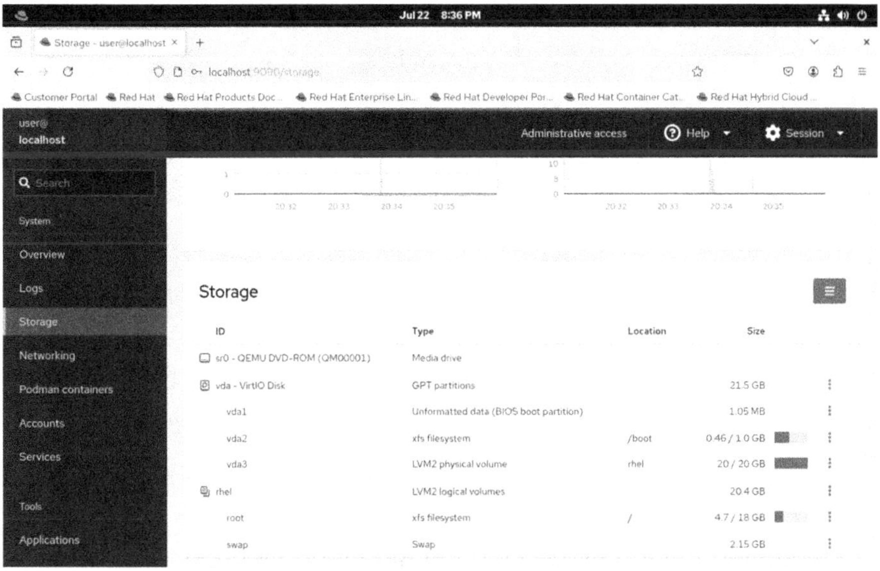

Figure 5-2. *Storage tab of the Cockpit web user interface on the virtual machine with BIOS*

There are two commonly used CLI tools to work with partitions in RHEL 10: `fdisk` and `parted`. The `fdisk` utility is part of the `util-linux` package.

This package is a base component of nearly all GNU/Linux distributions. It's a necessary collection of low-level system utilities that are crucial for a Linux system to function correctly. The `parted` tool is part of the GNU (GNU's Not Unix) project. It is a separate package, but the tool is more advanced than `fdisk`. Both `fdisk` and `parted` require root privileges, and you should avoid making partition changes on mounted partitions. Let's start looking at fdisk first.

Let's assume we have an extra disk in the VM. You can view all partitions on all disks by running fdisk with the -l option:

```
root@localhost:~# fdisk -l
Disk /dev/vda: 20 GiB, 21474836480 bytes, 41943040 sectors
Units: sectors of 1 * 512 = 512 bytes
Sector size (logical/physical): 512 bytes / 512 bytes
I/O size (minimum/optimal): 512 bytes / 512 bytes
Disklabel type: gpt
Disk identifier: 823D87A6-7859-4AB5-95D9-46525846DABD

Device       Start      End  Sectors Size Type
/dev/vda1     2048     4095     2048   1M BIOS boot
/dev/vda2     4096  2101247  2097152   1G Linux extended boot
/dev/vda3  2101248 41940991 39839744  19G Linux LVM

Disk /dev/sda: 20 GiB, 21474836480 bytes, 41943040 sectors
Disk model: QEMU HARDDISK
Units: sectors of 1 * 512 = 512 bytes
Sector size (logical/physical): 512 bytes / 512 bytes
I/O size (minimum/optimal): 512 bytes / 512 bytes
...
```

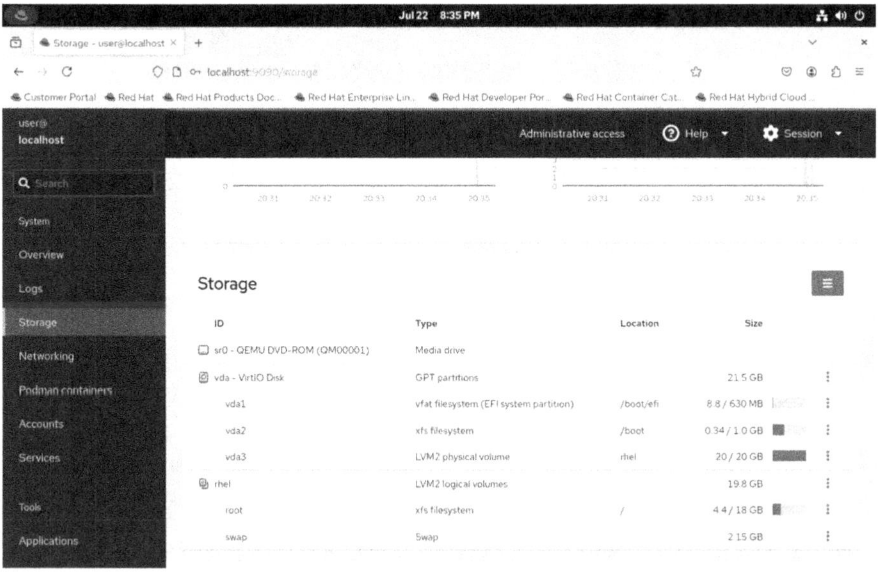

Figure 5-3. *Storage tab of the Cockpit web user interface on the virtual machine with UEFI*

We can see in the output that there are two disks: `/dev/vda` and `/dev/sda`. Both disks were 20 GiB. Both disks use 512-byte sectors. Logical sector size is the size of blocks that the operating system uses to address data on the disk. Physical sector size is the actual smallest unit of data that the disk hardware can handle in a single operation.

The disk `/dev/sda` has no partitions, but `/dev/vda` has three partitions. It is the same virtual machine with BIOS as in Figure 5-2.

`/dev/vda1` is a small partition required for systems that boot using a traditional BIOS but have a GPT-partitioned disk. `/dev/vda2` is a partition that will be mounted as /boot. `/dev/vda2` is a partition designated as "`Linux LVM`" (Logical Volume Manager) physical volume. Actual file systems are not directly on this partition; this is a layer of storage virtualization we will study later in this chapter. In the output, you will see `/dev/mapper/rhel-root` and `/dev/mapper/rhel-swap`. This is also another view on LVM volumes; we will skip this for now.

From the output, you can see that the `Disklabel type: gpt` for `/dev/vda`, but there is no information for `/dev/sda`. This means there is no partition table on `/dev/sda`.

The `fdisk` tool is designed as an interactive, dialog-driven utility. To start working with a particular block device, you need to provide its name:

```
root@localhost:~# fdisk /dev/sda

Welcome to fdisk (util-linux 2.40.2).
Changes will remain in memory only, until you decide to
write them.
Be careful before using the write command.

Device does not contain a recognized partition table.
Created a new DOS (MBR) disklabel with disk identifier
0xdebf441e.

Command (m for help):
```

Notice two statements `fdisk` provided before it shows its prompt. First, it is stated that until you save your changes, no changes will be made to the disk. It is always safe to press Ctrl+C or q and exit without any changes. To save changes, use the "w" command and press Enter. The second statement is that no partition table exists on the disk. By default, `fdisk` will propose an MBR layout. Again, the partition table was created in memory, but nothing had been written to the disk yet. As you can see in the prompt, you can use the command m to list commands supported by fdisk. Enter "m" and look for GPT partition table. We do not want to use MBR. You will find the "g" command:

```
Command (m for help): g
Created a new GPT disklabel (GUID: DD990F54-1B64-4690-
AA28-4EFFF42A3592).
```

Now we can create a couple of partitions:

```
Command (m for help): n
Partition number (1-128, default 1):
First sector (2048-41943006, default 2048):
Last sector, +/-sectors or +/-size{K,M,G,T,P} (2048-41943006,
default 41940991): +2G

Created a new partition 1 of type 'Linux filesystem' and of
size 2 GiB.

Command (m for help): n
Partition number (2-128, default 2):
First sector (4196352-41943006, default 4196352):
Last sector, +/-sectors or +/-size{K,M,G,T,P}
(4196352-41943006, default 41940991): +500M

Created a new partition 2 of type 'Linux filesystem' and of
size 500 MiB.
```

Creation of a partition requires three parameters: the number of partitions, the first sector of the partition, and the last sector. For the first two parameters, you can keep the default and press Enter. Then, `fdisk` proposes the first available number of partitions and the first free sector. For the last sector, it is easier to provide the size of the partition as I did. In the first example, I created a 2 GB partition, and in the second, a 500 MB partition.

We can verify results by printing the partition table:

```
Command (m for help): p
Disk /dev/sda: 20 GiB, 21474836480 bytes, 41943040 sectors
Disk model: QEMU HARDDISK
Units: sectors of 1 * 512 = 512 bytes
Sector size (logical/physical): 512 bytes / 512 bytes
I/O size (minimum/optimal): 512 bytes / 512 bytes
```

```
Disklabel type: gpt
Disk identifier: 0C8849FC-950C-414E-ACC1-B08CAF38A1FC

Device         Start     End Sectors  Size Type
/dev/sda1       2048 4196351 4194304    2G Linux filesystem
/dev/sda2    4196352 5220351 1024000  500M Linux filesystem
```

We can change the type of partition with the "t" command. Utility asked you alias or the type number. To list types or common aliases, you can enter L:

```
Command (m for help): t
Partition number (1,2, default 2): 1
Partition type or alias (type L to list all): L
  1 EFI System                       C12A7328-F81F-11D2-
                                     BA4B-00A0C93EC93B
  2 MBR partition scheme             024DEE41-33E7-11D3-9D69-
                                     0008C781F39F
  3 Intel Fast Flash                 D3BFE2DE-3DAF-11DF-BA40-
                                     E3A556D89593
  4 BIOS boot                        21686148-6449-6E6F-744E-
                                     656564454649
  ...
218 DragonFlyBSD HAMMER2             5CBB9AD1-862D-11DC-
                                     A94D-01301BB8A9F5
219 U-Boot environment               3DE21764-95BD-54BD-
                                     A5C3-4ABE786F38A8

Aliases:
   linux          - 0FC63DAF-8483-4772-8E79-3D69D8477DE4
   swap           - 0657FD6D-A4AB-43C4-84E5-0933C84B4F4F
   home           - 933AC7E1-2EB4-4F13-B844-0E14E2AEF915
   uefi           - C12A7328-F81F-11D2-BA4B-00A0C93EC93B
```

```
   raid           - A19D880F-05FC-4D3B-A006-743F0F84911E
   lvm            - E6D6D379-F507-44C2-A23C-238F2A3DF928
   xbootldr       - BC13C2FF-59E6-4262-A352-B275FD6F7172
```

Let's change type to LVM:

```
Partition type or alias (type L to list all): lvm

Changed type of partition 'Linux filesystem' to 'Linux LVM'.

Command (m for help): p
Disk /dev/sda: 20 GiB, 21474836480 bytes, 41943040 sectors
Disk model: QEMU HARDDISK
Units: sectors of 1 * 512 = 512 bytes
Sector size (logical/physical): 512 bytes / 512 bytes
I/O size (minimum/optimal): 512 bytes / 512 bytes
Disklabel type: gpt
Disk identifier: 0C8849FC-950C-414E-ACC1-B08CAF38A1FC

Device       Start     End Sectors  Size Type
/dev/sda1     2048 4196351 4194304    2G Linux LVM
/dev/sda2  4196352 5220351 1024000  500M Linux filesystem
```

At the end, we will delete the second partition and write data on the disk:

```
Command (m for help): d
Partition number (1,2, default 2): 2

Partition 2 has been deleted.

Command (m for help): p
Disk /dev/sda: 20 GiB, 21474836480 bytes, 41943040 sectors
Disk model: QEMU HARDDISK
Units: sectors of 1 * 512 = 512 bytes
Sector size (logical/physical): 512 bytes / 512 bytes
```

```
I/O size (minimum/optimal): 512 bytes / 512 bytes
Disklabel type: gpt
Disk identifier: 0C8849FC-950C-414E-ACC1-B08CAF38A1FC

Device      Start     End Sectors Size Type
/dev/sda1    2048 4196351 4194304   2G Linux LVM

Command (m for help): w
The partition table has been altered.
Calling ioctl() to re-read partition table.
Syncing disks.
```

The parted tool has interactive and non-interactive modes, with the latter mostly used for scripting. Entering interactive mode is the same as in `fdisk`: you need to provide the name of the disk. Then you can enter commands, like `print`, in the example:

```
root@localhost:~# parted /dev/sda
GNU Parted 3.6
Using /dev/sda
Welcome to GNU Parted! Type 'help' to view a list of commands.
(parted) print
Model: ATA QEMU HARDDISK (scsi)
Disk /dev/sda: 21.5GB
Sector size (logical/physical): 512B/512B
Partition Table: gpt
Disk Flags:

Number  Start   End     Size    File system  Name  Flags
 1      1049kB  2149MB  2147MB                     lvm

(parted)
```

Selected parted commands you can find in Table 5-2.

Table 5-2. *Selected parted commands*

Device	Description
mklabel gpt	Set the partitioning scheme GPT for the disk.
mkpart primary ext4 0% 10GB mkpart primary xfs 10GB 11GB	Create two new partitions. The first partition type is ext4, starting from 0%, i.e., the starting sector of the disk, and with a size of 10 GB. The second is type xfs, beginning at 10G (where the first ended) and ending at 11Gb, i.e., the size is 1Gb.
rm 2	Delete the second partition from the disk.
Quit	Quit parted.

Working with Logical Volume Management

Logical Volume Manager (LVM) is an implementation of an abstraction level of virtual volumes on top of physical volumes. It provides the system administrator with more flexibility, such as resizing volumes without disrupting services, taking snapshots, aggregating multiple disks, performing online data migration, striping, and mirroring.

LVM is a set of user-space tools that uses the Device Mapper (DM) to implement its functionality. The Device Mapper is a kernel driver that provides a framework for mapping physical block devices to virtual block devices in a generic manner.

As shown in Figure 5-4, LVM from the user's perspective consists of three main layers:

- **PVs (physical volumes)** - These are physical devices segmented into physical extents for future use as building blocks. As PV, you can use almost any block device, including a whole device, a single partition from a device, a RAID array, a loop device, or any other DM-backed volume.

- **VGs (volume groups)** – It is a pool of joint space from PVs that were built into this VG. One PV can belong only to one VG. VG can consist of logical volumes and unused space.
- **LVs (logical volumes)** – These are what applications and users consume. LV can be formatted and used to store files, much like a partition on a physical device. LVs consist of logical extents that map to physical extents.

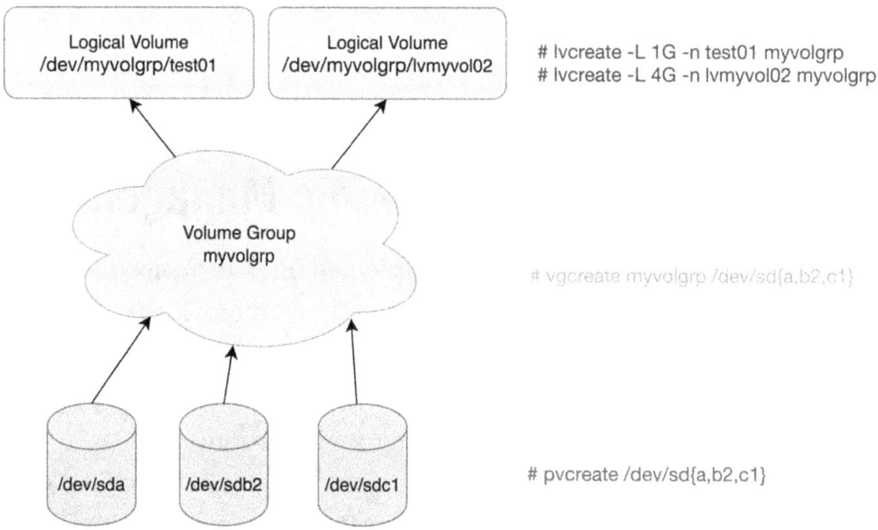

Figure 5-4. *Logical volume manager*

Figure 5-4 also illustrates the commands used at each stage of building logical volumes from a physical device. Let's try them, assuming you have a device with three Linux LVM partitions. If you don't have partitions, it is a `parted` command for a new empty device `/dev/sda`:

```
root@localhost:~# parted -s /dev/sda mklabel gpt \
mkpart primary 0% 30% set 1 lvm on \
mkpart primary 30% 60% set 2 lvm on \
mkpart primary 60% 100% set 3 lvm on
```

First, let's check the existing LVM setup by listing logical volumes, volume groups, and physical volumes:

```
root@localhost:~# lvdisplay
  --- Logical volume ---
  LV Path                /dev/rhel/swap
  LV Name                swap
  VG Name                rhel
  LV UUID                dVMTYu-957d-sj2N-JCcW-Dc7h-o2ft-XnLcCM
  LV Write Access        read/write
  LV Creation host, time localhost.localdomain, 2025-07-20
  14:18:50 +0200
  LV Status              available
  # open                 1
  LV Size                2.00 GiB
  Current LE             512
  Segments               1
  Allocation             inherit
  Read ahead sectors     auto
  - currently set to     256
  Block device           253:1

  --- Logical volume ---
  LV Path                /dev/rhel/root
  LV Name                root
  VG Name                rhel
  LV UUID                OJVOIU-9533-fCfd-ywOG-YhZ4-ien4-qNvF9a
  LV Write Access        read/write
  LV Creation host, time localhost.localdomain, 2025-07-20
  14:18:50 +0200
  LV Status              available
  # open                 1
  LV Size                <17.00 GiB
```

```
  Current LE             4351
  Segments               1
  Allocation             inherit
  Read ahead sectors     auto
  - currently set to     256
  Block device           253:0
```

What can we see from the output of the command? The system has two existing logical volumes: /dev/rhel/swap and /dev/rhel/root. We can see the status of the volumes, available; sizes, 2Gb and about 17 GB; the current number of logical extents, 512 and 4351; and that both volumes consist of single segments.

```
root@localhost:~# vgdisplay
  --- Volume group ---
  VG Name               rhel
  System ID
  Format                lvm2
  Metadata Areas        1
  Metadata Sequence No  3
  VG Access             read/write
  VG Status             resizable
  MAX LV                0
  Cur LV                2
  Open LV               2
  Max PV                0
  Cur PV                1
  Act PV                1
  VG Size               <19.00 GiB
  PE Size               4.00 MiB
  Total PE              4863
```

```
  Alloc PE / Size       4863 / <19.00 GiB
  Free  PE / Size       0 / 0
  VG UUID               yL36E7-fxrR-bZHL-ZPAo-Zu1I-drR3-h86huc
```

The only volume group is named `rhel`. It has only one physical volume, with a size of approximately 19GB. The size of each physical extent is 4 MiB, and there are a total of 4863 physical extents. However, it has zero free extents available for allocation to logical volumes.

```
root@localhost:~# pvdisplay
  --- Physical volume ---
  PV Name               /dev/vda3
  VG Name               rhel
  PV Size               <19.00 GiB / not usable 0
  Allocatable           yes (but full)
  PE Size               4.00 MiB
  Total PE              4863
  Free PE               0
  Allocated PE          4863
  PV UUID               xmpQog-sSQk-UABG-gUW4-40Zd-VwQi-8oCBcL
```

The last command, `pvdisplay`, shows the only existing physical volume created on the third partition of `/dev/vda`.

As we have three free LVM tagged partitions, we can create physical volumes from them and check the results:

```
root@localhost:~# pvcreate /dev/sda{1,2,3}
  Physical volume "/dev/sda1" successfully created.
  Physical volume "/dev/sda2" successfully created.
  Physical volume "/dev/sda3" successfully created.
root@localhost:~# pvdisplay | grep sda
  "/dev/sda1" is a new physical volume of "<6.00 GiB"
  PV Name               /dev/sda1
```

```
  "/dev/sda2" is a new physical volume of "6.00 GiB"
  PV Name               /dev/sda2
  "/dev/sda3" is a new physical volume of "<8.00 GiB"
  PV Name               /dev/sda3
```

The next step is creating a volume group from physical volumes:

```
root@localhost:~# vgcreate testvg01 /dev/sda{1,2,3}
  Volume group "testvg01" successfully created
root@localhost:~# vgdisplay testvg01
  --- Volume group ---
  VG Name               testvg01
  System ID
  Format                lvm2
  Metadata Areas        3
  Metadata Sequence No  1
  VG Access             read/write
  VG Status             resizable
  MAX LV                0
  Cur LV                0
  Open LV               0
  Max PV                0
  Cur PV                3
  Act PV                3
  VG Size               <19.99 GiB
  PE Size               4.00 MiB
  Total PE              5117
  Alloc PE / Size       0 / 0
  Free  PE / Size       5117 / <19.99 GiB
  VG UUID               bUXAEO-HOEC-DYzf-KmWA-pCM6-k9NC-RFkhpy
```

As you can see, all extents are free and can be allocated. The last step is the creation of logical volumes. Here are three examples of creating three volumes:

```
root@localhost:~# lvcreate -n lv1gb -L 1G testvg01
  Logical volume "lv1gb" created.
root@localhost:~# lvcreate -n lv100pe -l 100 testvg01
  Logical volume "lv100pe" created.
root@localhost:~# lvcreate -n lvall -l 100%FREE testvg01
  Logical volume "lvall" created.
```

The difference lies in the volume size definition: first, in gigabytes, and second, in extents. In the third command, we request all remaining space in the volume group.

Tip Take a look at the man page lvcreate(8) for lots of examples, and remember that all man pages are available to you during the exam.

We will discuss file systems in more detail in the next chapter. For now, it's essential to understand that creating a file system and mounting it are necessary to use a volume. Let's create an `ext4` file system on the `testvg01` and mount it temporarily:

```
root@localhost:~# mkfs.ext4 /dev/testvg01/lv1gb
root@localhost:~# mkdir /mnt/lvm
root@localhost:~# mount /dev/testvg01/lv1gb /mnt/lvm
```

Now, let's try to copy /usr/share directory into the new volume. Eventually, it will fail since the size of files within the source directory is more than 1Gb volume:

```
root@localhost:~# cp -r /usr/share/ /mnt/lvm/
...
cp: cannot create directory '/mnt/lvm/share/empty.sshd': No
space left on device
cp: cannot create directory '/mnt/lvm/share/dnsmasq': No space
left on device
```

We can confirm the file system is 100% full by the `df` command output:

```
root@localhost:~# df -h | grep lvm
/dev/mapper/testvg01-lv1gb  974M  958M     0 100% /mnt/lvm
```

We can free up space by deleting two other volumes or by adding a new physical volume to the volume group. Let's delete unused volumes:

```
root@localhost:~# lvremove /dev/testvg01/lvall
root@localhost:~# lvremove /dev/testvg01/lv100pe
```

We can check that the volume group has free physical extents now:

```
root@localhost:~# vgdisplay testvg01 | grep Free
  Free  PE / Size       4861 / <18.99 GiB
```

Now we can give all free space on the volume group to the logical volume with the `lvextend` command and then extend the `ext4` file system to the size of the underlying volume without unmounting:

```
root@localhost:~# lvextend -l +100%FREE /dev/testvg01/lv1gb
  Size of logical volume testvg01/lv1gb changed from 1.00 GiB
(256 extents) to <19.99 GiB (5117 extents).
  Logical volume testvg01/lv1gb successfully resized.
root@localhost:~# resize2fs /dev/testvg01/lv1gb
resize2fs 1.47.1 (20-May-2024)
Filesystem at /dev/testvg01/lv1gb is mounted on /mnt/lvm; on-
line resizing required
```

```
old_desc_blocks = 1, new_desc_blocks = 3
The filesystem on /dev/testvg01/lv1gb is now 5239808 (4k)
blocks long.
```

Tip In case of the XFS file system, you have to use `xfs_growfs /mount_point` as root.

The command `df` will confirm we have a lot of free space now:

```
root@localhost:~# df -h | grep lvm
/dev/mapper/testvg01-lv1gb   20G  958M   18G   5% /mnt/lvm
```

And in the volume group, there are no free extents:

```
root@localhost:~# vgdisplay testvg01 | grep Free
  Free  PE / Size       0 / 0
```

By adding and removing physical disks to LVM, we can migrate data from one physical disk to another. In our case, it would be virtual disks on a virtual machine, but you can do this with physical disks and a physical server.

Let's say a new disk is `/dev/sdb`. It should be equal to or larger than the source disk. We can create from the whole disk one physical volume and add it to the existing volume group:

```
root@localhost:~# pvcreate /dev/sdb
  WARNING: adding device /dev/sdb with idname
  Physical volume "/dev/sdb" successfully created.
root@localhost:~# vgextend testvg01 /dev/sdb
  Volume group "testvg01" successfully extended
```

Next, we will transfer data from all three existing physical volumes to the new one:

```
root@localhost:~# pvmove /dev/sda1 /dev/sdb
  /dev/sda1: Moved: 0.72%
  /dev/sda1: Moved: 100.00%
root@localhost:~# pvmove /dev/sda2 /dev/sdb
  /dev/sda2: Moved: 0.59%
  /dev/sda2: Moved: 100.00%
root@localhost:~# pvmove /dev/sda3 /dev/sdb
  /dev/sda3: Moved: 0.10%
  /dev/sda3: Moved: 100.00%
```

The last step is removing the old physical volumes from the group:

```
root@localhost:~# vgreduce testvg01 /dev/sda{1,2,3}
  Removed "/dev/sda1" from volume group "testvg01"
  Removed "/dev/sda2" from volume group "testvg01"
  Removed "/dev/sda3" from volume group "testvg01"
```

For deletion of LVs and VGs, you can use `lvremove` and `vgremove`.

Summary

This chapter covered the fundamental concepts of disk partitioning and Logical Volume Management in RHEL. We learned how to manage partitions with `parted` and `fdisk`.

We dived into Logical Volume Management (LVM), an essential skill for any Linux administrator. We learned about the three layers of LVM and studied practical examples to create PVs, VGs, and LVs. We also learned how to extend a logical volume to increase its size, a key benefit of LVM. The chapter concludes with a step-by-step guide on how to migrate data from an old physical disk to a new one without any downtime.

Exercises

1) Assuming you have a new, unpartitioned 20Gb disk named `/dev/sdb.` Use `fdisk /dev/sdb` to enter the interactive mode. Create a new DOS (MBR) partition table for the disk. Create one primary partition of 2 Gb and one extended partition. Within the extended partition, create two logical partitions of 500 MiB each.

2) Convert partitions to LVM type if you used any other. From the remaining space, create another partition.

3) Using the LVM partitions you created in a previous exercise, create physical volumes and include into the `vg01` group.

4) From the `vg01` volume group, create a new logical volume named `lv01` with a size of 3 GiB. Create a second logical volume named `lv02` that uses 40% of the remaining free space in the volume group.

5) Delete all LVs, VGs, and PVs.

CHAPTER 6

GNU/Linux File Systems

This chapter explores the essentials of RHEL 10 file systems, covering both local and network storage, special permissions, and swap space management. We'll start with a deep dive into the two primary local file systems: XFS (the default) and ext4.

Basics of File Systems

As we already know, for storing files on the logical volume or partition, you need to create a file system on it. The three most used local file systems in the GNU/Linux world and supported in RHEL 10 are XFS, ext4, and vfat. We will cover the Network File System (NFS) in this chapter later, but will start with an overview of local file systems.

XFS was initially developed more than 30 years ago by Silicon Graphics, Inc. (SGI), for the IRIX operating system (a non-existent today Unix-like operating system). In early 2000, the file system was released under the GNU General Public License (GPL) and ported to GNU/Linux. Since RHEL 7, it is the default file system for this distribution. In RHEL 6, it was ext4. Key features of XFS:

- Metadata journaling for file system integrity in case of accidental power off or similar issues. The journal keeps a record of operations that can be replayed after the system reboots.
- Supported file system size up to 1024 TiB.

A. Markelov, *Red Hat RHCSA 10 Study Companion*, Certification Study Companion Series,
https://doi.org/10.1007/979-8-8688-2226-1_6

- A large number of concurrent disk operations. XFS is focused on scalability and large data sets.
- Support for online file systems is growing (while mounted and in use).

The ext "extended" file system has been part of GNU/Linux since the early days. The first version of ext was created to overcome the limitations of the MINIX file system, which was initially used in early versions of GNU/Linux. The ext4 is the last generation of the file system and can read and write previous ext2 and ext3 versions. Here are some of the ext4 features:

- Supported file system size up to 50 TiB.
- Journal (was added in ext3).
- ext4 supports not only extending but also reducing the size.
- For small systems with limited I/O, ext4 might be a better fit.

VFAT (Virtual File Allocation Table) is a file system driver in Linux that supports compatibility with FAT32 (File Allocation Table) partitions that have long file names. You should not use it for local disks due to limitations like a lack of standard Unix file permissions, ownership, or symbolic links. The primary usage of VFAT is in USB drives, SD cards, and other removable media used to exchange data with different operating systems, digital cameras, and similar devices.

Tip This is not an exam topic, but if you are interested in support of the modern Windows NTFS file system in GNU/Linux, it is supported. You need to install the ntfs-3g and ntfsprogs packages from the EPEL repository. Red Hat does not officially support the EPEL repository, and using its software is at your own risk.

RHEL 10 also fully supports volume-managing file systems, also known as volume manager – Stratis. Stratis is a wrapper on top of LVM, XFS, and Device Mapper. It hides the complexity of the underlying components. Stratis falls outside the scope of the RHCSA 10 objectives.

You can easily create and mount file systems via the Cockpit web user interface, as shown in Figure 6-1, but we will look at how to do this from the command line.

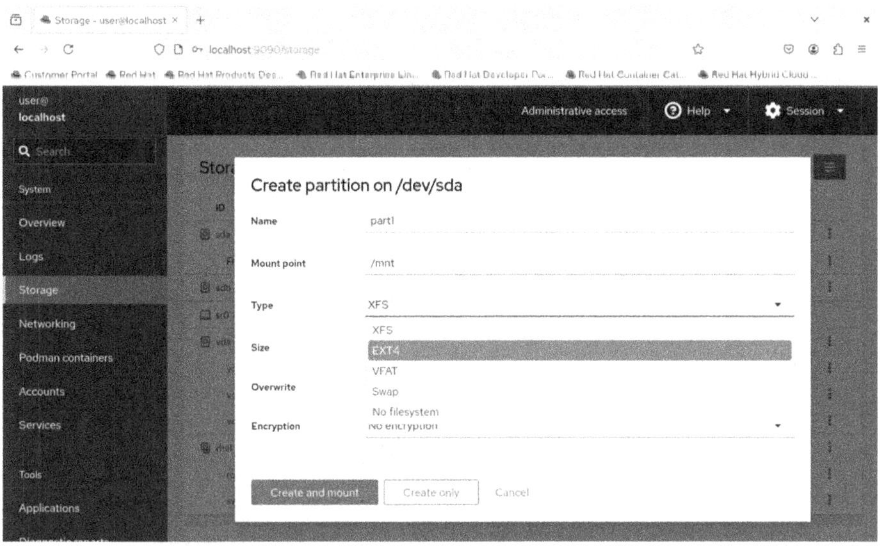

***Figure 6-1.** Creation of a file system dialog in the Cockpit web user interface*

It is easy to create a file system if you go with the default parameters for a file system. Type `mkfs` in the command line, and press the [Tab] key twice to see auto-completion options. You will get several proposals. We are primarily interested in three of them: `mkfs.xfs`, `mkfs.ext4`, and `mkfs.fat`. The `mkfs.vfat` is a symbolic link to `mkfs.fat`. By the way, `mkfs.ext4 mkfs.ext3`, `mkfs.ext2`, and `mke2fs` are also links, but hard links. To remember, just know `mkfs` dot and then the name of the file system.

The only necessary parameter for all mkfs commands is the name of the device; other options will be specific to a particular file system:

```
root@localhost:~# mkfs.ext4 /dev/sda1
...
root@localhost:~# mkfs.xfs /dev/sda2
...
root@localhost:~# mkfs.vfat /dev/sda3
...
```

As you already know, a file system that is to be used needs to be mounted. There are two commands: `mount` and `umount`.

For mounting a file system, we need an empty directory - a mount point. We can use a non-empty directory as well. Still, you usually do not want this, because the original content of the directory will not be accessible until you unmount the file system. Let's try with one of the newly created file systems:

```
root@localhost:~# mkdir /mnt/database
root@localhost:~# mount /dev/sda1 /mnt/database
root@localhost:~# mount | grep sda1
/dev/sda1 on /mnt/database type ext4 (rw,relatime,seclabel)
```

The first mount command has two parameters: what you want to mount (a device with a file system) and where you want to mount (the mount point). The second mount command in the example has no options - it will show all mounted file systems at this moment. As you can see, it displays the type of the file system - ext4 - and in square brackets several mount options. Most of the mount options are described in the sections FILESYSTEM-INDEPENDENT MOUNT OPTIONS and FILESYSTEM-SPECIFIC MOUNT OPTIONS of mount(8).

We can provide mount options with `-o` during the initial mount command, or we can remount an already-mounted file system by adding remount to the mount options. In the following example, we will remount our file system on the fly to make it read-only:

```
root@localhost:~# mount -o remount,ro /dev/sda1
root@localhost:~# mount | grep sda1
/dev/sda1 on /mnt/database type ext4 (ro,relatime,seclabel)
```

Because it is a one-to-one mapping between the file system and the mount point, this command will be equivalent:

```
root@localhost:~# mount -o remount,ro /mnt/database
```

Mounting File Systems at Boot

If I reboot the system right now, after the server is up, the file system mounted manually will not be mounted again. There is a special configuration file /etc/fstab that instructs the operating system to mount file systems during the boot-up process. We can investigate the existing /etc/fstab file that was created during the installation:

```
root@localhost:~# cat /etc/fstab
#
# /etc/fstab
# Created by anaconda on Sun Jul 20 12:18:51 2025
#
# Accessible filesystems, by reference, are maintained under
'/dev/disk/'.
# See man pages fstab(5), findfs(8), mount(8) and/or blkid(8)
for more info.
#
# After editing this file, run 'systemctl daemon-reload' to
update systemd
# units generated from this file.
```

```
#
UUID=28f624ef-3980-4347-9b8f-ded361026976
/                        xfs     defaults        0 0
UUID=f6656985-0ed2-4597-98ef-100d350a304a /
boot                     xfs     defaults        0 0
UUID=07379e89-b5f9-4ebe-9863-61957f7a1ae1
none                     swap    defaults        0 0
```

As you can see, only three non-comment lines are present in the file. Each line consists of six fields. The first is "what we want to mount", i.e., a device with a file system. You can put the LVM volume or partition name here, such as /dev/vda1 or /dev/sda2. However, Red Hat recommends using UUID (Universally Unique Identifier), a 128-bit number generated when a file system is created. In some scenarios, for example, in public clouds or by using a SAN (Storage Area Network) attached device, the names of devices can change after reboot. However, UUID will always be the same. To check what device has what UUID, you can use the `lsblk --fs` command:

```
root@localhost:~# lsblk --fs
NAME       FSTYPE      FSVER    LABEL
UUID                                     FSAVAIL FSUSE%
MOUNTPOINTS
sda
└─sda1      ext4        1.0              9d5628d4-e8e8-4eaf-
b071-0f1f3d8c63c9     18.5G      0% /mnt/database
sdb
sr0
vda
├─vda1
├─vda2      xfs                          f6656985-0ed2-4597-98ef-
100d350a304a    475.9M    50% /boot
```

```
└─vda3      LVM2_member LVM2 001        xmpQog-sSQk-UABG-gUW4-
40Zd-VwQi-8oCBcL
  ├─rhel-root
  │        xfs                          28f624ef-3980-4347-9b8f-
ded361026976        12G     29% /
  └─rhel-swap
           swap       1                07379e89-b5f9-4ebe-9863-
61957f7a1ae1                     [SWAP]
```

As we can see from this example, instead of /dev/sda1 in /etc/fstab or a manual mount command, we can use UUID=9d5628d4-e8e8-4eaf-b071-0f1f3d8c63c9.

The second field is the mount point. We can see that the first line is the root file system /, the second line is /boot, and the third line is none for Swap. A swap partition doesn't need a mount point. We will discuss the concept of swap at the end of this chapter. The next is a type of file system. In our case, it is xfs in the first two lines and swap in the third. You can find defaults in the following field for all three lines, which means default mounting options.

The last two fields have the number zero. The legacy dump tool uses the first number. It is not common for other backup tools to use this field. It is common for the field to be set to 0, indicating that the dump utility should not back up this partition. The last, sixth field sets up the order in which the fsck tool will verify that the file system is clean during the boot process. The XFS system does not use fsck. For ext2, 3, and 4, it is usually 1 for the root file system and 2 for others. Zero means do not run fsck.

A typo in a device name or a nonexistent mount point in a /etc/fstab file can prevent the system from finding critical partitions, such as the root file system. This error will halt the boot process, and you'll need to use a recovery mode to correct the typo. To save time for debugging after changes in the /etc/fstab, you can use the findmnt tool to check the configuration. Here is an example of output if you make a mistake in the UUID:

```
root@localhost:~# findmnt --verify
/
   [E] unreachable on boot required source:
UUID=18f624ef-3980-4347-9b8f-ded361026976
   [W] recommended root FS passno is 1 (current is 0)
   [W] your fstab has been modified, but systemd still uses the
old version;
       use 'systemctl daemon-reload' to reload

0 parse errors, 1 error, 2 warnings
```

After editing the/etc/fstab file, run the systemctl daemon-reload command to ensure all daemons use the new setup. You may also reboot the server instead.

Using Special Files Permissions

To continue learn about future topics, we need to review several special file system permissions beyond standard rwx. Two of them affect executable files (suid and sgid), while two others (sticky bit and sgid again) affect directories. First, we will look at the executable.

Suid, or set user ID on an executable file, allows a user to run that file with the permissions of the file's owner, not the user who calls it. With sgid, or set group ID, the executable file will run with the group affiliation of the group that owns this file. There are no effects of suid or sgid on non-executable files.

In the `ls -l` output, the owner's permission x is replaced with an s for suid, and the group's permission x is replaced with an s for sgid. If the file is not executable for the owner, you will see a capital S instead, and the same if the file is not executable for the group and no sgid is set. Take into account that S for files typically indicates a misconfiguration. Even if suid or sgid are set up, the lack of execution rights means it is useless.

A good example of suid is the passwd tool. It has the setuid bit, so when you run passwd, you can modify /etc/shadow, which is only writable by root:

```
user@localhost:~$ ls -l /usr/bin/passwd
-rwsr-xr-x. 1 root root 91584 Nov  4  2024 /usr/bin/passwd
```

The example of sgid on an executable is the plocate tool. plocate finds all files on the system matching the given pattern (you can use symlink locate as well). It uses the database /var/lib/plocate/plocate.db, which should not be readable by everyone, as it may contain sensitive information. So plocate has set sgid and belongs to the plocate group, and the database has read access for the plocate group:

```
user@localhost:~$ ls -l /usr/bin/plocate
-rwxr-sr-x. 1 root plocate 318224 Feb 14  2025 /usr/bin/plocate
user@localhost:~$ ls -l /var/lib/plocate/plocate.db
-rw-r-----. 1 root plocate 2816854 Aug 18 20:00 /var/lib/
plocate/plocate.db
```

You can set up suid by chmod u+s and sgid as chmod g+s. In numerical format to set up suid, you need to add 4 left to standard digit permissions, and for sgid 2, like in this example:

```
user@localhost:~$ ls -l file1
-rwsrwx---. 1 user user 0 Aug 18 20:18 file1
user@localhost:~$ chmod 2770 file1
user@localhost:~$ ls -l file1
-rwxrws---. 1 user user 0 Aug 18 20:18 file1
```

Now, let's talk about the effects of special permissions on directories.

Everything created within a directory with sgid will inherit the group ownership of the directory. This is useful for shared directories where a team needs to collaborate. In the next section of the chapter, we will discuss the shared directory using the Network File System. We will use sgid bit and a common group of users.

The sticky bit prevents regular users from deleting or renaming files within a directory with the sticky bit unless the user owns the file or the directory. The sticky bit is used in shared directories like `/tmp`. The `x` in the "other" permission field is replaced with a `t` in the `ls -l` output. If the "other" doesn't have execute permission, you will see a capital `T`.

```
user@localhost:~$ ls -ld /tmp/
drwxrwxrwt. 21 root root 4096 Aug 18 18:38 /tmp/
```

You can set up sticky bit by `chmod o+t`. To set up the sticky bit in numerical format, add `1` to the standard permissions.

In Table 6-1, you can find a summary of special permissions and their effects.

Table 6-1. *Special permissions effects*

Device	Files	Directories
SUID `chmod u+s`	The executable file will run as the user who owns this file, not the user who calls it. There are no effects on non-executable files. Example: `-rwsr-xr-x`	There are no effects on directories.
SGID `chmod g+s`	The executable file will run with the group affiliation of the group that owns this file. There are no effects on non-executable files. Example: `-rwxr-sr-x`	Everything created within that directory will inherit the group ownership of the directory. Example: `drwxrws---`
Sticky bit `chmod o+t`	There are no effects on files.	It prevents users from deleting or renaming files within a directory with the sticky bit unless the user owns the file or the directory. Example: `drwxrwxrwt`

Accessing NFS File Systems

Using the Network File System (NFS) protocol, you can mount shared directories from a network and use them as if they were local. This allows you to centralize resources on servers. RHEL 10 has a client and a server for NFS, but RHCSA covers only the client part.

Access rights for files and directories on NFS are determined by their file permissions for UID and GID. Once a remote host mounts the shared file system, these permissions are the only security protecting each file.

The `root` user on a client is mapped to the `nobody` account on the NFS server by default, which restricts its privileges. This behavior can be controlled using the `root_squash` mount option.

Although it is out of scope for the exam to install an NFS server, we will do so to ensure we can practice with the NFS client. You can use the same server for both client and server installation, but to make it more realistic, install an NFS server on a separate virtual machine.

To differentiate two virtual machines from each other, we will use the host names nfsserver and nfsclients. By the way, to change the name, you can use the `hostnamectl` command as root (the new hostname will be displayed in the prompt only for new sessions):

```
root@localhost:~# hostnamectl set-hostname nfsserver
```

First, install the `nfs-utils` package (it will need to be installed in the client as well):

```
root@nfsserver:~# dnf install -y  nfs-utils
```

Next, we need to edit `/etc/nfs.conf` to set fixed port numbers for some of the NFS components. It will help us to open specific ports on the firewall:

```
root@nfsserver:~# cat /etc/nfs.conf
...
[lockd]
```

```
port=5555
...
[statd]
port=6666
```

Next, we will need to create a directory to share files over the network. We will utilize group `users` and the sgid bit to facilitate collaboration:

```
root@nfsserver:~# mkdir -p /nfs/share
root@nfsserver:~# chmod 2770 /nfs/share/
root@nfsserver:~# chgrp users /nfs/share/
```

We need to add a shared directory as an export point to the `/etc/exports` configuration file. You have to use a proper network. In this example, 192.168.122.0/24 is used. It is the default NAT (Network Address Translation) network for virtual machines created with KVM (Kernel-based Virtual Machine) and QEMU – virtualization technologies used in RHEL:

```
root@nfsserver:~# cat /etc/exports
/nfs/share/ 192.168.122.0/24(rw)
```

We need to open NFS-related ports at the firewall by using the `firewall-cmd` command:

```
root@nfsserver:~# firewall-cmd --permanent --add-
service={nfs,rpc-bind,mountd}
success
root@nfsserver:~# firewall-cmd --permanent --add-port={5555/
tcp,5555/udp,6666/tcp,6666/udp}
root@nfsserver:~# firewall-cmd --reload
```

The last step is to start the server and enable it by default.

```
root@nfsserver:~# systemctl enable --now rpc-statd nfs-server
```

Do not worry if commands look unfamiliar to you. We will learn about services and the firewall in the following chapters.

We are now starting work with the NFS client, and this part is included in the exam requirements.

The only package we need to install is the `nfs-utils` package:

```
root@nfsclient:~# dnf install nfs-utils
```

Make sure the user you are working with is a member of the users group:

```
root@nfsclient:~# usermod -aG users user
user@nfsclient:~$ id
uid=1000(user) gid=1000(user) groups=1000(user),100(users) cont
ext=unconfined_u:unconfined_r:unconfined_t:s0-s0:c0.c1023
```

Now we can query available mounts at the NFSv3 server. If you followed the installation instructions, your server supports both NFSv3 and NFSv4 versions:

```
user@nfsclient:~$ showmount --exports nfsserver
Export list for nfsserver:
/nfs/share 192.168.122.0/24
```

You can use an IP address instead of `nfsserver`, or you can use the `/etc/hosts` file to map IP addresses to a hostname. You will learn more about `/etc/hosts` in the chapter about the network in RHEL.

In case of an NFSv4-only server, the command will fail after the timeout. NFSv4 introduced the concept of an export tree, eliminating the need for the specific path to a particular directory. You can mount the root of the tree. But if needed, you can still use the full path as with NFSv3.

As user root, we can mount NFS by using the format `<name of NFS server>:/path/to/directory`:

```
root@nfsclient:~# mkdir /mnt/nfs
root@nfsclient:~# mount nfsserver:/nfs/share /mnt/nfs
```

Let's try to copy any file to the NFS server:

```
user@nfsclient:~$ ls -ld /mnt/nfs/
drwxrws---. 2 root users 20 Aug 22 20:50 /mnt/nfs/
user@nfsclient:~$ cp /etc/passwd /mnt/nfs/
user@nfsclient:~$ ls -l /mnt/nfs/
total 4
-rw-r--r--. 1 user users 2587 Aug 22 20:50 passwd
```

You can create a file because you are part of the users group. If another user who is not part of the group tries to make a file, it fails. It applies to the root user as well, but not because he is not part of the users group. It is the effect of the default root_squash mount option:

```
root@nfsclient:~# cp /etc/passwd /mnt/nfs/passwd2
cp: cannot stat '/mnt/nfs/passwd2': Permission denied
```

To make mounting permanent, you need to update /etc/fstab:

```
user@nfsclient:~$ cat /etc/fstab
...
nfsserver:/nfs/share /mnt/nfs nfs defaults 0 0
```

Configure Automounter

Another topic of the exam is the autofs service or automounter. It can automatically mount file systems on demand and automatically unmount them if the file system is not in use. autofs was created to allow unprivileged users to mount file systems without needing root permissions. Mounting file systems with an automounter makes them accessible to all users by default. However, you can use access permissions to restrict who can access them.

Automounter can use fixed mount points (direct) and indirect mounts, where it doesn't have a fixed location until it's needed. A typical example is with remote home directories. The path of the mount point will depend on the particular user. Do not forget that the official Red Hat documentation is available during the exam, specifically the automounter described in the "Managing file systems" book. Apart from other examples, it includes an example of automounting home directories from the NFS server.

To start with automounter, you need to install the `autofs` package:

```
root@nfsclient:~# dnf -y install autofs
```

The master map file lists the directories controlled by `autofs` and points to other files or network locations that contain specific automount maps for those directories. With the package, you will get the default master map - `/etc/auto.master` - and several examples of map files:

```
root@nfsclient:~# ls /etc/auto.*
/etc/auto.master  /etc/auto.misc  /etc/auto.net  /etc/auto.smb

/etc/auto.master.d:
```

We will use our existing setup with an NFS server and an NFS client to demonstrate the usage of automounter. First, make sure you unmount the remote directory and delete the corresponding line from `/etc/fstab`. We can add a new line to the default master map, `/etc/auto.master`, which will have the link to `/etc/auto.nfs` map file that will serve the `/mnt` directory:

```
/mnt /etc/auto.nfs
```

The map file itself will look like

```
root@nfsclient:~# cat /etc/auto.nfs
nfs -fstype=nfs4 nfsserver:/nfs/share
```

The last step is to enable and start the service:

```
root@nfsclient:~# systemctl enable --now autofs
```

Now it is possible to test automounter:

```
user@nfsclient:~$ ls /mnt/nfs
passwd
user@nfsclient:~$ mount | grep mnt/nfs
nfsserver:/nfs/share on /mnt/nfs type nfs4 (rw,relatime,vers=4
.2,rsize=1048576,wsize=1048576,namlen=255,hard,proto=tcp,timeo
=600,retrans=2,sec=sys,clientaddr=192.168.122.153,local_lock=no
ne,addr=192.168.122.163)
```

Swap Managing

Swap, swap area, or swap partition is the dedicated space on the server's disk that acts as an extension of RAM. Indeed, hard drives or SSDs are much slower than RAM, and the server will use swap as a last resort. The Linux kernel will move inactive pages of memory to swap if it doesn't have enough space in RAM for active processes. Red Hat provides a recommendation on the optimal swap size based on the amount of RAM available. You can find them in the official documentation. For example, if RAM is between 2Gb and 8Gb, swap space should be the same as RAM, but if you want to use hibernation, which is typical for laptops, then swap space should be twice as big as RAM.

Swap space typically is a separate partition or an LVM logical volume, but for tests, you can even use a file. For sure, the file will be slower than the logical volume or partition because of another layer.

To check the total size of the swap and current usage, you can use the command `free` or `free -h` to make it more human-readable. The first line is about RAM, and we are interested in the second line only:

```
user@localhost:~$ free
               total        used        free      shared  buff/
cache   available
Mem:        23758692     1007096    22454904       29564
647900    22751596
Swap:        2097148           0     2097148
user@localhost:~$ free -h
               total        used        free      shared  buff/
cache   available
Mem:            22Gi       983Mi        21Gi
28Mi       632Mi        21Gi
Swap:          2.0Gi          0B       2.0Gi
```

Currently, the system has 2 Gb of swap and nothing in use.

Let's say we have a new disk `/dev/sda` and want to give half of it to swap. As an example, let's create a new partition interactively with `parted`. User input shown as bold text:

```
root@localhost:~# parted /dev/sda
GNU Parted 3.6
Using /dev/sda
Welcome to GNU Parted! Type 'help' to view a list of commands.
(parted) mklabel gpt
(parted) mkpart
Partition name?  []? swap
File system type?  [ext2]? linux-swap
Start? 0%
End? 50%
(parted) print
```

```
Model: ATA QEMU HARDDISK (scsi)
Disk /dev/sda: 21.5GB
Sector size (logical/physical): 512B/512B
Partition Table: gpt
Disk Flags:

Number  Start   End     Size    File system     Name  Flags
 1      1049kB  10.7GB  10.7GB  linux-swap(v1)  swap  swap

(parted) quit
Information: You may need to update /etc/fstab.
```

The next step is to write the swap signature. The mkswap command writes a single block of data with a signature to the beginning of a device, leaving the rest of the space unallocated. This allows the Linux kernel to use the device to store memory pages as a swap area.

```
root@localhost:~# mkswap /dev/sda1
Setting up swapspace version 1, size = 10 GiB
(10736365568 bytes)
no label, UUID=ab2286fd-60c3-46be-b167-1bfae8634d1f
```

Now it is possible to activate swap and check that the size will grow from the initial 2 Gb:

```
root@localhost:~# swapon /dev/sda1
root@localhost:~# free -h
              total        used        free      shared  buff/
cache   available
Mem:           22Gi       993Mi        21Gi
28Mi       653Mi        21Gi
Swap:          11Gi          0B        11Gi
```

The last step is to update /etc/fstab to make changes persistent. You need to add a new line by using a UUID or a device name:

```
UUID=ab2286fd-60c3-46be-b167-1bfae8634d1f none swap
defaults 0 0
```

or

```
/dev/sda1 none swap defaults 0 0
```

By using the option pri=<number>, you can define which swap partition will be used first. The smaller pri number means this partition will have higher priority:

```
UUID=b7733bb3-.. none swap pri=100 0 0
UUID=ab2286fd-.. none swap pri=200 0 0
```

To check all swap partitions in use, you can print swapon without any options:

```
root@localhost:~# swapon
NAME      TYPE      SIZE USED PRIO
/dev/dm-1 partition   2G   0B  100
/dev/sda1 partition  10G   0B  200
```

Summary

This chapter provides a comprehensive overview of local and network file systems, special permissions, and swap management. The chapter begins by introducing the main local file systems used in RHEL 10: XFS and ext4.

To make a file system usable, you must first create it with the mkfs command and then mount it to an empty directory using the mount command. Manually mounted file systems are temporary and are lost on reboot. To make a mount persistent, you must add an entry to the /etc/fstab configuration file.

The chapter details special permissions that extend beyond the standard read, write, and execute (rwx): SUID, SGID, and Sticky bit.

The Network File System (NFS) protocol allows you to mount and access shared directories from a network server as if they were local. The chapter covers the client side of NFS, which is an exam topic.

Swap space acts as an extension of a server's RAM, storing inactive memory pages on a disk when physical RAM is full. The chapter explains how to create and manage a swap partition using the parted command to create the partition and the `mkswap` command to prepare it.

Exercises

1) Use the `parted` command to create a new GPT partition table on a disk (e.g., `/dev/sdb`), and then create a new primary partition using 30% of the available space. Format this partition with the XFS file system.

2) Modify the `/etc/fstab` file to ensure the new XFS partition mounts automatically to `/mnt/newxfs` every time the system boots. Use the partition's UUID for the entry.

3) Use the `parted` command to create a new partition with LVM type using 50% of the available space. Add a partition to the existing LVM group, and extend / file system.

4) Use the `lsblk --fs` or `blkid` commands to list all file systems on your system and their corresponding UUIDs.

5) Create a directory `/tmp/shared_project` and a group named `devops`. Set the directory's group ownership to `devops`, and apply the SGID bit. Add your user to the `devops` group, and verify that any new files you create in that directory inherit the `devops` group ownership.

6) Create a 1 Gb file at `/tmp/swapfile` using `dd`. Use the `mkswap` command to format the file as a swap area. Activate the swap file with the `swapon` command, and verify the new total swap size with `free -h`.

CHAPTER 7

Operating Running Systems

Now, it's time to discuss the operation and lifecycle of an operating system. This chapter explores the practical aspects of managing a live GNU/Linux environment. We will begin by examining the startup and shutdown system. Then, you will learn how to identify and manage CPU- and memory-intensive processes, as well as methods for adjusting process scheduling. We study tuning profiles to optimize performance for specific workloads. Next, this chapter will empower you to locate and interpret system log files and journals. We will master starting, stopping, and checking the status of network services, a fundamental skill for any network administrator. The chapter concludes by examining secure methods for transferring files between systems, ensuring your data moves safely across your network.

Boot and Shut Down a System Gracefully

RHEL 10 has two approaches for lifecycle management of the operating system:

- Traditional, based on RPM packages, standard boot process, and a mutable system.
- Image mode is based on Container-Native Workflows for the operating system.

A. Markelov, *Red Hat RHCSA 10 Study Companion*, Certification Study Companion Series,
https://doi.org/10.1007/979-8-8688-2226-1_7

Here is the process of traditional booting RHEL in short:

- First, when the machine is powered on, either legacy BIOS or modern UEFI software runs the Power on Self Test (POST) to test and initialize the hardware.
- GRUB2 (GRand Unified Bootloader version 2) is the de facto standard for most general-purpose Linux distributions. In the case of BIOS, the very small first stage of the bootloader (`boot.img`), taken from MBR, loads stage 1.5 (`core.img`) from a dedicated 1M Boot partition. Once loaded, core.img gains enough intelligence to understand the file system, access the partition that is mounted as `/boot/`, and proceed with the booting process.
- In the case of modern UEFI, which is a BIOS replacement, the BIOS Boot partition does not exist. Instead of that, a FAT32-formatted EFI System Partition (ESP) is mounted to `/boot/efi/`, accessed, and the boot loader is stored in `/boot/efi/EFI/redhat/grubx64.efi` loaded.
- Next, GRUB2 loads its configuration from the `/boot/grub2/grub.cfg` file. For UEFI systems, it is `/boot/efi/EFI/redhat/grub.cfg`, but it also points to `/boot/grub2/grub.cfg`, if you will check the content. At that point, you can see a menu to select which kernel to boot. See Figure 7-1 for an example. You should not edit `/boot/grub2/grub.cfg` or `/boot/efi/EFI/redhat/grub.cfg`. Those files are generated from `/etc/default/grub` and `/etc/grub.d/` scripts.

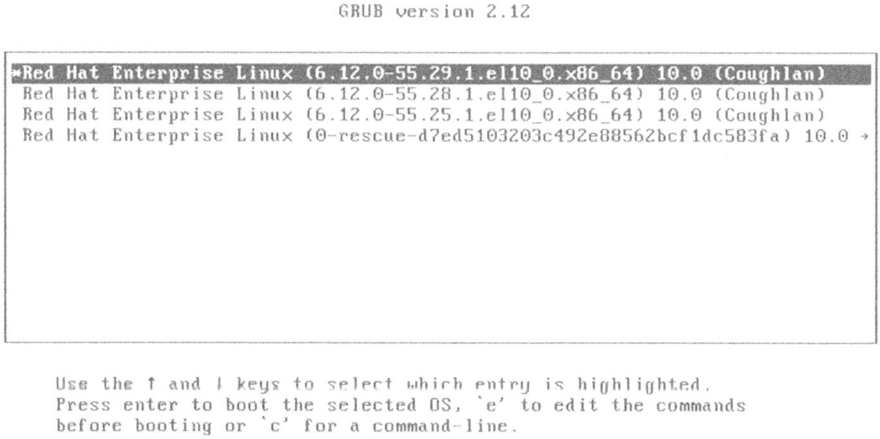

***Figure 7-1.** GRUB2 boot menu*

- Next, GRUB2 loads the kernel and the initramfs image into memory. You can find corresponding files in / boot/ directory. The command uname -r will print the kernel release:

```
root@localhost:/boot# ls /boot/vmlinuz-$(uname -r)
/boot/initramfs-$(uname -r).img
/boot/initramfs-6.12.0-55.22.1.el10_0.x86_64.img
/boot/vmlinuz-6.12.0-55.22.1.el10_0.x86_64
root@localhost:/boot# uname -r
6.12.0-55.22.1.el10_0.x86_64
```

- The initramfs image contains "initial RAM filesystem." It includes kernel modules (drivers) for hardware required during boot, file systems needed during the boot process, and a minimal set of user-space tools, such as mount, for example, and init scripts.

- The boot loader hands over to the kernel. Kernel initializes modules from initramfs and executes the first process with process ID number one by executing the initialization script `/sbin/init`. In fact, this is a symbolic link to `systemd` – System and Service Manager in RHEL and many other GNU/Linux distributions. The command `ps` below shows the process with a PID equal to one.

```
root@localhost:~# ls -l /sbin/init
lrwxrwxrwx. 1 root root 22 Mar 10 01:00 /sbin/init ->
../lib/systemd/systemd
root@localhost:~# ps -q 1
    PID TTY          TIME CMD
      1 ?        00:00:01 systemd
```

- systemd mounts file systems guided by `/etc/fstab` file into `/sysroot` directory and then pivots the root directory to `/sysroot`. Next, `systemd` starts or stops units, for example, system services based on the default target, which is configured by `/etc/systemd/system/default.target` or passed as an argument to the kernel. As you see, this file is a symbolic link, and it can be changed to other targets shipped as part of the system:

```
root@localhost:~# ls -l /etc/systemd/system/
default.target
lrwxrwxrwx. 1 root root 40 Jul 20 14:23 /etc/systemd/
system/default.target -> /usr/lib/systemd/system/
graphical.target
```

There are several available systemd targets. Every target is a set of systemd modules that need to be started or stopped. During boot up, the process mainly involves starting modules. Here are some of the most used:

- `graphical.target` is default for desktops and servers with a graphical environment. Apart from graphical logins, it provided text-based logins and supported multiple users. It is the modern equivalent of runlevel 5 in the traditional System V init system used in older Unix and Linux distributions (including RHEL until version 7).
- `multi-user.target` is the default for most servers. It supports multiple users with text-based logins only. It is the modern equivalent of runlevel 3.
- `rescue.target` is the primary target for server repairs in case of startup issues.
- `emergency.target` is more minimal than `rescue.target`. It should be chosen if the `rescue.target` unit fails to execute.

If you want to see all available targets in the system, you may use the following `systemctl` command:

```
root@localhost:~# systemctl list-units --type=target --all
  UNIT           LOAD    ACTIVE   SUB    DESCRIPTION >
  basic.target__loaded  active   active Basic System
...
```

To boot manually into another target, use the `systemctl isolate` command. Services not included in this target would be stopped, and required services will be started. Let's say you're now at the `graphical.target`, and to switch into text-only logins, target `multi-user.target`, you can use the command:

```
root@localhost:~# systemctl isolate multi-user.target
```

You can easily check and change the default target as well. It will be used at the next reboot:

```
root@localhost:~# systemctl get-default
graphical.target
root@localhost:~# systemctl set-default multi-user.target
Removed '/etc/systemd/system/default.target'.
Created symlink '/etc/systemd/system/default.target' → '/usr/
lib/systemd/system/multi-user.target'.
```

To gracefully reboot the system, you can use the command `systemctl reboot`, and to power off, `systemctl poweroff`.

The next topic related to the boot process is recovering the root password. You need to reboot the server, and when the GRUB2 menu appears, press the key `e`, which means edit. The moment when you need to press the `e` key is shown in Figure 7-1. After that, you will see several lines related to this particular Linux kernel. You need to add `init=/bin/bash` to the end of the kernel command line, as shown in Figure 7-2. That means the system will run the Bash shell instead of systemd, and the boot process will stop before systemd runs into any target or starts any service.

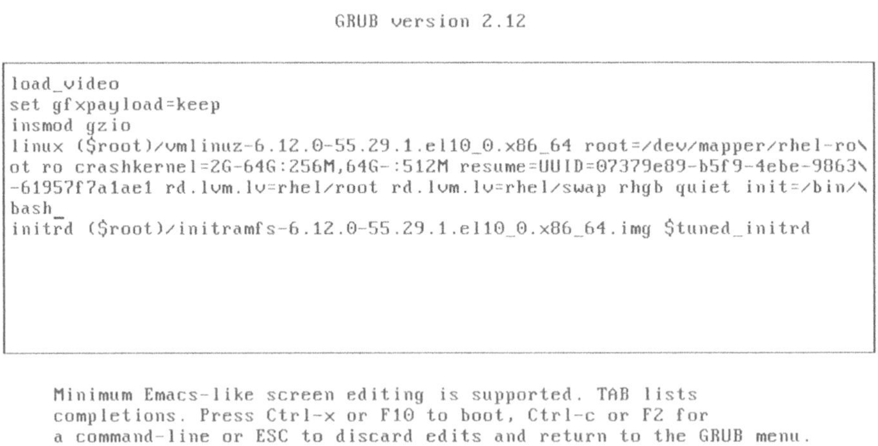

Figure 7-2. *GRUB2 boot menu*

Then press Ctrl+X to boot. In a few seconds, you will receive a shell prompt, but the root file system will be mounted read-only. You need to remount it with the rw option:

```
sh-5.2# mount -o remount,rw /
```

Now it is possible to change the root password:

```
sh-5.2# passwd root
```

The last step before rebooting the system is to create a file named /.autorelabel. It is necessary because the /etc/shadow file, which we re-created with the passwd command just now, will lack the proper SELinux label. In case /.autorelabel exists during boot, it will force re-labeling of the file system. We will discuss SELinux in the chapter related to security.

```
sh-5.2# touch /.autorelabel
```

That is all. You can reboot the system and log in with a new root password.

Linux Processes

The process in GNU/Linux is a running instance of the program. It is one of the fundamental concepts in the operating system. The Linux kernel is responsible for managing resources between processes. More precisely, the Linux scheduler is in charge. Each of the processes is tracked by PID (Process ID), and all processes are linked into a reversed tree growing from the first system process, which in RHEL 10 is systemd, as we discussed earlier. You can see the process hierarchy by using the command pstree:

```
root@localhost:~# pstree -p
systemd(1)─┬─ModemManager(1091)─┬─{ModemManager}(1097)
           │                    ├─{ModemManager}(1098)
           │                    └─{ModemManager}(1100)
           ├─NetworkManager(1104)─┬─{NetworkManager}(1113)
           │                      ├─{NetworkManager}(1114)
           │                      └─{NetworkManager}(1115)
           ├─accounts-daemon(1022)─┬─{accounts-daemon}(1067)
           │                       ├─{accounts-daemon}(1068)
           │                       └─{accounts-daemon}(1070)
           ├─at-spi-bus-laun(1742)─┬─dbus-daemon(1748)
           │                       ├─{at-spi-bus-laun}(1743)
           │                       ├─{at-spi-bus-laun}(1744)
           │                       ├─{at-spi-bus-laun}(1745)
           │                       └─{at-spi-bus-laun}(1747)
           ├─at-spi2-registr(1816)─┬─{at-spi2-registr}(1817)
...
```

Besides PID and parent ID (PPID), every process has other characteristics. Some of them are

- Process state
- Security properties (ownership, SELinux attributes, etc)
- Address space of allocated memory
- Environment, like global and local variables, and the current scheduling context
- Resources such as open files, network connections, and CPU time

A process can have different states managed by the scheduler:

- Running (R) – The process is currently executing.

- Sleeping (S) – The process is waiting for an external event, such as user input or reading or writing data to a disk.
- Stopped (T) – The process has been paused, usually by a user (e.g., Ctrl+Z).
- Zombie (Z) – A process that does not exist and has released its resources, but its entry still exists in the kernel's process table.

In fact, you can interact with processes and get information via the virtual file system `/proc`. Virtual means this is not a file stored somewhere; it is a representation of kernel memory structures. If you look into `/proc`, you will find numerous subdirectories with numbers, and each number corresponds to the PID of the associated process. For example, you can retrieve a command line with the options used to call the process from the `cmdline` virtual file:

```
root@localhost:~# cat /proc/1/cmdline
/usr/lib/systemd/systemd--switched-root--system--
deserialize=47rhgb
```

You can obtain information about the CPU, memory, and other attributes of the process. However, it is not very convenient, so we will use CLI tools from the `procps-ng` suite. We will examine the `top`, `ps`, and `kill`.

The example of `top` output is shown in Figure 7-3. The first several lines indicated load averages, a summary of processes, and memory consumption. Memory consumption is quite similar to the output of the `free` command, and load averages, and uptime is the same as the output of the `uptime` command. Load averages are a measure of the average system workload over the last minute, the last 5 minutes, and the previous 15 minutes. A lower number indicates an idle system, while a higher number indicates a busy system. Linux determines load average by showing how many processes are ready to run on a CPU and how many processes are waiting for input and output (I/O) to complete. It is not a measurement of the CPU alone, but of the entire system.

```
user@localhost:~ - top

top - 14:38:54 up 6 min,  2 users,  load average: 0.20, 0.08, 0.02
Tasks: 334 total,   1 running, 333 sleeping,   0 stopped,   0 zombie
%Cpu(s):  0.5 us,  0.1 sy,  0.0 ni, 99.3 id,  0.0 wa,  0.1 hi,  0.0 si,  0.0 st
MiB Mem :  23201.8 total,  20888.8 free,   1756.0 used,    920.2 buff/cache
MiB Swap:  12287.0 total,  12287.0 free,      0.0 used.  21445.9 avail Mem

    PID USER      PR  NI    VIRT    RES    SHR S  %CPU  %MEM     TIME+ COMMAND
   3375 user      20   0 4281932 300532 106804 S   2.7   1.3   0:03.80 ptyxis
   2597 user      20   0 5896692 371844 129252 S   1.3   1.6   0:05.29 gnome-shell
   3538 user      20   0  231580   5420   3244 R   0.3   0.0   0:00.09 top
      1 root      20   0   49520  41156  10236 S   0.0   0.2   0:02.55 systemd
      2 root      20   0       0      0      0 S   0.0   0.0   0:00.01 kthreadd
      3 root      20   0       0      0      0 S   0.0   0.0   0:00.00 pool_workqueue_re+
      4 root       0 -20       0      0      0 I   0.0   0.0   0:00.00 kworker/R-rcu_gp
      5 root       0 -20       0      0      0 I   0.0   0.0   0:00.00 kworker/R-sync_wq
      6 root       0 -20       0      0      0 I   0.0   0.0   0:00.00 kworker/R-slub_fl+
      7 root       0 -20       0      0      0 I   0.0   0.0   0:00.00 kworker/R-netns
      9 root       0 -20       0      0      0 I   0.0   0.0   0:00.00 kworker/0:0H-even+
     10 root      20   0       0      0      0 I   0.0   0.0   0:00.03 kworker/0:1-mm_pe+
     11 root      20   0       0      0      0 I   0.0   0.0   0:00.00 kworker/u32:0-eve+
     12 root       0 -20       0      0      0 I   0.0   0.0   0:00.00 kworker/R-mm_perc+
     13 root      20   0       0      0      0 I   0.0   0.0   0:00.00 kworker/u32:1-ipv+
     14 root      20   0       0      0      0 I   0.0   0.0   0:00.00 rcu_tasks_kthread
     15 root      20   0       0      0      0 I   0.0   0.0   0:00.00 rcu_tasks_rude_kt+
     16 root      20   0       0      0      0 I   0.0   0.0   0:00.00 rcu_tasks_trace_k+
     17 root      20   0       0      0      0 S   0.0   0.0   0:00.00 ksoftirqd/0
     18 root      20   0       0      0      0 I   0.0   0.0   0:00.08 rcu_preempt
     19 root      20   0       0      0      0 S   0.0   0.0   0:00.00 rcu_exp_par_gp_kt+
```

Figure 7-3. *top tool*

At the bottom, you can find the table of processes that are refreshed every three seconds by default. Here is an explanation of the default columns:

- PID – Process ID.
- USER – Owner of the process.
- PR – Priority of the process. The lower number means higher priority. If the top displays "rt", it means the process is real-time.

- NI - The niceness value of the process. A regular user can change the niceness value for their own processes (decrease only). A regular user cannot change a priority. This is how the user can influence the priority of the process. Niceness can be from -20 to +19. A lower means a higher priority. For non-real-time processes, the kernel calculates priority using the formula: PR = 20 + NI. For example, a nice value of 0 maps to a priority of 20.
- VIRT - The amount of virtual memory used by the process.
- RES - The amount of resident memory used by the process. This is the actual physical RAM used by the process.
- SHR - The amount of shared memory used by the process. This memory can be or already is shared with other processes. For example, if it is a common library.
- S - State of the process.
- %CPU - The percentage of CPU time the process has used at the moment of screen update.
- %MEM - The percentage of physical memory the process has used at the moment of screen update.
- COMMAND - The command started the process.
- TIME+ - It is a CPU time consumed by all threads of a process, so for a multi-threaded process, it flows faster than real time.

To get help with keystrokes in the top, you can press ?. Some of the most commonly used:

q - Quit.

`f` - Change columns. You can turn off the default and add additional ones, like PPID or Group.

`Shift + p` - Sort processes by CPU utilization.

`Shift + m` - Sort processes by memory utilization.

`k` - Kill a process. You need to enter the PID and the signal (will be covered later).

`r` - Change the niceness value. You need to enter the PID and the value.

Tip `htop` is a modern, enhanced, and more user-friendly alternative to the classic `top`. You can check Figure 7-4. It offers a more visually appealing and interactive interface. It's color-coded and uses graphical bar meters for CPU, memory, and swap usage. You can install `htop` from the EPEL repository at home for testing purposes, but this repository and tool are not available during the exam.

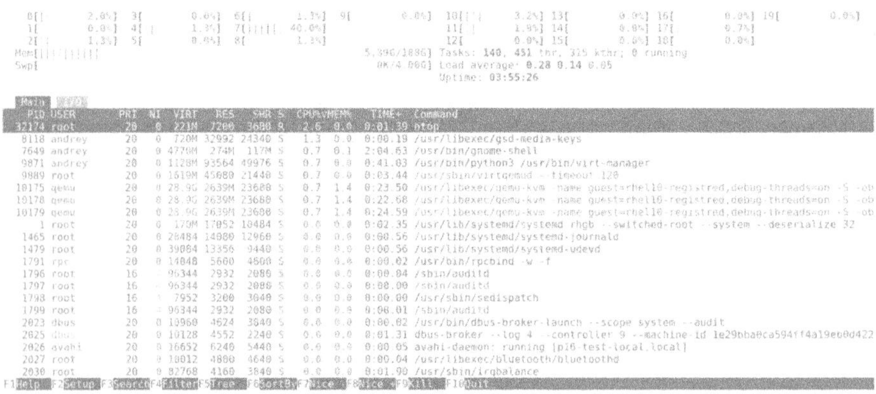

***Figure 7-4.** htop tool*

Another command that allows you to list processes is ps. It is commonly used with the option aux. It will print all processes in the system:

```
[~]$ ps aux
USER           PID %CPU %MEM    VSZ   RSS TTY      STAT
START   TIME COMMAND
root             1  0.1  0.3 175216 13676 ?        Ss   12:28
0:02 /usr/lib/systemd/systemd --switched-root --s
root             2  0.0  0.0      0     0 ?        S    12:28
0:00 [kthreadd]
root             3  0.0  0.0      0     0 ?        I<   12:28
0:00 [rcu_gp]
root             4  0.0  0.0      0     0 ?        I<   12:28
0:00 [rcu_par_gp]
```

The columns in the default outputs are the same as in the top. The only thing not familiar to you is TTY – a terminal to which a process is attached.

You can sort output by using codes from the section STANDARD FORMAT SPECIFIERS of ps(1). By default, the sort order is from lowest to highest, but you can use the minus symbol to specify a descending sort order. Here is an example of how to get the top ten memory-consuming processes by adding the head command to the standard output of ps:

```
root@localhost:~# ps aux --sort -%mem | head -n 11
USER           PID %CPU %MEM    VSZ   RSS TTY      STAT
START   TIME COMMAND
user          2597  4.4  1.5 5892768 379164 ?      Ssl  14:38
0:24 /usr/bin/gnome-shell
user          3375  3.7  1.5 4283092 370536 ?      Ssl  14:38
0:20 /usr/bin/ptyxis --gapplication-service
user          2794  0.6  0.7 1394880 166860 ?      Sl   14:38
0:03 /usr/bin/gnome-software --gapplication-service
...
```

And the following example is for the top CPU-consuming processes:

```
root@localhost:~# ps aux --sort -%cpu | head -n 11
USER         PID %CPU %MEM    VSZ   RSS TTY      STAT
START   TIME COMMAND
root        4984  100  0.0 230696  4012 pts/1    R+   14:48
0:00 ps aux --sort -%cpu
user        2597  3.9  1.5 5897888 379164 ?      Ssl  14:38
0:24 /usr/bin/gnome-shell
user        3375  3.7  1.5 4299484 370792 ?      Ssl  14:38
0:23 /usr/bin/ptyxis --gapplication-service
user        2794  0.5  0.7 1394880 166860 ?      Sl   14:38
0:03 /usr/bin/gnome-software --gapplication-service
...
```

We mentioned signals already but did not explain the meaning. A signal is a software interrupt that can be applied to a process. Every signal has a short name and a number. The number may vary across different hardware platforms, but the names remain the same. You can send a signal to process by using the command `kill`. The name is `kill` because this tool is often used to terminate a process, and the default signal that the command sends is `SIGTERM` ("polite" way to ask a process to terminate). You can change the signal by adding the `-s` option. Some of the well-known signals with numbers for x86_64 systems:

- `SIGKILL (9)` – Forceful termination of the process. It cannot be ignored and helps stop unresponsive processes.
- `SIGTERM (15)` – Standard way to terminate a process. It allows a process to shut down gracefully.
- `SIGINT (2)` – Typical signal sending by pressing `Ctrl+C`. It also allows a process to shut down gracefully.
- `SIGHUP (1)` – Widely used to request service reload configuration files, for example, when you updated them.

You can use `kill -l` to list all available signals.

Let's say I want to kill the `top` tool running in another terminal. First, I need to find the process number:

```
root@localhost:~# ps aux | grep top
user        18879  0.3  0.0 231588  5320 pts/0    S+   16:52
0:00 top
root        18889  0.0  0.0 227688  2084 pts/1    S+   16:52
0:00 grep --color=auto top
```

Then I can use the `kill` command and check if the process no longer exists:

```
root@localhost:~# kill 18879
root@localhost:~# ps aux | grep top
root        18984  0.0  0.0 227688  2032 pts/1    S+   16:52
0:00 grep --color=auto top
```

By default, regular processes start, as shown in the `top` output, with a priority of 20. You can adjust the priority by setting the niceness value, also known as "nice." As you already know, a regular user can decrease the niceness value for their own processes, but as root, you can increase it as well. We can adjust the nice value for the running process and start a process using a non-default nice value. Let's start with existing processes.

Let's start, in one terminal window, any process that will run for a significant amount of time, for example, sending one thousand ICMP packets to any reachable IP address with `ping`, and then switch to another terminal:

```
user@localhost:~$ ping -c 1000 192.168.122.1
PING 192.168.122.1 (192.168.122.1) 56(84) bytes of data.
64 bytes from 192.168.122.1: icmp_seq=1 ttl=64 time=0.455 ms
64 bytes from 192.168.122.1: icmp_seq=2 ttl=64 time=0.578 ms
...
```

To print priority and nice value of processes, we need to use `lax` options in `ps` instead of `aux`. Option `l` instead of `u` will mean "long" listing instead of "user-friendly." And "lax" is also salmon in the Swedish language, but this will not be tested on the exam, so don't worry.

We can confirm that by default, the process has priority 20 and niceness 0:

```
user@localhost:~$ ps lax | grep 192.168.122.1
0  1000   19547   19181  20   0 228876  2548 skb_wa S+
pts/1      0:00 ping -c 1000 192.168.122.1
0  1000   19562   19254  20   0 227828  2036 pipe_r S+
pts/2      0:00 grep --color=auto 192.168.122.1
```

As a regular user, we can increase the nice value to decrease priority. The following command will change niceness from 0 to 11, which means priority will be changed from the default 20 to 31:

```
user@localhost:~$ renice -n 11 19547
19547 (process ID) old priority 0, new priority 11
user@localhost:~$ ps lax | grep 192.168.122.1
0  1000   19547   19181  31  11 228876  2548 skb_wa
SN+  pts/1      0:00 ping -c 1000 192.168.122.1
0  1000   19567   19254  20   0 227828  2076 pipe_r S+
pts/2      0:00 grep --color=auto 192.168.122.1
```

But if a regular user tries to change the nice value back, it will fail. Decreasing is allowed only for the `root`. The `root` account can even make negative niceness:

```
user@localhost:~$ renice -n 0 19547
renice: failed to set priority for 19547 (process ID):
Permission denied
user@localhost:~$ sudo renice -n 0 19547
[sudo] password for user:
```

```
19547 (process ID) old priority 11, new priority 0
user@localhost:~$ ps lax | grep 192.168.122.1
0  1000   19547   19181  20   0 228876  2548 skb_wa S+
pts/1      0:00 ping -c 1000 192.168.122.1
0  1000   19576   19254  20   0 227828  2152 pipe_r S+
pts/2      0:00 grep --color=auto 192.168.122.1
user@localhost:~$ sudo renice -n -1 19547
19547 (process ID) old priority 0, new priority -1
user@localhost:~$ ps lax | grep 192.168.122.1
0  1000   19547   19181  19  -1 228876  2548 skb_wa
S<+  pts/1      0:00 ping -c 1000 192.168.122.1
0  1000   19582   19254  20   0 227828  2032 pipe_r S+
pts/2      0:00 grep --color=auto 192.168.122.1
```

With nice command, you can start up a new program with a nice value different from the default zero:

```
user@localhost:~$ nice -n 15 ping 192.168.122.1
```

Performance Management with TuneD

The GNU/Linux system has numerous tunable parameters in various subsystems. Default settings are suitable for generic workloads. For fine-tuning the kernel, it is essential to have a thorough understanding of how the Linux Kernel works, including the parameters and their impact on performance and interaction with each other. However, it is possible to define typical workload profiles and set typical settings for them or even monitor the system and dynamically change tunables. Red Hat achieved this with the system service TuneD, and switching TuneD workload profiles is one of the exam topics.

The initial release of RHEL 10 has 15 profiles out of the box. Some of them are

- `balanced` - This is the standard power-saving profile, designed to balance performance and energy use. It automatically adjusts and optimizes settings as needed. It is the default profile in RHEL 10.
- `desktop` - The profile is based on `balanced` and includes extra optimization for interactive applications, typical of a workstation.
- `throughput-performance` - The server optimized profile for high-throughput workloads.
- `virtual-guest` - The profile for systems running in Hypervisors such as VMWare or KVM. It is based on `throughput-performance`.
- `oracle` and `mssql` - Profiles optimized for particular databases.
- `powersave` - The profile for maximum power saving performance to minimize power consumption, for example, for a laptop running on batteries.

Before using TuneD, you may need to install, enable, and start it, depending on the configuration chosen during the operating system's deployment. The corresponding commands are

```
root@localhost:~# dnf install tuned
root@localhost:~# systemctl enable --now tuned
```

Now we can check what profile is active:

```
root@localhost:~# tuned-adm active
Current active profile: throughput-performance
```

To obtain the complete list of available profiles, use the `tuned-adm list` command:

```
root@localhost:~# tuned-adm list
Available profiles:
- accelerator-performance     - Throughput performance based
tuning with disabled higher latency STOP states
- aws                         - Optimize for aws ec2 instances
- balanced                    - General non-specialized
tuned profile
...
```

To change the active profile, you can use the `profile` subcommand:

```
root@localhost:~# tuned-adm profile desktop
root@localhost:~# tuned-adm active
Current active profile: desktop
```

System Journals

System journals play a crucial part in troubleshooting and monitoring of the operating system and its services. Like many other Linux distributions and various hardware devices, such as routers and switches, RHEL utilizes the syslog protocol. Syslog is a standard for sending and receiving log messages.

There are two services that process syslog messages in RHEL 10:

- `systemd-journald` daemon collects event messages from the Linux Kernel, the early stages of the boot process, the `STDOUT` and `STDERR` of daemons as they start up and run, and syslog events. It collects events into a binary journal that by default does not persist across reboots. The default location is `/run/log/journal/` on virtual file system tmpfs.

- `rsyslog` service reads and processes syslog messages from `systemd-journald` and writes them into persistent files in `/var/log` directory.

To retrieve and display messages from the binary `systemd-journald` journal, you can use the `journalctl` command. By default, it shows all messages, but you can use different options to specify queries. Some of them you may find in Table 7-1.

Table 7-1. *journalctl options*

Options	Description
`-b`	Shows logs for the last boot.
`-k`	Shows kernel logs.
`-u _SYSTEMD_UNIT=<name.service>`	Show logs for the specified systemd service.
`-n <number>`	Show the last <number> lines of the log.
`-f`	Shows the most recent journal entries and continuously outputs new ones. It is similar to the command `tail` with a file name.
`-p <priority>`	Shows logs with specified priority and higher.
`--since, --until`	Shows logs with specified time restrictions. For examples of how to define time, see systemd.time(7).

For example, show Kernel logs from 9:00 to 18:00 on September 6 with the err priority or higher:

```
root@localhost:~# journalctl -k --since "2025-09-06 9:00"
--until "2025-09-06 18:00" -p err
Sep 06 12:35:48 localhost kernel: Warning: Unmaintained driver
is detected: ip_set
```

Now, let's examine rsyslog and its associated log files. Some of the log files are

- `/var/log/boot.log` – Startup logs
- `/var/log/secure` – Logs related to security and authentication
- `/var/log/maillog` – Logs related to the mail server
- `/var/log/cron` – Cron jobs logs
- `/var/log/messages` – All other syslog messages

In the `/var/log/`, you may find other directories and files related to individual services.

Syslog messages have priority and facility. You may find a list of priorities in Table 7-2. The facility is a subsystem that produces logs, for example, kernel or mail logs. Priorities provided according to `syslog(2)`.

Table 7-2. *Syslog priorities*

Level value	Description
0 – emerg	The system is unusable
1 – alert	Action must be taken immediately
2 – crit	Critical conditions
3 – err	Error conditions
4 – warning	Warning conditions
5 – notice	Normal but significant condition
6 – info	Informational
7 – debug	Debug-level messages

The main configuration file of rsyslog is `rsyslog.conf`. Also, individual services can have configuration files in `/etc/rsyslog.d` directory. The purpose of these configuration files is to send messages to a specific destination based on priority and facility. We can look at some of the rules RHEL provides by default in the `/etc/rsyslog.conf`:

```
#### RULES ####

# Log all kernel messages to the console.
# Logging much else clutters up the screen.
#kern.*   /dev/console

# Log anything (except mail) of level info or higher.
# Don't log private authentication messages!
*.info;mail.none;authpriv.none;cron.none /var/log/messages

# The authpriv file has restricted access.
authpriv.* /var/log/secure

# Log all the mail messages in one place.
mail.*     /var/log/maillog
```

There are four rules in this example. First, it is commented, but if uncommented, it will send all messages from the kernel facility, regardless of priority, to the console. Star means all, and a dot separates the facility from the priorities field. The second rule sends messages from all facilities with priority `info` and higher to `/var/log/messages`. At the same time, messages from `mail`, `authpriv`, and `cron` facilities are excluded. The last two rules are in charge of sending all authpriv and mail to their own log files.

For real-time monitoring of logs, `tail` is often used. The command `tail -f /var/log/messages` will show the last ten lines of the messages file and will continue to show new arriving messages until you press `Ctrl+C`. Another helpful command `logger` can send a message to `rsyslog` manually:

```
user@localhost:~$ logger -p local0.notice "The new NOC shift is on duty."
```

In that case, the local0 facility was used. Facilities local0-local7 are reserved for user usage.

We can see how log files look like:

```
user@localhost:~$ sudo tail -n 5 /var/log/messages
Sep  7 12:08:55 localhost systemd[1]: Starting systemd-
hostnamed.service - Hostname Service...
Sep  7 12:08:55 localhost systemd[1]: Started systemd-
hostnamed.service - Hostname Service.
Sep  7 12:08:58 localhost su[6042]: (to user) root on pts/0
Sep  7 12:09:03 localhost user[6071]: The new NOC shift is on duty.
Sep  7 12:09:28 localhost systemd[1]: systemd-hostnamed.
service: Deactivated successfully.
```

Every new message starts on a new line. First is the date and time, then the host name. The rsyslog service can receive and send messages over the network if properly configured. The following fields are the process name, its PID, and the message itself.

The logrotate command manages log files to keep them from getting too big and filling up the /var/log directory:

```
root@localhost:~# ls -l /var/log
...
-rw-------. 1 root   root    500895 Sep  7 12:14 messages
-rw-------. 1 root   root    592320 Jul 20 12:30
messages-20250720
-rw-------. 1 root   root    643441 Aug 18 16:45
messages-20250818
-rw-------. 1 root   root    801402 Aug 24 13:41
messages-20250824
-rw-------. 1 root   root   1036460 Sep  3 14:47
messages-20250903
...
```

The logrotate renames a log file with a date-based extension, essentially archiving and compressing the old file. While most logs are rotated weekly, the frequency can be adjusted.

Checking the Status of Services

As we have already learned, the systemd daemon is responsible for controlling the startup of system services in RHEL 10. The systemd daemon replaced SysV init, the traditional init system for Linux, including RHEL versions before RHEL 7. For a short time, RHEL 6 also used another init system called Upstart before fully transitioning to systemd.

You can use the command systemctl list-units --type=service to list all loaded services. To check the status of an individual service, you can use the command systemctl status and the name of the service:

```
root@localhost:~# systemctl status  sshd.service
● sshd.service - OpenSSH server daemon
     Loaded: loaded (/usr/lib/systemd/system/sshd.service;
enabled; preset: enabled)
     Active: activating (auto-restart) (Result: exit-code)
since Sun 2025-09-07 13:15:36 CEST; 2s ago
 Invocation: 724e7f7b6ac7410db0882fee700ee298
       Docs: man:sshd(8)
             man:sshd_config(5)
    Process: 1889 ExecStart=/usr/sbin/sshd -D $OPTIONS
(code=exited, status=255/EXCEPTION)
   Main PID: 1889 (code=exited, status=255/EXCEPTION)
   Mem peak: 1.1M
        CPU: 13ms
```

From the output, we can see that the OpenSSH server daemon is enabled, which means it will start after reboot, and the status is `activating (auto-restart) (Result: exit-code)`. This is an example of a service with a faulty configuration file, preventing it from starting. Let's say you corrected a mistake in the config. You can restart the service and check the status again:

```
root@localhost:~# systemctl restart sshd.service
root@localhost:~# systemctl status sshd.service
● sshd.service - OpenSSH server daemon
     Loaded: loaded (/usr/lib/systemd/system/sshd.service;
enabled; preset: enabled)
     Active: active (running) since Sun 2025-09-07 13:17:00
CEST; 25s ago
 Invocation: 104efae5f01d43778737a760cf2801ad
       Docs: man:sshd(8)
             man:sshd_config(5)
   Main PID: 1905 (sshd)
      Tasks: 1 (limit: 60200)
     Memory: 1M (peak: 1.3M)
        CPU: 16ms
     CGroup: /system.slice/sshd.service
             └─1905 "sshd: /usr/sbin/sshd -D [listener] 0 of
10-100 startups"
```

That is better. You can start service with `start` and stop with `stop`:

```
root@localhost:~# systemctl stop sshd.service
root@localhost:~# systemctl status sshd.service
○ sshd.service - OpenSSH server daemon
     Loaded: loaded (/usr/lib/systemd/system/sshd.service;
enabled; preset: enabled)
```

```
     Active: inactive (dead) since Sun 2025-09-07 13:25:45
CEST; 7s ago
...
root@localhost:~# systemctl start sshd.service
root@localhost:~# systemctl status sshd.service
● sshd.service - OpenSSH server daemon
     Loaded: loaded (/usr/lib/systemd/system/sshd.service;
enabled; preset: enabled)
     Active: active (running) since Sun 2025-09-07 13:26:14
CEST; 2s ago
...
```

You can enable and disable the service, meaning they will be started or stopped after a reboot. If you disable the running service, it will continue to be active, but will not start after a reboot:

```
root@localhost:~# systemctl disable sshd.service
Removed '/etc/systemd/system/multi-user.target.wants/sshd.
service'.
root@localhost:~# systemctl status sshd.service
● sshd.service - OpenSSH server daemon
     Loaded: loaded (/usr/lib/systemd/system/sshd.service;
disabled; preset: enabled)
     Active: active (running) since Sun 2025-09-07 13:26:14
CEST; 3min 23s ago
...
root@localhost:~# systemctl enable sshd.service
Created symlink '/etc/systemd/system/multi-user.target.wants/
sshd.service' → '/usr/lib/systemd/system/sshd.service'.
```

By adding -now, you can enable and start the service at the same time.

Files Transfer Between Systems

The last topic for this chapter is how to transfer files between systems securely. Over the decades, the FTP (File Transfer Protocol) protocol was the default choice for transferring files. RHEL 10 has server and FTP clients, but if you check the Red Hat documentation, you can find

> *"... FTP clients and servers software are deprecated and will be removed in the future major version of RHEL... These FTP protocol implementations are no longer under active development..."*
>
> —Release Notes for Red Hat Enterprise Linux 10.0

The primary reason for its deprecation is that FTP transmits data, including usernames and passwords, in plain text.

One of the recommended replacements is the `scp` command - Secure Copy. SCP uses the SFTP protocol over an SSH connection for data transfer and provides the same authentication and security as a login session.

Tip In RHEL versions before RHEL 9, `scp` utilized a less flexible SCP protocol.

The `scp` command is similar to the `cp` command. You need to specify the source and then the destination. A remote system can be a source or a destination. The format for a file or directory for a remote system is `username@servername_or_ip:/path/to/file`. For example, I want to copy a directory recursively to a remote system with IP address 192.168.122.153 as user2:

```
user@localhost:~$ scp -r /usr/share/doc/openssh
user2@192.168.122.153:/home/user2/
user2@192.168.122.153's password:
```

```
CREDITS                          100% 5494      6.2MB/s   00:00
ChangeLog                        100%  283KB   60.9MB/s   00:00
OVERVIEW                         100% 6333     23.7MB/s   00:00
...
```

Summary

This chapter covers the practical management of a running RHEL 10 system, focusing on its operational lifecycle. It details the system boot process, from hardware tests to the GRUB2 bootloader and the initiation of the `systemd` daemon. It also explains how to gracefully shut down the system and even recover a lost root password.

The chapter explains how to manage processes, which are running programs. It introduces tools like `top` and `ps` to monitor resource usage and `kill` to terminate processes. The concept of niceness is presented as a way to adjust a process's priority.

For performance tuning, the chapter highlights the use of the TuneD service, which applies predefined profiles to optimize the system for different workloads. It also covers system logging, explaining that `systemd-journald` collects logs while `rsyslog` writes them to permanent files in `/var/log`.

Finally, the chapter discusses how to manage system services using `systemctl` to check their status and start or stop them. It also mentions the use of SFTP secure protocols for file transfers.

Exercises

1) Use systemctl to find the default systemd target on your system. Use systemctl to temporarily switch your system to multi-user.target.

2) Follow the chapter's steps to reset the root password on your test system.

3) Examine the output of journalctl -b to review the messages from the most recent system boot.

4) Use the ps command to identify the top three processes consuming the most CPU and memory.

5) Start a new process with a non-default nice value using the nice command, and then verify the change with ps.

6) Use renice to change the niceness of a running process, and then confirm the change with ps.

7) Use tuned-adm active to determine which performance profile is currently active on your system. Switch the active TuneD profile to throughput-performance using the tuned-adm profile command.

8) Practice stopping and then starting a non-critical service, such as the firewalld service, using systemctl stop and systemctl start.

CHAPTER 8

Configure Systems

In this chapter, we will explore some aspects of configuring RHEL 10 systems that are covered in the exam. In the previous chapter, we provided an example using the `logrotate` tool, which runs periodically for log file housekeeping. Now it is time to see how to configure recurring tasks or run a program at a specified future moment. We will then explore jobs and job management. A crucial part of system administration is keeping local time synchronized across the network. It is essential for log correlation in distributed systems. The last topic in this chapter is configuring the OpenSSH server and key-based authentication for SSH.

Bash Jobs Managing

Job management in Bash enables users to execute and control multiple commands within a single shell. This feature is used for interactive sessions and for parallel execution in shell scripts as well.

It can be one foreground job that controls the terminal and many background jobs. One of the background jobs can be switched to the foreground, and then the current foreground job will become a background job. A job can consist of one process or a pipeline of processes. All processes in the pipeline will be the same job.

A. Markelov, *Red Hat RHCSA 10 Study Companion*, Certification Study Companion Series,
https://doi.org/10.1007/979-8-8688-2226-1_8

You can directly start projects in the background by adding ampersand (&) at the end of the command line:

```
user@localhost:~$ sleep 3600 &
[1] 5880
user@localhost:~$ jobs
[1]+  Running                 sleep 3600 &
```

The `sleep` command will delay for a specified amount of time. By default, the number in the command is in seconds. After you started the job in the foreground shell, it printed the job number and process number. The command `jobs` will print all jobs in the foreground. Let's add two more jobs:

```
user@localhost:~$ sleep 7200 &
[2] 5886
user@localhost:~$ sleep 9000 &
[3] 5887
user@localhost:~$ jobs
[1]   Running                 sleep 3600 &
[2]-  Running                 sleep 7200 &
[3]+  Running                 sleep 9000 &
```

As you can see in the output of the `jobs` command, we have three background jobs. Symbol plus means current job, and minus is previous job. If you do not specify the job number in job control commands, the current job is assumed. If I want to switch the current background job to the foreground, I can use the `fg` command:

```
user@localhost:~$ fg
sleep 9000
```

As you see, the current job is now in the foreground, but the Bash prompt does not appear since the job is still running and controls the terminal. For sure, I can interrupt it by pressing Ctrl+C, but what if I want to send it back to the background without interruption? I can stop it first by pressing Ctrl+Z and then send it to the background with bg, where it will continue to execute:

```
user@localhost:~$ fg
sleep 9000
^Z
[3]+  Stopped                 sleep 9000
user@localhost:~$ jobs
[1]   Running                 sleep 3600 &
[2]-  Running                 sleep 7200 &
[3]+  Stopped                 sleep 9000
user@localhost:~$ bg 3
[3]+ sleep 9000 &
user@localhost:~$ jobs
[1]   Running                 sleep 3600 &
[2]-  Running                 sleep 7200 &
[3]+  Running                 sleep 9000 &
```

You can use the command kill not only with a process number, but with a job number preceded by a percent sign:

```
user@localhost:~$ kill %2
user@localhost:~$ jobs
[1]-  Running                 sleep 3600 &
[3]+  Running                 sleep 9000 &
```

Tip There are other ways to control multiple tasks from a single terminal – terminal multiplexers. One of these types of programs that came with RHEL 10 is tmux. If you choose to use tmux, you can start a new session with the command tmux new. If the connection to the remote server is lost, you can rejoin a session with the `tmux attach` command. Table 8-1 lists the most common shortcuts for `tmux` commands. Figure 8-1 shows the user interface for `tmux`. Terminal multiplexers are not part of the exam topics. This information is for your convenience only.

Table 8-1. *tmux commands*

Command key bindings	Action
Ctrl+b ?	Show the screen with help.
Ctrl+b d	Detach from the session.
Ctrl+b s	List sessions.
Ctrl+b c	Create a new window.
Ctrl+b n	Change to the next window.
Ctrl+b p	Change to the previous window.
Ctrl+b 0…9	Select windows 0 through 9.
Ctrl+b %	Create a horizontal pane.
Ctrl+b "	Create a vertical pane.
Ctrl+b ↑↓→←	Move to pane.

***Figure 8-1.** The user interface for tmux*

Deferred Execution of Commands with at

GNU/Linux, like other Unix-like operating systems, has mechanisms for delayed execution of scripts and another for recurring tasks, such as log rotation. We will start from deferred execution of commands with the `at` command. This is quite a common task when a system administrator needs to run a script at a specific time, for example, during the weekend night, for some housekeeping when no one is working with the system.

The system daemon `atd` is installed and working by default in most configurations. In case it was missed, you can install it from the `at` package. Managing the software with RPM packages will be covered in the next chapter.

Tool at allows fairly complex time specifications to specify time. Then, the user can view their own queue of planned tasks using the atq command. The root user can view all queues.

Here are some examples:

```
user@localhost:~$ at now + 30 min
warning: commands will be executed using /bin/sh
at Sun Sep 28 13:08:00 2025
at> echo Test
at> Ctrl+d <EOT>
job 1 at Sun Sep 28 13:08:00 2025
user@localhost:~$ at 19:00 September 29
warning: commands will be executed using /bin/sh
at Mon Sep 29 19:00:00 2025
at> echo Test2
at> Ctrl+d <EOT>
job 2 at Mon Sep 29 19:00:00 2025
user@localhost:~$ at 10:00 tomorrow
warning: commands will be executed using /bin/sh
at Mon Sep 29 10:00:00 2025
at> echo Test3
at> Ctrl+d <EOT>
job 3 at Mon Sep 29 10:00:00 2025
user@localhost:~$ at teatime + 1000 days
warning: commands will be executed using /bin/sh
at Sat Jun 24 16:00:00 2028
at> echo Test4
at> Ctrl+d <EOT>
job 4 at Sat Jun 24 16:00:00 2028
user@localhost:~$ atq
```

```
1      Sun Sep 28 13:08:00 2025 a user
2      Mon Sep 29 19:00:00 2025 a user
3      Mon Sep 29 10:00:00 2025 a user
4      Sat Jun 24 16:00:00 2028 a user
```

With the command `atrm`, you can remove a job from the queue:

```
user@localhost:~$ atrm 2
user@localhost:~$ atq
1      Sun Sep 28 13:08:00 2025 a user
3      Mon Sep 29 10:00:00 2025 a user
4      Sat Jun 24 16:00:00 2028 a user
```

Also, you can provide a command to the script:

```
user@localhost:~$ at midnight < database_backup.sh
warning: commands will be executed using /bin/sh
job 5 at Mon Sep 29 00:00:00 2025
```

Recurrent Execution of Commands with cron

The `crond` daemon is another form of automation that you will likely find in almost all Unix-like operating systems. By using the standard format, you can describe when you want the system to start a command or script. Format is so well-known that it is used even in software other than operating systems, for example, in the container orchestration platform Kubernetes.

You do not need to remember this format because the main system-wide configuration file has its description in comments:

```
user@localhost:~$ cat /ctc/crontab
SHELL=/bin/bash
PATH=/sbin:/bin:/usr/sbin:/usr/bin
MAILTO=root
```

```
# For details see man 4 crontabs

# Example of job definition:
# .---------------- minute (0 - 59)
# |  .------------- hour (0 - 23)
# |  |  .---------- day of month (1 - 31)
# |  |  |  .------- month (1 - 12) OR jan,feb,mar,apr ...
# |  |  |  |  .---- day of week (0 - 6) (Sunday=0 or 7) OR
sun,mon,tue,wed,thu,fri,sat
# |  |  |  |  |
# *  *  *  *  * user-name  command to be executed
```

Every user has their own `crontab` file, empty by default, plus the operating system itself has a system configuration file and directories. The syntax will be the same, so we can start experimenting with a regular user's file.

To create or edit a user's crontab file, use the command `crontab -e`. This will open the default editor that is set by the `$VISUAL` or `$EDITOR` environment variables. If neither set, then `vi` will be open by default. To open with nano use:

```
user@localhost:~$ export EDITOR=nano; crontab -e
```

The configuration line consists of five fields: minutes, hours, day of month, month, and day of week. The sixth field is the command itself. This differs from the system crontab file we saw earlier. Before the command, it has the user's name with which the privileges command will start.

The symbol star (*) means every possible instance of the field. Star divided by number X means "every X instance of this field." For example, enter this line and save:

```
*/30 * * * * /home/user/bin/test.sh
```

This will run the test.sh script every 20 minutes. The next example will run the script only on working days at 17:25:

```
25 17 * * 1-5 /home/user/bin/test2.sh
```

This example means run the script every second Sunday at 9:00:

```
0 9 * * 0 /home/user/bin/test3.sh
```

Run the script on Monday and Thursday at 13:00 but not during the summer:

```
0 13 * 1-5,9-12 1,4 /home/user/bin/test4.sh
```

Users' `crontab` files will be stored in the directory `/var/spool/cron/`. The standard output of running commands will be redirected to the user's local mailbox if the mail system is configured.

Best practice for system crontab files is to place them in /etc/cron.d/ directory to avoid overwriting of `/etc/crontab`. There are also four additional directories that exist: `/etc/cron.monthly`, `/etc/cron.weekly`, `/etc/cron.daily`, and `/etc/cron.hourly`. In these directories, place the executable scripts themselves, not crontab configuration files, to run them at the specified frequency indicated in the directory name.

Configure Time Service Clients

Keeping local time synchronized across the network is essential for log correlation in distributed systems. The most common and sufficient for regular IT systems is Network Time Protocol (NTP). In RHEL 10, the NTP service is implemented by `chrony`. During the interactive installation of RHEL, you were asked about time synchronization, and your virtual machine is likely already receiving accurate time information from public NTP services. The `timedatectl` from the Systemd suite can show you the current status and overview of time-related information:

```
user@localhost:~$ timedatectl
               Local time: Sun 2025-09-28 15:31:51 CEST
           Universal time: Sun 2025-09-28 13:31:51 UTC
                 RTC time: Sun 2025-09-28 13:31:51
                Time zone: Europe/Stockholm (CEST, +0200)
System clock synchronized: yes
              NTP service: active
          RTC in local TZ: no
```

As you see from the output, the NTP service is active. What you should know is how to change the server to get the precise time, for example, in an isolated network with no access to public NTP servers. Check the line that starts with pool in `/etc/chrony.conf`:

```
root@localhost:~# grep pool /etc/chrony.conf
# Use public servers from the pool.ntp.org project.
# Please consider joining the pool (https://www.pool.ntp.org/
join.html).
pool 2.rhel.pool.ntp.org iburst
```

Instead of the public server `2.rhel.pool.ntp.org`, you need to put the local server name or IP address. Then, you need to restart the chronyd service. To check that the machine is synchronized to the proper server, use the command:

```
root@localhost:~# chronyc sources -v

  .-- Source mode  '^' = server, '=' = peer, '#' = local clock.
 / .- Source state '*' = current best, '+' = combined, '-'
= not combined,
| /             'x' = may be in error, '~' = too variable, '?'
= unusable.
||                                                 .-
xxxx [ yyyy ] +/- zzzz
```

```
||      Reachability register (octal) -.           |  xxxx =
adjusted offset,
||      Log2(Polling interval) --.      |          |  yyyy =
measured offset,
||                                \     |          |  zzzz =
estimated error.
||                                 |    |           \
MS Name/IP address         Stratum Poll Reach LastRx
Last sample
===============================================================
================
^* 172.16.10.10                 3   6   377
36  +1661us[+1661us] +/-   29ms
```

Configuring OpenSSH

The last topic for this chapter is some aspects of working with OpenSSH. We already know how to connect via SSH and how to copy files with SCP using a username and password. Now, let's discuss SSH key-based authentication.

SSH implemented security by public-key encryption. When you first connect to a new server, its public keys are stored in your home directory:

```
user@localhost:~$ ssh user@192.168.122.153
The authenticity of host '192.168.122.153 (192.168.122.153)'
can't be established.
ED25519 key fingerprint is SHA256:TD/
J4ROk61Zp92JpKgCMFuX419OBwwuncKJ6XSLD69U.
This key is not known by any other names.
Are you sure you want to continue connecting (yes/no/
[fingerprint])? yes
Warning: Permanently added '192.168.122.153' (ED25519) to the
list of known hosts.
```

```
user@192.168.122.153's password:
Last login: Sat Sep 27 17:35:55 2025
```

The file where the key is stored on the machine from which you are doing the connection is `.ssh/known_hosts`:

```
user@localhost:~$ cat .ssh/known_hosts
192.168.122.153 ssh-ed25519 AAAAC3Nza...
192.168.122.153 ssh-rsa AAAAB3NzaC1yc...
```

If the key is changed and you know that no one has reinstalled the server or regenerated the server's key pair, it may be a sign of a man-in-the-middle attack.

```
user@localhost:~$ ssh user@192.168.122.153
@@@@@@@@@@@@@@@@@@@@@@@@@@@@@@@@@@@@@@@@@@@@@@@@@@@@@@@@@@@
@    WARNING: REMOTE HOST IDENTIFICATION HAS CHANGED!     @
@@@@@@@@@@@@@@@@@@@@@@@@@@@@@@@@@@@@@@@@@@@@@@@@@@@@@@@@@@@
IT IS POSSIBLE THAT SOMEONE IS DOING SOMETHING NASTY!
Someone could be eavesdropping on you right now (man-in-the-
middle attack)!
It is also possible that a host key has just been changed.
The fingerprint for the ED25519 key sent by the remote host is
SHA256:m2lBvajLvRCttrFBhBo3VxGHpsIM29Qyivb8medOsnI.
Please contact your system administrator.
Add correct host key in /home/user/.ssh/known_hosts to get rid
of this message.
Offending ECDSA key in /home/user/.ssh/known_hosts:3
Host key for 192.168.122.153 has changed and you have requested
strict checking.
Host key verification failed.
```

To solve that, you can delete either the corresponding entry in `~/.ssh/known_hosts` or the entire file – it will be populated as you connect to VMs over SSH. Do that only if you're certain that this is not an MITM attack!

There is also a system-wide file `/etc/ssh/ssh_known_hosts` where the root user can add public keys for remote servers.

Instead of typing a password during connection to a remote server, you can use key-based authentication for ssh. In that case, you generate your personal key pair and store your public key in a special file within the home directory of the remote user on the remote server. The public key is not secret, but the fact that it is stored on the server allows you to connect.

First, you need to generate a key pair by using the `ssh-keygen` command:

```
user@localhost:~$ ssh-keygen
Generating public/private ed25519 key pair.
Enter file in which to save the key (/home/user/.ssh/id_
ed25519):
Enter passphrase for "/home/user/.ssh/id_ed25519" (empty for no
passphrase):
Enter same passphrase again:
Your identification has been saved in /home/user/.ssh/
id_ed25519
Your public key has been saved in /home/user/.ssh/id_
ed25519.pub
The key fingerprint is:
SHA256:MnM5W5JANJMOnVwMqfOuZIaH6aj4kkpIDtZkto9FtKw user@
localhost
The key's randomart image is:
+--[ED25519 256]--+
|     oB+oO.      |
|     ..+B o      |
|   o ... +       |
```

```
|  + . +.oo         |
|.o . .+ES .        |
|*     +o=.=        |
|.+   + =o.         |
|=   o =   .        |
|=+o . ..           |
+----[SHA256]-----+
```

Alternatively, you can provide a password to encrypt the key and protect it. In my case, I twice pressed Enter when I was asked for a passphrase and did not use password protection. The output command will show you the names of the files with private and public keys:

```
user@localhost:~$ ls .ssh
id_ed25519  id_ed25519.pub  known_hosts
```

Now you can copy the public key as the user you will use in the future to the corresponding server. Use option `-i` to point the `ssh-copy-id` command to the public key:

```
user@localhost:~$ ssh-copy-id -i .ssh/id_ed25519.pub
user@192.168.122.153
/usr/bin/ssh-copy-id: INFO: Source of key(s) to be installed:
".ssh/id_ed25519.pub"
/usr/bin/ssh-copy-id: INFO: attempting to log in with the new
key(s), to filter out any that are already installed
/usr/bin/ssh-copy-id: INFO: 1 key(s) remain to be installed --
if you are prompted now it is to install the new keys
user@192.168.122.153's password:

Number of key(s) added: 1
```

```
Now try logging into the machine, with: "ssh -i .ssh/id_ed25519
'user@192.168.122.153'"
and check to make sure that only the key(s) you wanted
were added.
```

Now you can test that you will not be asked for a password:

```
user@localhost:~$ ssh  user@192.168.122.153
Last login: Fri Oct  3 21:15:02 2025 from 192.168.122.163
```

The main configuration file of the OpenSSH server is stored in the file /etc/ssh/sshd_config. Some of the essential options you should be aware of are presented in Table 8-2.

Table 8-2. *OpenSSH server configuration options*

Options by default	Explanation
Port 22	By default, the OpenSSH server uses port 22.
ListenAddress 0.0.0.0	0.0.0.0 means the OpenSSH server is listening for connections on all IP addresses of this server.
PermitRootLogin yes	This setting depends on what you chose during the installation. It can be No as well. It is recommended not to permit root direct login.
PasswordAuthentication yes	It is recommended to use key-based authentication and turn off this setting.

Summary

In this chapter, we delved into core RHEL 10 system configuration topics essential for any aspiring system administrator, focusing on automation, synchronization, and security – all key areas of the RHEL certification exam.

We first explored job management in Bash, learning how to run commands in the foreground and background.

Next, we covered command scheduling. For single, deferred tasks, we used the `at` utility, which allows for flexible time specifications (e.g., now + 30 min, tomorrow, teatime). For recurrent tasks, we focused on the `cron` daemon.

The chapter then shifted to maintaining time synchronization across the network using the Network Time Protocol (NTP), which is critical for log correlation.

Finally, we addressed essential aspects of OpenSSH configuration. We reinforced the importance of the host key fingerprint in `~/.ssh/known_hosts` for preventing man-in-the-middle attacks. The highlight of this section was setting up key-based authentication for SSH, a more secure alternative to password login.

Exercises

1) Execute the `sleep 1200` command in the background. Immediately verify it is running, and then note its job number.

2) Start a `ping 127.0.0.1` process in the foreground. Stop it using the appropriate key sequence, and then send the stopped process to the background so it resumes running.

3) Schedule a command using at to execute five minutes from now. The command should redirect the output of date to a file named `~/test_output.txt`.

4) Immediately after scheduling the job, use the command to view the job queue.

5) Edit your user's crontab file to run the command `/bin/echo "Cron!" > ~/cron.log` every day at 9:00.

6) Use the Systemd utility to display the current system time, time zone, and the status of the NTP service.

7) Generate a new key pair. Use a strong passphrase for security. What are the names of the two files created in your `~/.ssh/` directory?

8) You need to enable key-based authentication for the user root on the local server 127.0.0.1. Use the specialized utility to securely copy your users' public key to the server.

9) Which two lines would you modify in the main OpenSSH server configuration file (`/etc/ssh/sshd_config`) to disable password authentication and prevent the `root` user from logging in directly?

CHAPTER 9

Managing Software

Now, it's time to discuss software management in Red Hat Enterprise Linux. In this chapter, we will discuss only the traditional and most commonly used methods of managing software required for the RHCSA exam: RPM packages and Flatpak. We will not talk about RHEL bootc images, which is a new feature in RHEL 10. But it is not required for the exam and definitely not widely adopted at the time of writing this book.

Updating Software with a GUI

Before we delve into the command line, let's examine the graphical tools available to users in RHEL. You don't need any extra knowledge to search for new software in already configured repositories and update existing software. In GNOME, you have a GUI tool named Software, where you can simply check for updates and apply them. In Figures 9-1 and 9-2, you can see what a notification about new updates looks like and how to check the details of the updated packages.

A. Markelov, *Red Hat RHCSA 10 Study Companion*, Certification Study Companion Series,
https://doi.org/10.1007/979-8-8688-2226-1_9

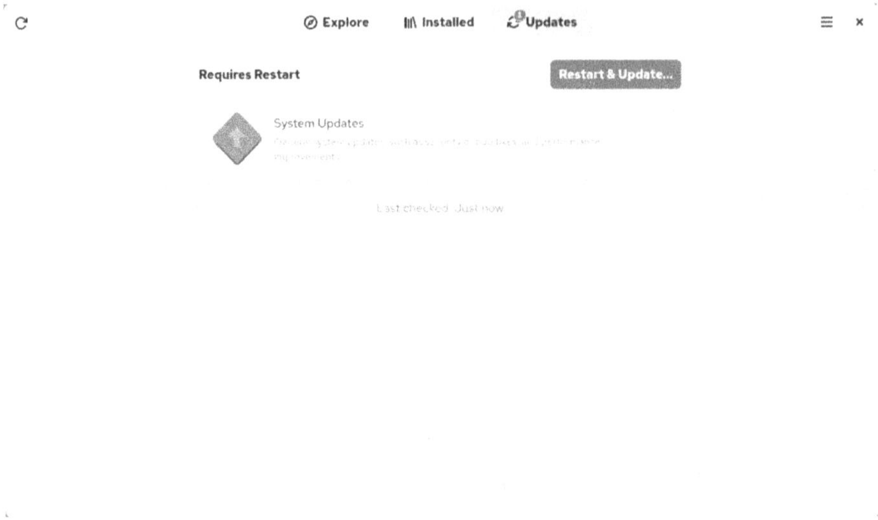

Figure 9-1. *Software GUI tool updates*

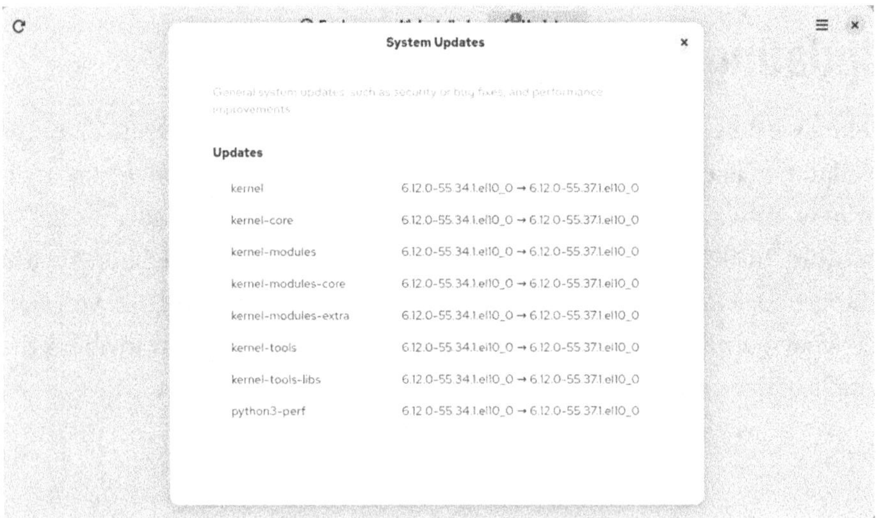

Figure 9-2. *Software GUI tool update details*

Another graphical tool with more advanced capabilities is the Cockpit Web UI, which you are already aware of. It has two tabs: Application and Software updates related to software management. In the Software updates tab, you can not only update packages, but also enable automatic updates. You can see this tab in Figure 9-3.

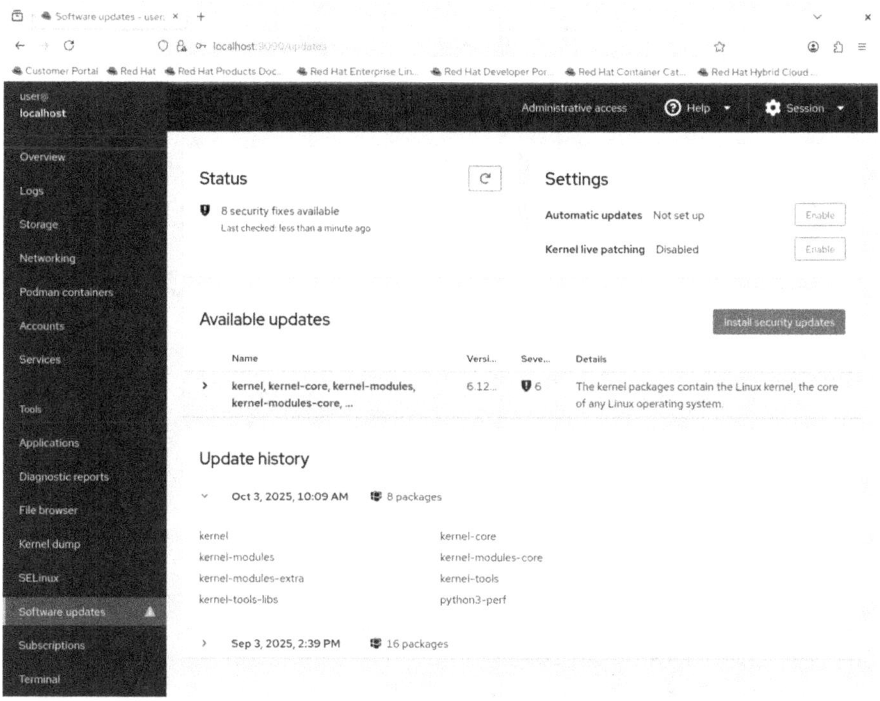

***Figure 9-3.** Cockpit Software updates page*

In Web-UI, you can find the third tab – Subscriptions – which is related to getting software updates from restricted Red Hat repositories, but managing subscriptions is out of scope for the exam. How to subscribe to your lab's VMs is described in Appendix A.

Working with RPM

One way to classify Linux distributions is by the package manager they use. First, it is distributions that use .deb packages, the APT (Advanced Package Tool), and the `dpkg` package management systems. Examples of such distributions are Debian, Ubuntu, and Linux Mint. Another common package type is .rpm, and the package management tool is `rpm`, which is used by `dnf` under the hood. Examples of RPM-based distributions are RHEL, CentOS, Fedora, SUSE Linux Enterprise Server (SLES), and openSUSE. We will start from the RPM tool and then continue with dnf.

RPM is originally an acronym for Red Hat Package Manager, now a recursive acronym for RPM Package Manager.

If you mount the RHEL installation DVD, you will find approximately one thousand RPM packages in the `BaseOS/Packages` directory at the root of the disk:

```
root@localhost:~# mount /dev/cdrom /media/
root@localhost:~# ls /media/BaseOS/Packages
accel-config-4.1.8-2.el10.x86_64.rpm
accel-config-libs-4.1.8-2.el10.x86_64.rpm
...
zsh-5.9-15.el10.x86_64.rpm
zstd-1.5.5-9.el10.x86_64.rpm
```

The name of the file with the RPM package consists of several parts:

```
name-version.el10.architecture.rpm
```

For example, let's look at two packages:

```
root@localhost:~# ls /media/BaseOS/Packages/ | grep bash
bash-5.2.26-6.el10.x86_64.rpm
bash-completion-2.11-16.el10.noarch.rpm
```

bash and bash-completion are names of the packages; 5.2.26-6 and 2.11-16 are versions. el10 stands for Enterprise Linux 10. For example, for Fedora Linux, it can be fc43 for Fedora Linux version 43. Previously, Fedora Linux was known as Fedora Core, which is why it is abbreviated as fc. Next part of the name is x86_64 when the package contains files specific to the 64-bit instruction set extension of x86 (most modern Intel or AMD CPUs) or noarch if this package is common for all architectures.

Tip When you use the dnf tool later, you need to provide only the package name. In that case, the latest version will be installed.

You can install or update a package with rpm; however, you will more often use the dnf tool instead of using rpm directly. dnf uses rpm as its back end but adds features such as handling dependencies and repositories.

Here is an example of installing a package with rpm:

```
root@localhost:/media/BaseOS/Packages# rpm -ivh zsh-5.9-15.
el10.x86_64.rpm
Verifying...              ################################# [100%]
Preparing...              ################################# [100%]
Updating / installing...
   1:zsh-5.9-15.
el10                      ################################# [100%]
```

Here is another example:

```
root@localhost:/media/BaseOS/Packages# rpm -ivh krb5-
server-1.21.3-7.el10.x86_64.rpm
error: Failed dependencies:
    krb5-libs(x86-64) = 1.21.3-7.el10 is needed by krb5-
server-1.21.3-7.el10.x86_64
    krb5-pkinit(x86-64) = 1.21.3-7.el10 is needed by krb5-
server-1.21.3-7.el10.x86_64
...
```

As you can see, the installation failed. The reason is that the `rpm` tool cannot manage dependencies by itself. Most likely, you will use the rpm tool for queries. Let's see some examples. Get detailed information about the package:

```
user@localhost:~$ rpm -qi bash
Name        : bash
Version     : 5.2.26
Release     : 6.el10
Architecture: x86_64
Install Date: Sun 20 Jul 2025 02:19:22 PM CEST
Group       : Unspecified
Size        : 8542552
License     : GPL-3.0-or-later
Signature   : RSA/SHA256, Wed 19 Feb 2025 04:16:57 PM CET, Key
              ID 199e2f91fd431d51
Source RPM  : bash-5.2.26-6.el10.src.rpm
Build Date  : Tue 29 Oct 2024 04:00:19 PM CET
Build Host  : x86-64-02.build.eng.rdu2.redhat.com
Packager    : Red Hat, Inc. <http://bugzilla.redhat.com/
              bugzilla>
Vendor      : Red Hat, Inc.
URL         : https://www.gnu.org/software/bash
Summary     : The GNU Bourne Again shell
Description :
The GNU Bourne Again shell (Bash) is a shell or command
language interpreter that is compatible with the Bourne shell
(sh). Bash incorporates useful features from the Korn shell
(ksh) and the C shell (csh). Most sh scripts can be run by bash
without modification.
```

List all files included in the package:

```
user@localhost:~$ rpm -ql bash
/etc/skel/.bash_logout
/etc/skel/.bash_profile
/etc/skel/.bashrc
/usr/bin/alias
/usr/bin/bash
...
```

What package is providing the specific file:

```
user@localhost:~$ rpm -qf /usr/sbin/useradd
shadow-utils-4.15.0-5.el10.x86_64
```

List all configuration files included in the package:

```
user@localhost:~$ rpm -qc shadow-utils
/etc/default/useradd
/etc/login.defs
/etc/pam.d/passwd
```

List all documentation files included in the package:

```
user@localhost:~$ rpm -qd shadow-utils
/usr/share/doc/shadow-utils/HOWTO
/usr/share/doc/shadow-utils/NEWS
...
```

The RPM package itself is an archive that contains files, metadata, and scripts that run during the installation or uninstallation of the package. To see scripts, you can use this query:

```
user@localhost:~$ rpm -q --scripts dnf
postinstall scriptlet (using /bin/sh):

if [ $1 -eq 1 ] && [ -x "/usr/lib/systemd/systemd-update-
helper" ]; then
    # Initial installation
    /usr/lib/systemd/systemd-update-helper install-system-units
dnf-makecache.timer || :
fi
preuninstall scriptlet (using /bin/sh):
...
```

And finally, deleting the package:

```
root@localhost:~# rpm -evh zsh
Preparing...          ################################# [100%]
Cleaning up / removing...
   1:zsh-5.9-15.
el10                  ################################# [100%]
```

To extract files from the package, you can use a combination of rpm2cpio and cpio tools:

```
root@localhost:~# rpm2cpio zsh-5.9-15.el10.x86_64.rpm | cpio -id
16665 blocks
```

This is not an exam objective, so you don't have to memorize this.

Working with DNF

DNF is a user-friendly tool used for installing, updating, removing, and getting information about RPM packages and their dependencies. It works with local or remote repositories from Red Hat or third-party vendors.

Tip DNF is an abbreviation of Dandified YUM. YUM was used in RHEL until version 8, but was replaced by DNF, which is faster and uses less memory. RHEL has a symlink `yum` pointed to `dnf`. If you are interested, YUM stands for Yellowdog Updater Modified. And Yellow Dog was the name of a GNU/Linux distribution that no longer exists, more than ten years ago.

Let's check what repositories Red Hat provides for RHEL by default:

```
root@localhost:~# dnf repolist
Updating Subscription Management repositories.
repo id                             repo name
rhel-10-for-x86_64-appstream-rpms   Red Hat Enterprise Linux 10
for x86_64 - AppStream (RPMs)
rhel-10-for-x86_64-baseos-rpms      Red Hat Enterprise Linux 10
for x86_64 - BaseOS (RPMs)
```

There are two enabled repositories:

- **BaseOS** - Core set of operating system functionality
- **AppStream** - Additional user-space applications, runtime languages, and databases

Another repository available with all RHEL subscriptions is CodeReady Linux Builder. It provides additional packages for developers. Let's enable it via the command line:

```
root@localhost:~# dnf config-manager --enable codeready-
builder-for-rhel-10-x86_64-rpms
Updating Subscription Management repositories.
root@localhost:~# dnf repolist
Updating Subscription Management repositories.
```

```
repo id                                       repo name
codeready-builder-for-rhel-10-x86_64-rpms Red Hat CodeReady
Linux Builder for RHEL 10 x86_64 (RPMs)
rhel-10-for-x86_64-appstream-rpms         Red Hat Enterprise
Linux 10 for x86_64 - AppStream (RPMs)
rhel-10-for-x86_64-baseos-rpms            Red Hat Enterprise
Linux 10 for x86_64 - BaseOS (RPMs)
```

We enabled the repo definition, which is already present in the system. All Red Hat repositories are described in the file `/etc/yum.repos.d/redhat.repo`. There are more than a hundred repositories in this file. To access many of them, you will require an additional subscription from Red Hat.

Let's add a formally non-Red Hat repository, EPEL, from the Fedora community. EPEL stands for Extra Packages for Enterprise Linux, and it provides additional packages not included and not supported by Red Hat. EPEL packages are based on Fedora Linux packages and should not conflict with base RHEL packages.

Open the page `https://docs.fedoraproject.org/en-US/epel/` in the browser, and use the instructions for EL10. See Figure 9-4.

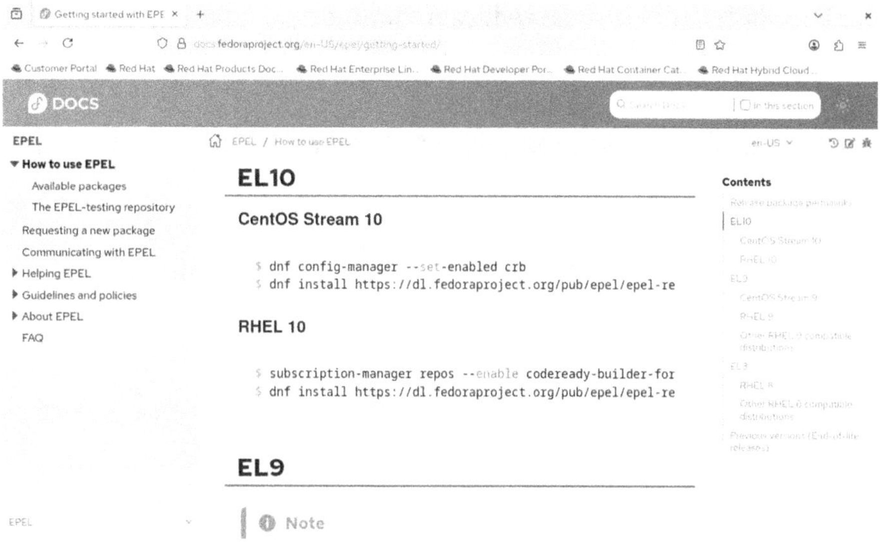

Figure 9-4. *EPEL landing page*

Now we can check /etc/yum.repos.d/ again:

```
root@localhost:~# ls /etc/yum.repos.d/
epel.repo  epel-testing.repo  redhat.repo
```

As you can see, two additional files were added with a new repo description. We can take a close look at the content of epel.repo file:

```
[epel]
name=Extra Packages for Enterprise Linux $releasever -
$basearch
# It is much more secure to use the metalink, but if you wish
to use a local mirror
# place its address here.
#baseurl=https://download.example/pub/
epel/$releasever${releasever_minor:+z}/Everything/$basearch/
```

```
metalink=https://mirrors.fedoraproject.org/
metalink?repo=epel${releasever_minor:+-z}-
$releasever&arch=$basearch
gpgkey=file:///etc/pki/rpm-gpg/RPM-GPG-KEY-EPEL-
$releasever_major
gpgcheck=1
repo_gpgcheck=0
metadata_expire=24h
countme=1
enabled=1
...
```

There are several mandatory and optional parameters for the repository:

- [epel] - The repository ID. This is where the repository description begins. The repository ID should be unique on the particular server.
- name - A human-readable description. It can be any text.
- metalink - This is a dynamic URL that returns an up-to-date list of geographically close and currently operational mirrors.
- baseurl - This is used instead of metalink. Direct URL of the repo.
- gpgkey - Path to GPG public key used to verify the authenticity of packages.
- gpgcheck - If set to 1, dnf will verify packages using a GPG public key.

- `metadata_expire` – Repository's metadata is refreshed from the remote server once every 24 hours.
- `enabled` – If set to 1, dnf will use this repo. You can trigger this with the dnf config-manager command as I showed earlier, or you can edit the file directly.

To create a minimal required file pointed to some example URL, you need just several lines in the existing or new .repo file:

```
[my-repo]
name=My Minimal Custom Repo. You can put any text here.
baseurl=http://myserver/repo
enabled=1
gpgcheck=0 # not recommended, but it is fine for tests.
```

Now we can try the most used dnf commands you need to know for an exam. First, update all installed packages:

```
root@localhost:~# dnf update
...
Dependencies resolved.
================================================================
============================
 Package       Arch       Version
Repository                                 Size
================================================================
============================
Installing:
 kernel        x86_64    6.12.0-55.38.1.el10_0    ...
Removing:
 kernel        x86_64    6.12.0-55.30.1.el10_0    @rhel-10-for-
x86_64-baseos-rpms      0
 ...
```

```
Transaction Summary
================================================================
==============================
Install  5 Packages
Upgrade  6 Packages
Remove   5 Packages

Total download size: 94 M
Is this ok [y/N]: y
Downloading Packages:
(1/11): kernel-6.12.0-55.38.1.el10_0.x86_64.rpm              ...
----------------------------------------------------------------
--------------------------
Total
9.8 MB/s |  94 MB     00:09
Running transaction check
...
Complete!
```

You can add option -y if you don't want to answer yes to questions interactively. It is a valuable option, especially for scripts.

For search by package names and descriptions, use dnf search:

```
root@localhost:~# dnf search mutt
...
================= Name Exactly Matched: mutt ==================
mutt.x86_64 : A text mode mail user agent
================ Name & Summary Matched: mutt =================
mutter-common.noarch : Common files used by mutter and forks
of mutter
mutter-devel.x86_64 : Development package for mutter
===================== Name Matched: mutt ======================
mutter.x86_64 : Window and compositing manager based on Clutter
```

The command `dnf install` will resolve dependencies and install the required package:

```
root@localhost:~# dnf install httpd
...
Dependencies resolved.
============================================
============================================================
 Package        Arch     Version
Repository                                  Size
============================================
============================================================
Installing:
 httpd          x86_64   2.4.63-1.el10_0.2
rhel-10-for-x86_64-appstream-rpms          49 k
Installing dependencies:
 apr            x86_64   1.7.5-2.el10
rhel-10-for-x86_64-appstream-rpms         132 k
 apr-util       x86_64   1.6.3-21.el10
...
Transaction Summary
============================================
============================================================
Install  11 Packages

Total download size: 2.1 M
Installed size: 6.0 M
Is this ok [y/N]: y
```

The command `dnf remove` will do the opposite, and dependencies are included in the removal:

```
root@localhost:~# dnf remove httpd
..
Remove  11 Packages
```

Some of the packages are grouped together, and you can install or remove the entire group at once. To list, install, and remove use verbs with the group:

```
root@localhost:~# dnf group list
Updating Subscription Management repositories.
Last metadata expiration check: 1:33:42 ago on Thu 09 Oct 2025
05:59:19 PM CEST.
Available Environment Groups:
   Server
   Minimal Install
   Workstation
   Custom Operating System
   Virtualization Host
Installed Environment Groups:
   Server with GUI
Installed Groups:
   Container Management
   Headless Management
Available Groups:
   Legacy UNIX Compatibility
   Smart Card Support
   Scientific Support
   Security Tools
   Graphical Administration Tools
   RPM Development Tools
```

```
   Development Tools
   Network Servers
   Console Internet Tools
   .NET Development
   System Tools
root@localhost:~# dnf group install "Development Tools"
...
Install  127 Packages
Total download size: 143 M
Installed size: 475 M
...
```

To check the history of dnf operations, you can use `dnf history`:

```
root@localhost:~# dnf history
Updating Subscription Management repositories.
ID     | Command line                                    |
Date and time    | Action(s)      | Altered
---------------------------------------------------------------
------------------------------------------
    10 | remove httpd                                    |
2025-10-09 19:09 | Removed        |   11
     9 | install httpd                                   |
2025-10-09 18:53 | Install        |   11
     8 | install https://dl.fedoraproject.org/pub/epel/epel |
2025-10-05 16:45 | Install        |    1 EE
     7 | install postfix                                 |
2025-09-28 14:22 | Install        |    2
     6 | install mutt                                    |
2025-09-28 14:21 | Install        |    4
     5 | update                                          |
2025-09-27 17:05 | C, E, I, U     |   86 EE
```

```
     4 | install -y nfs-utils                                 |
2025-08-13 12:50 | Install        |    7 EE
     3 | update                                               |
2025-08-10 11:59 | I, U           |   91 EE
     2 | update                                               |
2025-07-22 18:36 | I, U           |  176 E<
     1 |                                                      |
2025-07-20 14:18 | Install        | 1263 >E
```

The last dnf command for this section is info. You can use it with a group or directly for one particular package:

```
root@localhost:~# dnf info bash
...
Installed Packages
Name         : bash
Version      : 5.2.26
Release      : 6.el10
Architecture : x86_64
Size         : 8.1 M
Source       : bash-5.2.26-6.el10.src.rpm
Repository   : @System
From repo    : anaconda
Summary      : The GNU Bourne Again shell
URL          : https://www.gnu.org/software/bash
License      : GPL-3.0-or-later
Description  : The GNU Bourne Again shell (Bash) is a shell or
command language
             : interpreter that is compatible with the Bourne
               shell (sh). Bash
             : incorporates useful features from the Korn shell
               (ksh) and the C shell
```

```
                   : (csh). Most sh scripts can be run by bash
                     without modification.

root@localhost:~# dnf group info "Development Tools"
...
Group: Development Tools
 Description: A basic development environment.
 Mandatory Packages:
   autoconf
   automake
...
 Default Packages:
   asciidoc
   byacc
...
 Optional Packages:
   cmake
   expect
...
```

Working with Flatpak

Installation of applications with Flatpak is a new topic for the RHCSA exam. Before version ten, Flatpak was not required knowledge for a system administrator from Red Hat's point of view. You probably cannot meet it if you are not using a desktop application on GNU/Linux. The first Flatpak SDK was introduced in RHEL 8.2 and has been installed by default since RHEL 9.

Flatpak is a framework for packaging and distributing desktop applications across different GNU/Linux distributions. Instead of packaging the same application in different types of packages, such as .rpm or .deb, and for various distribution versions, the developer can publish a single Flatpak application that works across all Linux distributions. GNOME Software and KDE Discover support Flatpak out of the box, allowing you to install applications via the Flatpak CLI or through native desktop tools.

Flatpak targets mainly desktop applications by design. In a Flatpak sandbox, applications are restricted from elevating privileges, accessing `/proc`, or creating sub-namespaces. By default, when you install an application, it will be installed for all users, but it is possible to install it only for the current user.

You don't need to know the technologies Flatpak uses under the hood for an exam, but I would recommend you to read the article about its architecture available at the Flatpak site: `https://docs.flatpak.org/en/latest/under-the-hood.html`.

The `https://flathub.org` is the main repository, essentially an "App Store for Linux." Repos in Flatpak are named remotes. You can see a screenshot of Flathub in Figure 9-5.

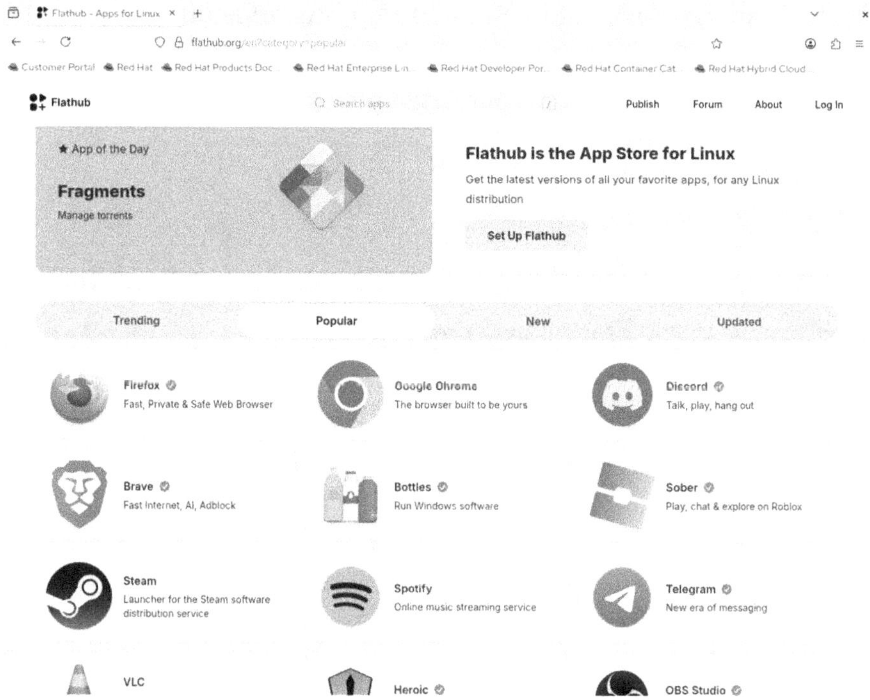

Figure 9-5. *Flathub website*

We can add Flathub by using the command `flatpak remote-add`:

```
user@localhost:~$ flatpak remote-add --if-not-exists flathub
https://dl.flathub.org/repo/flathub.flatpakrepo
```

You will be asked for the root password, and the repository will be added system-wide. By using the option `--user`, you can restrict this to the current user.

Now you can check the list of configured remotes:

```
user@localhost:~$ flatpak remote-list
Name    Options
flathub system
rhel    system,oci,no-gpg-verify
```

The Flathub we added just now and `rhel` was configured out of the box.

Red Hat provides the Firefox browser as an RPM and a Flatpak app. First, let's remove RPM:

```
root@localhost:~# dnf -y remove firefox
```

Now we can search for a Flatpak app:

```
user@localhost:~$ flatpak search firefox
Name                    Description
Application ID                        Version     Branch Remotes
Firefox                 Fast, Private & Safe Web Browser
org.mozilla.firefox                    143.0.4     stable
flathub,rhel
...
```

A Flatpak Application ID is a unique, three-part identifier used to name every application and runtime, like `com.developer.appname`. In the case of Firefox, it is `org.mozilla.firefox`. As you can see, it is available from `Flathub` and from `rhel` remotes.

To install from `rhel` remote, we need to provide its name and then the Application ID. Two notes: Run this command from the terminal in the desktop environment itself, not via SSH. You will also be prompted for the username and password you registered on RedHat.com.

```
user@localhost:~$ flatpak install rhel org.mozilla.firefox
Looking for matches...
Required runtime for org.mozilla.firefox/x86_64/stable
(runtime/com.redhat.Platform/x86_64/el10) found in remote rhel
Do you want to install it? [Y/n]: y

org.mozilla.firefox permissions:
...
```

```
     ID                      Branch    Op   Remote    Download
 1.  com.redhat.Platform     el10      i    rhel      < 395.2 MB
 2.  org.mozilla.firefox     stable    i    rhel      < 145.2 MB

Proceed with these changes to the system installation? [Y/n]: y
Login required remote rhel (realm https://registry.redhat.io/)
User: Your username at redhat.com
Password: password
        ID                      Branch  Op    Remote    Download
 1. [✓] com.redhat.Platform     el10    i     rhel      437.1 MB /
                                                        395.2 MB
 2. [✓] org.mozilla.firefox     stable  i     rhel      153.0 MB /
                                                        145.2 MB

Installation complete.
```

As you can see, com.redhat.Platform was installed as well. It is the shared libraries required by Flatpak apps built by Red Hat. You can check information by using flatpak info:

```
user@localhost:~$ flatpak info com.redhat.Platform

Red Hat Platform - Shared libraries

          ID: com.redhat.Platform
         Ref: runtime/com.redhat.Platform/x86_64/el10
        Arch: x86_64
      Branch: el10
...
```

To see all installed apps, you can use

```
user@localhost:~$ flatpak list
Name                        Application
ID              Version        Branch       Installation
Red Hat Platform            com.redhat.Platform        10
el10          system
Firefox                     org.mozilla.
firefox         140.3.0        stable       system
```

To run the application, use the application icon in the desktop environment or `flatpak run org.mozilla.firefox` command.

Some other useful flatpak subcommands:

- `update` – Update applications.
- `uninstall Application ID` – Uninstall the application.
- `remote-delete Remote` – Remove the remote repository from the local system.

Summary

This chapter focused on the essential and RHCSA-required methods for software management in Red Hat Enterprise Linux, primarily utilizing RPM packages through the command line and exploring the modern Flatpak framework.

The core of RHEL software management lies in the RPM Package Manager, which uses the .rpm file format. While the rpm command itself is fundamental for queries, its limitation in dependency management means system administrators primarily use the DNF (Dandified YUM) utility.

The chapter concluded with the introduction of Flatpak, a modern, sandboxed framework for distributing desktop applications independently of the underlying Linux distribution. Flatpak is now an explicit requirement for the RHCSA exam.

Exercises

1) Use DNF to search for packages related to the **"network"** term, listing only packages that are not yet installed.
2) Install the zsh package using DNF, ensuring the installation proceeds without any interactive prompts.
3) Remove the **zsh** package and any dependencies that are no longer needed, using a single DNF command.
4) Display a detailed description and list of packages (mandatory, default, and optional) included in the "Legacy UNIX Compatibility" package group.
5) Determine which installed RPM package owns the /etc/filesystems file.
6) Use the rpm command to list all files included in the installed bash package.
7) Use the dnf config-manager utility to enable the codeready-builder-for-rhel-10-x86_64-rpms repository.

8) Install the virt-manager package.

9) Write the flatpak command to add the Flathub remote repository only for the current user, without system-wide privileges, and only if the remote doesn't already exist.

10) Install Gimp from Flathub.

CHAPTER 10

Manage Basic Networking

In this chapter, we will discuss three basic network skills tested on the RHCSA exam: IP address configuration, hostname resolution configuration, and network firewall configuration. Since this book is dedicated to helping readers pass the RHCSA exam, the author assumes readers already know the fundamental, generic concepts of network adapter (interface), IP addresses, network ports, the Domain Name System, and hostnames.

IP Address Configuration

Before we get into the details, let's review some concepts you already need to know:

- **IPv4 address** – A 32-bit number usually written for human readability as four 8-bit decimal octets divided by a period. Example: `192.168.1.1`.
- **IPv6 address** – A 128-bit number usually expressed as eight hexadecimal groups divided by a colon. Leading zeros in groups can be omitted. If several groups consist only of zero numbers, they can be

A. Markelov, *Red Hat RHCSA 10 Study Companion*, Certification Study Companion Series,
https://doi.org/10.1007/979-8-8688-2226-1_10

combined into two columns. Example: `fe80 : 0000 : 0000 : 0000 : 5054 : 00ff : fefa : f86e`, the fully expanded form; `fe80::5054:ff:fefa:f86e`, the compressed form.

- **Netmask** – Indicates how many bits of the address belong to the subnet. IPv4 addresses can be written in older forms where the network part is "masked" with "1" in binary format. For human readability, it is also written as four 8-bit decimal octets separated by a period. Modern, CIDR syntax is shorter, and it specifies how many leading bits in the address belong to the network part. In that case, the netmask is specified in one decimal number. IPv6 addresses use only CIDR notation. Examples: `255.255.255.0`, old form; `/24`, CIDR form.
- **Routing table** – Each host in the network has a routing table that guides how to send traffic to other networks. It can include specific entries for specific networks and a default route for traffic that is not matched to a specific destination. If it is not directly connected to a network, the entry in the routing table will have a router IP address (gateway) of the particular host that will forward traffic.
- **Network interface** – Software representation of a physical interface (network adapter, network interface card, or NIC). It can also be virtual network interfaces that do not directly represent a particular NIC.

- **Local interface (loopback interface)** – An example of a virtual interface used for a system to communicate with itself (localhost). It is always assigned the IP address `127.0.0.1`, and network traffic sent to this interface stays within the host.
- **TCP/IP network model** – A four-layered set of abstractions that defines how traffic flows from one host to another and how different protocols interact.

Now it is time to look at the interfaces and IP addresses information. You can use the command `ip link show` (shortcut `ip l`) to see network interfaces, or you can use `ip addr show` (shortcut `ip a`) to see network interfaces and IP addresses.

Tip In older guides, you may have found tools like `ifconfig`, `route`, and others from the `net-tools` package. Most of them are obsolete, although included in RHEL 10. The `ip` tool and others included in the `iproute` package are a modern replacement.

```
root@localhost:~# ip a
1: lo: <LOOPBACK,UP,LOWER_UP> mtu 65536 qdisc noqueue state
UNKNOWN group default qlen 1000
    link/loopback 00:00:00:00:00:00 brd 00:00:00:00:00:00
    inet 127.0.0.1/8 scope host lo
       valid_lft forever preferred_lft forever
    inet6 ::1/128 scope host noprefixroute
       valid_lft forever preferred_lft forever
2: enp1s0: <BROADCAST,MULTICAST,UP,LOWER_UP> mtu 1500 qdisc
fq_codel state UP group default qlen 1000
    link/ether 52:54:00:fa:f8:6e brd ff:ff:ff:ff:ff:ff
    altname enx525400faf86e
```

```
    inet 192.168.122.153/24 brd 192.168.122.255 scope global
dynamic noprefixroute enp1s0
       valid_lft 2622sec preferred_lft 2622sec
    inet6 fe80::5054:ff:fefa:f86e/64 scope link noprefixroute
       valid_lft forever preferred_lft forever
```

Let's review the major parts of the command output. We can see two network interfaces. First, lo is the loopback interface. It has been assigned the IPv4 address 127.0.0.1/8 and the IPv6 address ::1/128. The interface is UP (active), and the physical layer (LOWER_UP) is also up. In fact, there is no corresponding physical interface for lo, so LOWER_UP is here more for the unification of output than for real meaning. The Maximum Transmission Unit is set to 65536 bytes (mtu 65536), a huge size typical for loopback. It is also not important for the virtual interface.

The second interface is a physical network card interface named enp1s0. In fact, this is a virtual machine, so the interface is virtual, but from the operating system's perspective, it is physical. This is an Ethernet NIC (wired). In the past, GNU/Linux used eth0, eth1, etc., for Ethernet cards, but in modern distributions, Predictable Network Interface Names are used. See systemd.net-naming-scheme(7) for more information. In our example, the prefix en is for Ethernet. p1 is the number of the PCI bus the device is connected to (PCI bus 1). And s0 is slot number 0 on the PCI bus. In case of WLAN interfaces, their name will start with wl.

We can see that the interface supports sending broadcast and multicast traffic (BROADCAST,MULTICAST), and is currently UP. The MTU is 1500 bytes. This is the standard minimum for Ethernet networks and is compatible with most devices' default settings.

The link/ether 52:54:00:fa:f8:6e is a hardware, physical (MAC) address for the NIC. The first three numbers identify the NIC vendor, and the last three should be unique to physical devices made by that vendor. Altname enx525400faf86e is secondary, persistent, and an alternative name that is derived directly from the device's MAC address. You can use it in the command instead of enp1s0. The IP address of the interface is `192.168.122.153`, and the netmask is `/24`. From the `scope global dynamic`, we can see that the address is globally reachable and was assigned dynamically (e.g., via the DHCP protocol). The Dynamic Host Configuration Protocol (DHCP) is a network protocol that automatically assigns IP addresses and other network parameters to devices. The IPv6 address is `fe80::5054:ff:fefa:f86e/64`. This is a link-local IPv6 address. It is only valid for communication on the local network segment. The lines `valid_lft` are related to the DHCP lease of the IP address.

Before making changes to the IP configuration in the command line, we can look at the graphical tools. First is, as usual, the setting in the GNOME desktop environment. As shown in Figure 10-1, pressing the configuration button near an interface opens a pop-up window with several tabs.

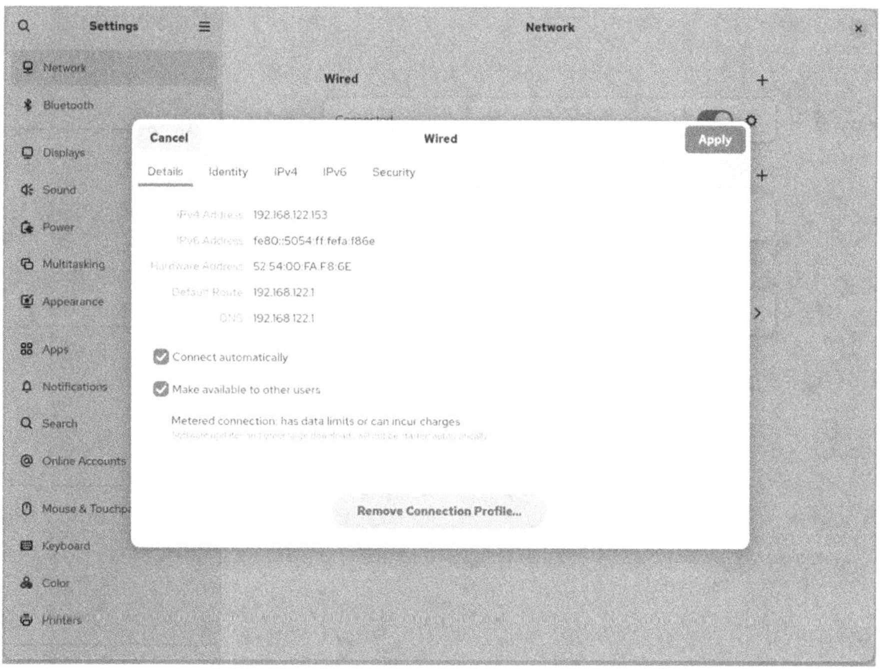

Figure 10-1. *Network settings in the GNOME desktop environment*

The first tab shows a summary of the interface. To change IPv4 or IPv6 addresses, click on the corresponding tabs.

A more advanced local graphical tool, oriented to system administrators rather than end users, is `nm-connection-editor`. It is an official graphical frontend explicitly built to interact with the NetworkManager daemon. We will talk about NetworkManager very soon.

The next familiar tool is Cockpit's web interface. In Figure 10-2, you can see the Networking overview page. From this page, you can edit firewall rules, add virtual interfaces, and, by clicking on the physical interface name, view and adjust interface configuration. Figure 10-3 shows the interface details. The interface name "Red Hat, Inc. Virtio 1.0" was derived from the first digits of the MAC address.

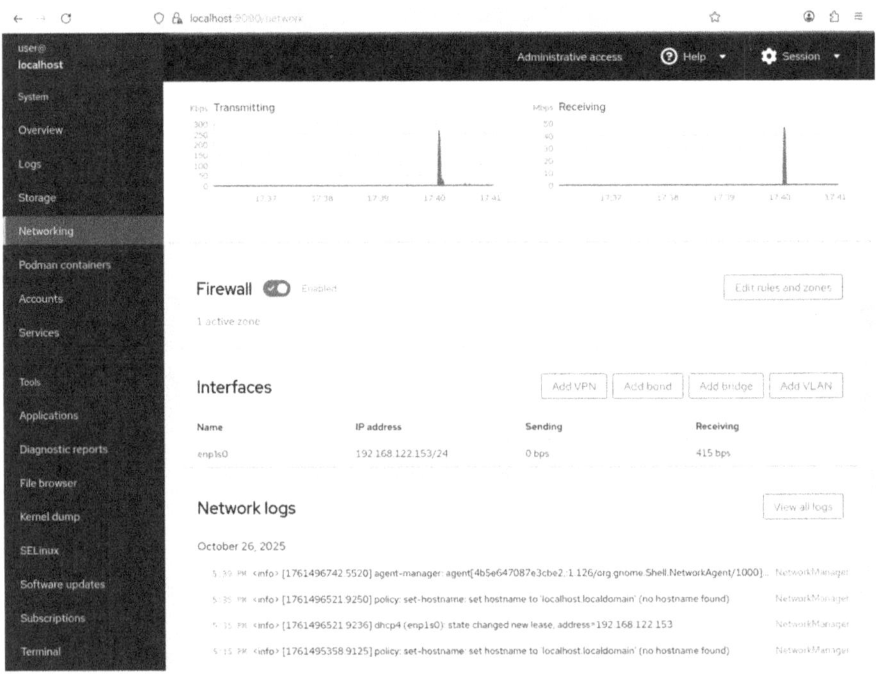

Figure 10-2. *Web console Networking overview page*

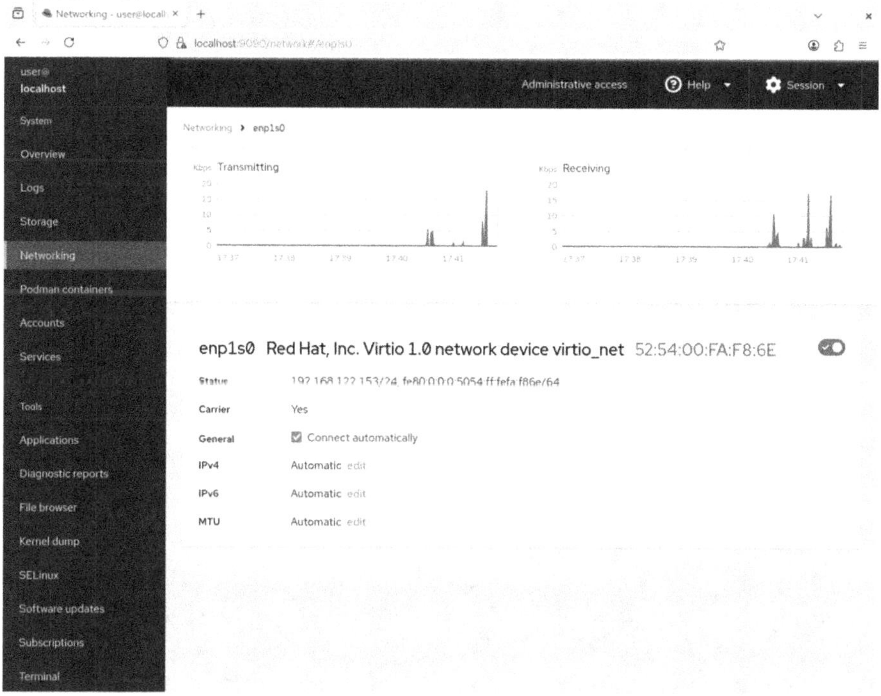

***Figure 10-3.** Network Interface details*

If you click Edit near IPv4, you will open a window similar to the one shown in Figure 10-4, where you can edit settings.

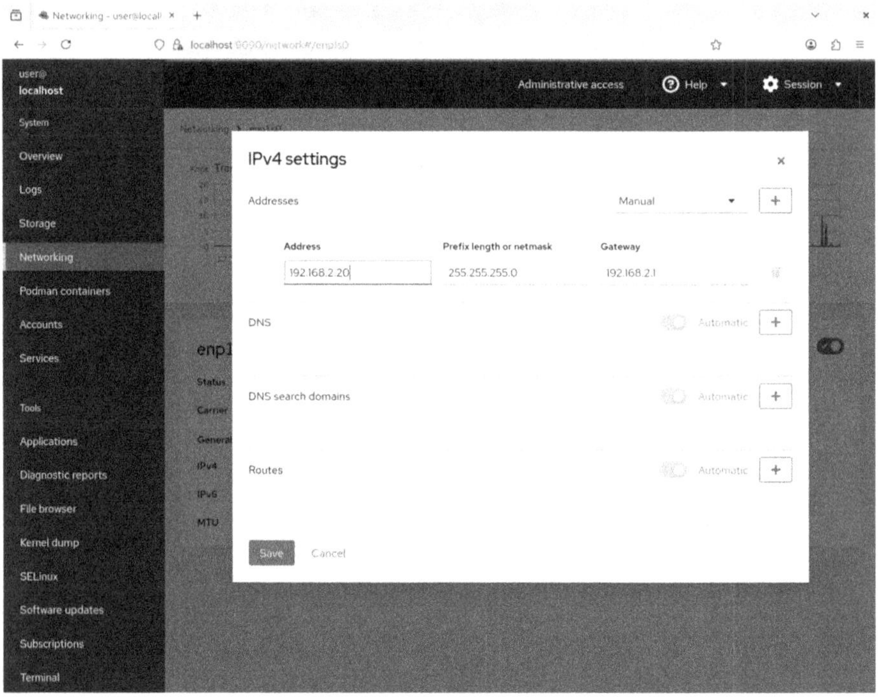

Figure 10-4. *Network Interface IPv4 settings editing*

Another user-friendly, easy-to-use tool you can explore is `nmtui`, which lets you configure connections via a text-based user interface. You can see it's the user interface in Figure 10-5. That means you can use this pseudo graphic tool via SSH connection from the terminal. As `nm-connection-editor`, it is also part of NetworkManager.

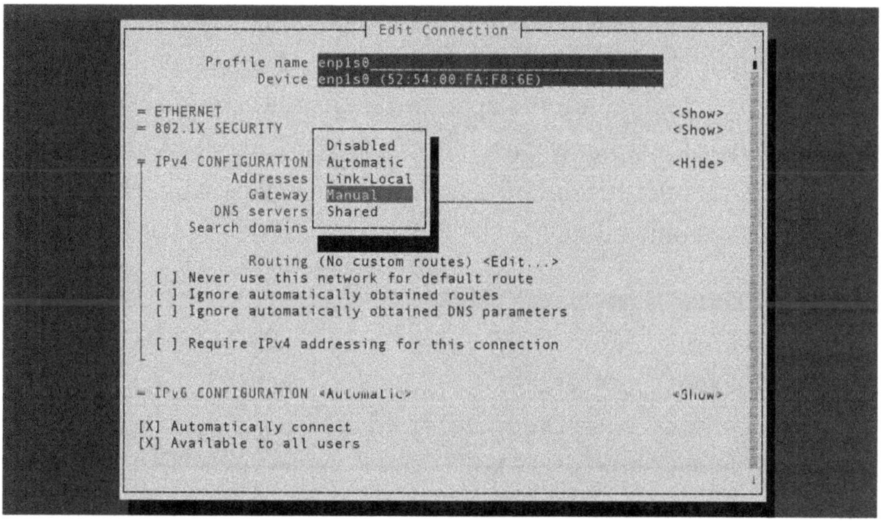

Figure 10-5. *The* `nmtui` *text-based user interface*

NetworkManager, the standard GNU/Linux network configuration tool suite, ensures that each Ethernet adapter has its own connection profile, with default settings that rely on DHCP for IPv4 and IPv6 configuration.

Tip Old ifcfg-* network configuration files stored in `/etc/sysconfig/network-script/` inherited from the network service are not presented anymore. Network configuration is now primarily handled by NetworkManager using key files located in the `/etc/NetworkManager/system-connections/` directory.

The primary CLI tool to change NetworkManager settings is `nmcli`. It is used to create, display, edit, delete, activate, and deactivate network connections. Two useful man pages you can refer to are `nmcli(1)` and `nmcli-examples(7)`.

When working with NetworkManager, keep in mind two concepts: devices and connections. The device is a network interface, and the connection is the settings that can be attached to the device (active) or can exist unattached. For example, your laptop has one connection for work and one connection for home. Depending on where your laptop will be used, the network adapter will use a dedicated connection. A connection can be active for only one device at a time, and a device cannot have more than one active connection.

```
root@localhost:~# nmcli dev status
DEVICE  TYPE     STATE                  CONNECTION
enp1s0  ethernet connected              enp1s0
lo      loopback connected (externally) lo
enp8s0  ethernet disconnected           --
enp9s0  ethernet disconnected           --
```

In this example, we can see a virtual machine with three devices, but only one, `enp1s0`, has an active connection. Connection is also named `enp1s0`. We can ignore the virtual `lo` device and connection. This is a list of connections:

```
root@localhost:~# nmcli con show
NAME    UUID                                 TYPE     DEVICE
enp1s0  eeee584a-4691-3522-a987-43943cd7f0f6 ethernet enp1s0
lo      6aa0fadd-c2e5-403b-a615-4837991aec86 loopback lo
```

If we want to activate a second device, we need to add a new connection and mark it as dedicated to the second device. Let's name the new connection `second`:

```
root@localhost:~# nmcli con add con-name second type ethernet
ifname enp8s0
Connection 'second' (51453b26-2b39-4175-81df-80e94e5f5cf5)
successfully added.
```

Now we can recheck the list of devices and connections:

```
root@localhost:~# nmcli dev status
DEVICE  TYPE      STATE                    CONNECTION
enp1s0  ethernet  connected                enp1s0
enp8s0  ethernet  connected                second
lo      loopback  connected (externally)   lo
enp9s0  ethernet  disconnected             --
root@localhost:~# nmcli con show
NAME    UUID                                  TYPE      DEVICE
enp1s0  eeee584a-4691-3522-a987-43943cd7f0f6  ethernet  enp1s0
second  51453b26-2b39-4175-81df-80e94e5f5cf5  ethernet  enp8s0
lo      6aa0fadd-c2e5-403b-a615-4837991aec86  loopback  lo
```

As we can see, enp8s0 now has an active connection, and the list of connections includes a new one named second. Now we can check devices with the ip command:

```
root@localhost:~# ip a
1: lo: <LOOPBACK,UP,LOWER_UP> mtu 65536 qdisc noqueue state
UNKNOWN group default qlen 1000
    link/loopback 00:00:00:00:00:00 brd 00:00:00:00:00:00
    inet 127.0.0.1/8 scope host lo
       valid_lft forever preferred_lft forever
    inet6 ::1/128 scope host noprefixroute
       valid_lft forever preferred_lft forever
2: enp1s0: <BROADCAST,MULTICAST,UP,LOWER_UP> mtu 1500 qdisc
fq_codel state UP group default qlen 1000
    link/ether 52:54:00:fa:f8:6e brd ff:ff:ff:ff:ff:ff
    altname enx525400faf86e
    inet 192.168.122.153/24 brd 192.168.122.255 scope global
dynamic noprefixroute enp1s0
       valid_lft 2271sec preferred_lft 2271sec
```

```
    inet6 fe80::5054:ff:fefa:f86e/64 scope link noprefixroute
       valid_lft forever preferred_lft forever
3: enp8s0: <BROADCAST,MULTICAST,UP,LOWER_UP> mtu 1500 qdisc
fq_codel state UP group default qlen 1000
    link/ether 52:54:00:0e:9b:8e brd ff:ff:ff:ff:ff:ff
    altname enx5254000e9b8e
    inet 192.168.122.39/24 brd 192.168.122.255 scope global
dynamic noprefixroute enp8s0
       valid_lft 2272sec preferred_lft 2272sec
    inet6 fe80::3ea3:efa7:cdc1:b7f0/64 scope link noprefixroute
       valid_lft forever preferred_lft forever
4: enp9s0: <BROADCAST,MULTICAST,UP,LOWER_UP> mtu 1500 qdisc
fq_codel state UP group default qlen 1000
    link/ether 52:54:00:42:d9:c2 brd ff:ff:ff:ff:ff:ff
    altname enx52540042d9c2
```

As you can see, enp8s0 has an assigned IP address from the DHCP server. But why does this happen? We can check the details of the connection:

```
root@localhost:~# nmcli con show second
connection.id:                          second
...
connection.type:                        802-3-ethernet
connection.interface-name:              enp8s0
connection.autoconnect:                 yes
connection.autoconnect-priority:        0
...
ipv4.method:                            auto
...
ipv6.method:                            auto
...
```

The connection is set to automatically connect when the interface becomes available, and IPv4 and IPv6 addressing are configured to use automatic methods. Priorities can typically be set from -999 (lowest priority) to 999 (highest priority).

Now we can create a second connection for the same interface, but with higher priority and manual settings.

```
root@localhost:~# nmcli con add con-name second-pri10 ifname
enp8s0 type ethernet  ipv4.method manual ipv4.addresses
10.10.10.1/24 connection.autoconnect-priority 10
Connection 'second-pri10' (72d9781f-3223-47b4-9cad-9c0f7f1
0646d) successfully added.
```

For now, enp8s0 is using "old" connection:

```
root@localhost:~# nmcli con show
NAME          UUID                                  TYPE      DEVICE
enp1s0        eeee584a-4691-3522-a987-43943cd7f0f6  ethernet  enp1s0
second        51453b26-2b39-4175-81df-80e94e5f5cf5  ethernet  enp8s0
lo            421cd4c9-251a-42fb-b420-c7ee8a8fe631  loopback  lo
second-pri10  72d9781f-3223-47b4-9cad-9c0f7f10646d  ethernet  --
```

What will happen if we turn the connection second off?

```
root@localhost:~# nmcli con down second
Connection 'second' successfully deactivated (D-Bus active
path: /org/freedesktop/NetworkManager/ActiveConnection/3)
root@localhost:~# nmcli dev status
DEVICE  TYPE      STATE                   CONNECTION
enp1s0  ethernet  connected               enp1s0
enp8s0  ethernet  connected               second-pri10
lo      loopback  connected (externally)  lo
enp9s0  ethernet  disconnected            --
```

Both connections for enp8s0 have autoconnection enabled, but those with manual IP address assignment have a higher priority. That is why second-pri10 is active.

```
root@localhost:~# ip a show enp8s0
3: enp8s0: <BROADCAST,MULTICAST,UP,LOWER_UP> mtu 1500 qdisc
fq_codel state UP group default qlen 1000
    link/ether 52:54:00:0e:9b:8e brd ff:ff:ff:ff:ff:ff
    altname enx5254000e9b8e
    inet 10.10.10.1/24 brd 10.10.10.255 scope global
    noprefixroute enp8s0
       valid_lft forever preferred_lft forever
    inet6 fe80::556b:b7e4:e45d:d725/64 scope link noprefixroute
       valid_lft forever preferred_lft forever
```

If we want to turn off the network interface, we need to disable the interface itself:

```
root@localhost:~#  nmcli dev dis enp8s0
Device 'enp8s0' successfully disconnected.
```

To enable the interface, activate one of the related connections:

```
root@localhost:~# nmcli con up second
```

Take into account that after the server's reboot, the active connection will be second-pri10. It is essential in the context of the exam, since your work will be checked after the system's reboot, as stated on the exam page:

> *As with all Red Hat performance-based exams, configurations must persist after reboot without intervention.*

You also need to know how to set up the default gateway and static routes. For the default gateway, you need to use keys ipv4.gateway and ipv6.gateway during creation or modification of the connection. To modify the connection, use nmcli con mod. For example, we can change the IPv4 gateway:

```
root@localhost:~# nmcli con mod second-pri10 ipv4.gateway
10.10.10.1
root@localhost:~# nmcli con show second-pri10 | grep
ipv4.gateway
ipv4.gateway:                           10.10.10.1
```

To check the routing table, you can use the `ip route` command:

```
root@localhost:~# ip route
default via 192.168.122.1 dev enp1s0 proto dhcp src
192.168.122.153 metric 100
default via 10.10.10.1 dev enp8s0 proto static metric 101
10.10.10.0/24 dev enp8s0 proto kernel scope link src 10.10.10.1
metric 101
192.168.122.0/24 dev enp1s0 proto kernel scope link src
192.168.122.153 metric 100
```

In most cases, the server has only one default gateway. The host where we added the new default gateway already has one. NetworkManager is smart enough to add a second gateway with a lower priority (i.e., a higher metric number). It will be used as a failback.

You can add or delete static routes with nmcli by using the syntax: `nmcli con mod connection_name +|-ipv4.routes "<route>"`. To add a route, use the plus sign, and to remove it, use the minus sign.

For example:

```
root@localhost:~# nmcli con mod enp1s0 +ipv4.routes
"172.16.0.0/12 192.168.122.20"
```

Re-activate the connection:

```
root@localhost:~# nmcli con up enp1s0
Connection successfully activated (D-Bus active path: /org/
freedesktop/NetworkManager/ActiveConnection/4)
```

```
root@localhost:~# ip route
...
172.16.0.0/12 via 192.168.122.20 dev enp1s0 proto static
metric 102
...
```

To check network connectivity, you can use the `ping` and `ping6` commands.

Configure Hostname Resolution

We already mentioned in Chapter 6 that for changing the hostname of the server, you can use the `hostnamectl` command as root:

```
root@localhost:~# hostnamectl set-hostname server1.local.test
```

The hostname is stored in the file `/etc/hostname`. This change is local; for external systems, nothing will change. In the same manner, you can have local mapping of hostnames to external systems' IP addresses in the local file `/etc/hosts`.

At the beginning of the Internet (ARPANET), it was the primary method for resolving hostnames to IP addresses before the Domain Name System (DNS) was developed. You can use it for now, most likely in small lab environments or in exceptional cases. It will be checked before querying DNS by default. The default `/etc/hosts` file looks like this in the example:

```
user@server1:~$ cat /etc/hosts
# Loopback entries; do not change.
# For historical reasons, localhost precedes localhost.
localdomain:
127.0.0.1   localhost localhost.localdomain localhost4
localhost4.localdomain4
```

```
::1          localhost localhost.localdomain localhost6
localhost6.localdomain6
# See hosts(5) for proper format and other examples:
# 192.168.1.10 foo.example.org foo
# 192.168.1.13 bar.example.org bar
```

You can add more lines if needed by using the format specified in the default examples. First, put the IP address and then the name or names.

Setting up the DNS server is not part of the RHCSA exam requirements, but you should be able to configure a DNS client. In all Unix-like systems, the /etc/resolv.conf file manages the list of DNS servers and their priorities. Priority is meant from the first to the last. Here is how it can look with only a DNS server:

```
user@server1:~$ cat /etc/resolv.conf
# Generated by NetworkManager
search local.test
nameserver 192.168.122.1
```

In this example, local.test is the search domain. It means that if you try to resolve a hostname without any dots, like server2, the DNS resolver will automatically append .local.test to the name and attempt to resolve server-a.local.test.

You are limited to three nameserver entries. On RHEL10, as on most modern GNU/Linux distributions, the /etc/resolv.conf file should not be changed manually.

Here is an example of how to add two more DNS servers to the existing connection:

```
root@server1:~# nmcli con mod enp1s0 ipv4.dns "8.8.8.8 8.8.4.4"
root@server1:~# nmcli con up enp1s0
Connection successfully activated (D-Bus active path: /org/
freedesktop/NetworkManager/ActiveConnection/3)
```

```
root@server1:~# cat /etc/resolv.conf
# Generated by NetworkManager
search local.test
nameserver 8.8.8.8
nameserver 8.8.4.4
nameserver 192.168.122.1
```

As you can see, we can see `192.168.122.1` acquired via DHCP at the end of the list. To remove it, we can turn off getting DNS servers from DHCP:

```
root@server1:~# nmcli con mod enp1s0 ipv4.ignore-auto-dns yes
root@server1:~# nmcli con up enp1s0
Connection successfully activated (D-Bus active path: /org/
freedesktop/NetworkManager/ActiveConnection/4)
root@server1:~# cat /etc/resolv.conf
# Generated by NetworkManager
search local.test
nameserver 8.8.8.8
nameserver 8.8.4.4
```

Restricting Network Access with a firewalld

The fundamental role of a network firewall is to protect a server by controlling the flow of data from and to external networks. It operates by applying rules to sort network traffic, deciding which connections are safe to allow and which to block. In RHEL 10, `firewalld` is a firewall management daemon. You can create, modify, and remove rules on the fly without restarting the `firewalld` service, ensuring uninterrupted network protection.

`firewalld` is recommended as the front end for the Netfilter framework in the Linux kernel, which does the job in the background. `firewalld` replaces the deprecated old `iptables`.

You can interact with `firewalld` by using `firewall-cmd` CLI, `firewall-config` GUI, or Cockpit web console. The `firewall-config` tool may not be installed by default, and you will need to install the package with the same name.

Tip In most scenarios, including exams, `firewalld` is more than sufficient. If you want to have full control of rules and cover more sophisticated examples, use the `nftables` framework. The usage of `nftables` is covered in the "Configuring firewalls and packet filters" book from the RHEL 10 documentation set.

`firewalld` has several concepts:

- **Zone** – A logically separated network based on the level of trust. It can be trusted and allows all traffic by default. Network interfaces and sources of traffic can be assigned to a zone. Specific traffic cannot ingress or egress more than one zone. By default, all traffic within a single zone is allowed, while traffic between different zones is denied. `firewalld` has several predefined zones stated in Table 10-1.

Table 10-1. *Default settings for predefined zones*

Zone	Default settings
block	Any traffic is rejected with an ICMP prohibited message back. The exception is traffic related to the egress connection.
drop	The same as block, but no ICMP notification will be sent back.
trusted	All incoming connections are accepted.
external	Best suited for external untrusted connections when the server acts as a router. Incoming traffic is rejected unless it is related to outgoing traffic. Outgoing IPv4 traffic is masqueraded. Masquerading means that outgoing traffic appears to originate from the IP address of the outgoing interface. Incoming SSH traffic is allowed.
dmz	By default, the only difference with `external` is that outgoing traffic is not masqueraded. Best suited for external, untrusted connections when your server has services exposed to the external world (known as a demilitarized zone, i.e., dmz). You can allow such services in this zone. Incoming traffic is rejected unless it is related to outgoing traffic. Incoming SSH traffic is allowed.
home and internal	Initially, they are the same. Incoming traffic is rejected unless it is related to outgoing traffic, except SSH, cockpit, mdns, samba-client, or dhcpv6-client.
public	Default zone. It instructs NetworkManager to add a new connection to this zone. You can change the default zone to any other. Incoming traffic is rejected unless it is related to outgoing traffic or matches the SSH, cockpit, or dhcpv6-client predefined services.
work	Incoming traffic is rejected unless it is related to outgoing traffic or matches the SSH, cockpit, or dhcpv6-client predefined services. The difference with the `public` zone is that the `work` zone is not the default.

- **Policies** - Rules to allow or deny traffic between zones.
- **Services** - A predefined set of rules covers incoming traffic from one specific network service. For example, the `samba` service requires more than one port, and the corresponding `firewalld` service will have all of them.

You can investigate any zone by using the `firewalld-cmd` command:

```
root@server1:~# firewall-cmd --zone=public --list-all
public (default, active)
  target: default
  ingress-priority: 0
  egress-priority: 0
  icmp-block-inversion: no
  interfaces: enp1s0
  sources:
  services: cockpit dhcpv6-client ssh
  ports:
  protocols:
  forward: yes
  masquerade: no
  forward-ports:
  source-ports:
  icmp-blocks:
  rich rules:
```

The public zone appears in the `firewall-config` GUI and the Cockpit web console, as shown in Figures 10-6 and 10-7.

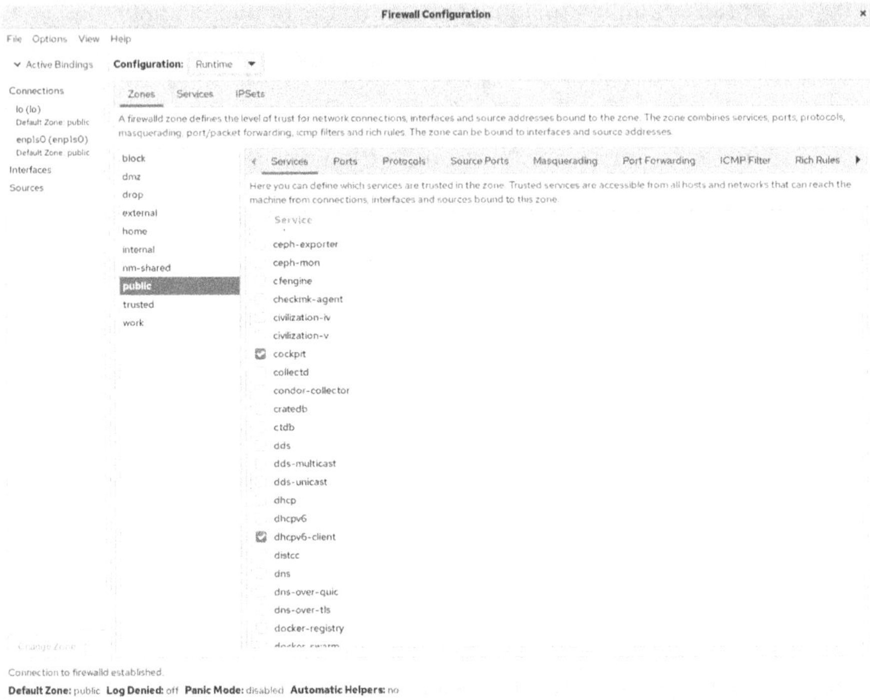

Figure 10-6. *The `firewall-config` user interface*

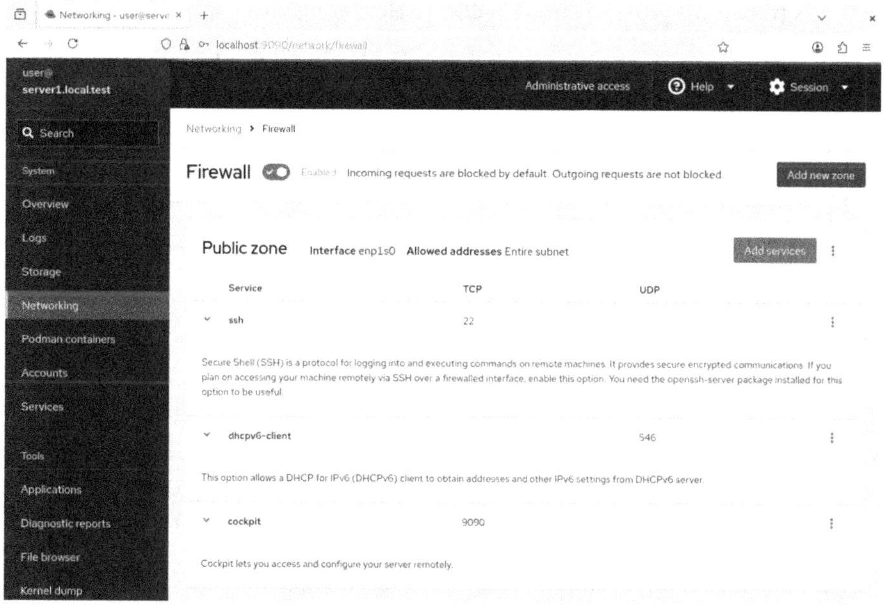

Figure 10-7. *Firewall settings in the Cockpit web console*

RHEL 10 comes with more than 250 predefined services. You can check the list of them by using the `firewall-cmd --get-services` command. If needed, you can add your own.

In Figure 10-6, you can see a drop-down switch labeled "Configuration." You can choose between Runtime and Permanent. `firewalld` uses two sets of rules: a runtime configuration and a permanent configuration (saved to disk). You can make runtime-only changes, but they will be lost after the `firewalld` service is reloaded or the host is restarted. When `firewalld` starts up, it always loads the rules from the permanent configuration. If you are using `firewall-cmd`, changes require the `--permanent` option to be saved across reboots, followed by `--reload` to activate them in the runtime configuration.

Let's play a bit with `firewall-cmd` to demonstrate its basic commands. First, we can retrieve active zones. We should get all zones with network interfaces and the default zone:

```
root@server1:~# firewall-cmd --get-active-zones
public (default)
  interfaces: enp1s0
```

Following commands list all zones:

```
root@server1:~# firewall-cmd --get-zones
block dmz drop external home internal nm-shared public
trusted work
```

As the next step, I want to change the interface `enp1s0` from zone `public` to `external`. But first, let's see the property `connection.zone` of connection `enp1s0` with `nmcli`:

```
root@server1:~# nmcli -g connection.zone con show enp1s0
public
```

As you see, NetworkManager is aware of `firewalld` zones. Now we can change the zone for the interface with `--change-interface`. If I were to add a new interface that does not belong to any zone, I would use the `--add-interface` option.

```
root@server1:~# firewall-cmd --change-interface=enp1s0
--zone=external --permanent
The interface is under the control of NetworkManager, setting
the zone to 'external'.
success
```

Let's see the property `connection.zone` of connection `enp1s0` again:

```
root@server1:~# nmcli -g connection.zone con show enp1s0
external
```

If we list active zones, we can still see public as the default zone:

```
root@server1:~# firewall-cmd --get-active-zones
external
  interfaces: enp1s0
public (default)
```

If you are changing the default zone, you don't need the --permanent option. It will be changed in the runtime and in the permanent configuration:

```
root@server1:~#  firewall-cmd --set-default-zone=external
success
root@server1:~#  firewall-cmd --get-active-zones
external (default)
  interfaces: enp1s0
```

If we want to drop all source traffic from a specific network, we can add it to the zone drop:

```
root@server1:~# firewall-cmd --add-source=10.10.10.0/24
--zone=drop --permanent
success
root@server1:~#  firewall-cmd --get-active-zones
external (default)
  interfaces: enp1s0
```

I added the source successfully, but the zone drop is not shown. This is because I added the source to the permanent configuration, but asked to show the runtime configuration. I need to reload the permanent configuration to the runtime:

```
root@server1:~#  firewall-cmd --reload
success
root@server1:~#  firewall-cmd --get-active-zones
drop
```

```
  sources: 10.10.10.0/24
external (default)
  interfaces: enp1s0
```

To remove the source, you can use the `--remove-source` option. Remember that all configurations in the exam should be persistent. Additionally, if the `--zone` option is not specified, the default zone is used.

If you want to give access to some of the network services (daemons) working on your host, your first option should be to search for existing `firewalld` services. If you are using something less common or your daemon uses a non-standard port, you need to specify both the port and the transport layer protocol, rather than the service. Let's see some examples. Here is how to add the samba service permanently and to runtime:

```
root@server1:~# firewall-cmd --add-service=samba --permanent
success
root@server1:~# firewall-cmd --reload
success
```

Here is how to add a specific UDP port permanently and to runtime:

```
root@server1:~# firewall-cmd --add-port=17057/udp --permanent
success
root@server1:~# firewall-cmd --reload
success
```

Here is how to remove changes from permanent configuration (they will be in runtime until `firewall-cmd --reload` or server reboot):

```
root@server1:~# firewall-cmd --remove-service=samba --permanent
success
root@server1:~# firewall-cmd --remove-port=17057/udp --permanent
success
```

In the examples above, we do not specify a zone, which means changes were made to the default.

Summary

You learned NetworkManager service and that `nmcli` are your primary command-line tools for it. We explored the critical distinction between network devices and connections and used `nmcli` to create new connection profiles, set static IP addresses, and configure default gateways and static routes.

Next, we covered hostname resolution. You saw how to set a persistent system hostname using `hostnamectl`. For name resolution, we discussed the role of the local `/etc/hosts` file and, more importantly, the correct method for configuring DNS clients.

Finally, we secured the system using `firewalld`. We introduced the core concepts of zones and services. You learned to use the `firewall-cmd` utility to manage these, including assigning interfaces to zones, adding services, and opening specific ports.

Exercises

1) Use the ip a command to list all network interfaces. Identify the IP address, netmask (in CIDR format), and MAC address for your primary Ethernet interface.

2) Use the ip route show command to display the system's current routing table. Identify the default gateway and its associated metric.

3) Use nmcli con show to list all available NetworkManager connection profiles. Identify which connections are currently active and on which devices.

4) Use nmcli to display all properties for your primary active connection. Note the `ipv4.method` value.

5) Add a new, persistent NetworkManager connection named lab-dhcp for your *second* (likely disconnected) Ethernet interface. Ensure it is configured to get an IP address automatically via DHCP and to autoconnect.

6) Create a new, persistent connection named `static1` for your primary interface. Configure it with the following manual settings:

   - **IP address** – 192.168.122.55/24
   - **Gateway** – 192.168.122.1
   - **DNS server** – 8.8.8.8
   - **Autoconnect** – No

7) Bring the `static1` connection up. Use `ip a` and `ip route` to verify that the static IP and new default gateway are active.

8) Add a *second* IP address, `10.10.10.55/24`, to your active `static1` connection. Do *not* remove the original `192.168.122.55/24` address. Verify with `ip a` that the interface now has both IP addresses.

9) Change your system's persistent hostname to `server15.test.local`.

10) Edit the `/etc/hosts` file to add a new entry. The entry should map the IP address `192.168.122.55` to the hostnames `web55.test.local` and `web55`.

11) Modify your active connection profile to use the static DNS servers `8.8.8.8` and `8.8.4.4`

12) Modify the same connection profile to set `ipv4.ignore-auto-dns` to `yes`. Reactivate the connection, and then inspect the `/etc/resolv.conf` file to ensure *only* your manually set DNS servers are present.

13) Add the `http` service to the default zone's runtime configuration. Verify it is listed. Then, reload the firewall using `firewall-cmd --reload`, and verify that the http service is now gone (because it was not permanent).

14) Permanently add TCP port 8080 to the public zone. Reload the firewall, and verify that the port is now active in the runtime configuration.

CHAPTER 11

Manage Security with SELinux

In this chapter, we will explore the basics of SELinux (Security-Enhanced Linux), an implementation of mandatory access control (MAC) that runs after the "traditional" discretionary access control (DAC) system.

What Is SELinux?

Within the DAC framework, we face a fundamental limitation in separating user access to resources: access is determined by user permissions. These are the classic `rwx` permissions at three levels: owner, owning group, and others. Additionally, there are POSIX ACLs, which only expand the number of levels at which permissions can be defined, but nothing more.

Therefore, any application running with `user1` permissions can do anything with all the data to which `user1` has access. It doesn't matter, for example, that this application is an email program that only needs access to `user1`'s emails. This program will also have access to, say, `user1`'s video files and `user1`'s pictures. And not only does the program itself have access, but it can also make all this data accessible to others. Things get much worse when `user1` has UID=0 (i.e., `root`). We run into the classic "superuser problem." In this case, we only have two levels of access: root

A. Markelov, *Red Hat RHCSA 10 Study Companion*, Certification Study Companion Series,
https://doi.org/10.1007/979-8-8688-2226-1_11

and regular users. In other words, it becomes impossible to implement access using the minimum necessary privileges.

In MAC, access rights are determined by the system itself using specially defined policies. In the implementation under consideration, SELinux, such policies operate at the system call level and are enforced by the Linux Kernel itself (but can also be implemented at the application level). The U.S. National Security Agency originally developed SELinux, and now it is an open source project included in the standard "vanilla" Linux Kernel. Commercial support has been available since RHEL 4.

SELinux is working after the classic Unix security model is applied. In other words, SELinux cannot allow anything that is denied through user/group permissions. Policies are described using a specialized access rule language. In most cases, SELinux rules are transparent to applications and require no modification.

Resources and processes in RHEL have SELinux labels, also named SELinux contexts. SELinux policy describes what processes with specific labels can do with resources that have their own specific labels.

The SELinux context has four parts: user, role, type, and security level. Of these, *type* is the most crucial component of the policy. This is because the policy rules that enforce access control (what a process can touch) are overwhelmingly based solely on the type field, not the full context.

Basic Operations

Let's start with experimenting. For that, we will use the Apache web server. We need to install the RPM package `httpd` and start the service, and then, using `curl`, we can check on the `localhost` web server, which will provide a test page:

```
root@server1:~# dnf -y install httpd
root@server1:~# systemctl start httpd
root@server1:~# curl http://localhost
```

```
<!DOCTYPE html PUBLIC "-//W3C//DTD XHTML 1.1//EN" "http://www.
w3.org/TR/xhtml11/DTD/xhtml11.dtd">

<html xmlns="http://www.w3.org/1999/xhtml" xml:lang="en">
    <head>
        <title>Test Page for the HTTP Server on Red Hat
Enterprise Linux</title>
...
```

Apache, by default, will serve the files we put in the /var/www/html directory via HTTP. For our demonstration of SELinux capabilities, we can create two files in the home directory: file1 and file2, each with its own content. Next, we will copy to the root directory of Apache file1 and move file2:

```
root@server1:~# echo "file1" > file1
root@server1:~# echo "file2" > file2
root@server1:~# cp file1 /var/www/html/
root@server1:~# mv file2 /var/www/html/
```

If you now try to access both files, you will find the first one you copied is accessible, but the second one you moved is not accessible:

```
root@server1:~# curl http:/localhost/file1
file1
root@server1:~# curl http:/localhost/file2
<!DOCTYPE HTML PUBLIC "-//IETF//DTD HTML 2.0//EN">
<html><head>
<title>403 Forbidden</title>
</head><body>
<h1>Forbidden</h1>
<p>You don't have permission to access this resource.</p>
</body></html>
```

Two files with the same permissions, but with such different behavior. Since this is an SELinux demonstration, we can look into SELinux logs. You can find them in the file `/var/log/audit/audit.log`; the log type is `AVC`, which stands for Access Vector Cache. This cache is where SELinux policy decisions are stored:

```
root@server1:~# tail /var/log/audit/audit.log | grep AVC
type=AVC msg=audit(1764701914.825:281): avc:  denied  { getattr
} for  pid=3201 comm="httpd" path="/var/www/html/file2"
dev="dm-0" ino=34144328 scontext=system_u:system_r:httpd_t
:s0 tcontext=unconfined_u:object_r:admin_home_t:s0 tclass=file
permissive=0
```

How to read this message? The number `1764701914` is Unix Epoch time, the number of seconds since January 1, 1970, 00:00:00 UTC. Next, you can read that it was denied to read the file's metadata: `avc: denied { getattr }`. It was denied for process with PID=3201 and command name `httpd`. The file to which access was denied is `/var/www/html/file2` on device `dm-0`, and the index descriptor of the file is `34144328`.

The next two parts are the most important. It is source context and target context. Source context in our case is `system_u:system_r:httpd_t:s0`, and `httpd_t` is the type on which the policy is based. This is the SELinux type for the Apache process. And target context is the context of the file with SELinux type `admin_home_t`. It is obvious that SELinux policy doesn't grant the web server access to files with type "this belongs to the admin home directory".

The last two parts of the message are the class of the target object (a regular file), and `permissive=0` indicates that, at the moment, SELinux was in enforcing mode, not in permissive. In enforcing mode, restrictions are applied, and in permissive mode, only logged in the audit log.

Let's first confirm that Apache processes have the `httpd_t` type. For that, we need option `Z` of the `ps` command:

```
root@server1:~# ps auxZ | grep httpd
system_u:system_r:httpd_t
:s0     root          3198  0.0  0.0  18428 10824 ?        Ss
19:54   0:00 /usr/sbin/httpd -DFOREGROUND
system_u:system_r:httpd_t
:s0     apache        3199  0.0  0.0  18100  5232
?         S     19:54   0:00 /usr/sbin/httpd -DFOREGROUND
system_u:system_r:httpd_t:s0    apache       3200  0.0  0.0
2419380 8256 ?        Sl   19:54   0:00 /usr/sbin/httpd
-DFOREGROUND
system_u:system_r:httpd_t:s0    apache       3201  0.0  0.0
2222708 7996 ?        Sl   19:54   0:00 /usr/sbin/httpd
-DFOREGROUND
...
```

Next, we can check the SELinux file types in /var/www/html/. For the command ls, the same option Z can be used:

```
root@server1:~# ls -lZ /var/www/html/
total 8
-rw-r--r--. 1 root root unconfined_u:object_r:httpd_sys_
content_t:s0 6 Dec  2 19:57 file1
-rw-r--r--. 1 root root unconfined_u:object_r:admin_
home_t:s0        6 Dec  2 19:57 file2
```

Why do file1 and file2 have different SELinux contexts? While moving a file within a single file system, it keeps the original metadata, including the SELinux label. When a file is copied or moved between two different file systems, a new file is actually created with the SELinux context of the target directory. Yes, part of the SELinux policy includes default labels for different directories.

To check the current mode, you can use getenforce, and to set it, use setenforce. Take into account that these changes will not be permanent:

```
root@server1:~# getenforce
Enforcing
root@server1:~# setenforce 0
root@server1:~# getenforce
Permissive
root@server1:~# curl http:/localhost/file2
file2
root@server1:~# setenforce 1
root@server1:~# curl http:/localhost/file2
<!DOCTYPE HTML PUBLIC "-//IETF//DTD HTML 2.0//EN">
<html><head>
<title>403 Forbidden</title>
...
```

The exam requires that all changes be permanent, so you should know how to do this with enforcement settings as well. For that file `/etc/sysconfig/selinux` is in charge. You need to edit the `SELINUX` line and set it to enforcing, permissive, or disabled. This file has instructions in the comments:

```
root@server1:~# cat /etc/sysconfig/selinux
# This file controls the state of SELinux on the system.
# SELINUX= can take one of these three values:
#     enforcing - SELinux security policy is enforced.
#     permissive - SELinux prints warnings instead of
enforcing.
#     disabled - No SELinux policy is loaded.
...
SELINUX=enforcing
```

Managing Labels and Booleans

The easiest way to change labels on files and directories is the `restorecon` tool. It will restore SELinux context to the default as defined by policy. Let's fix our `file2` and check now SELinux won't prevent access:

```
root@server1:~# restorecon -Rv /var/www/html/
Relabeled /var/www/html/file2 from unconfined_u:object_r:admin_
home_t:s0 to unconfined_u:object_r:httpd_sys_content_t:s0
root@server1:~# curl http:/localhost/file2
file2
```

But this will not work for custom directories that are unknown to the policy. If SELinux was disabled, new files were created without labels. In permissive mode, users can create files with incorrect labels. To make sure files on the system have correct labels, create a special file in the root directory and reboot the server:

```
root@server1:~# touch /.autorelabel; reboot
```

During the reboot process, files will be relabeled.

To list SELinux contexts that are covered in the policy, you can use the `semanage` tool:

```
root@server1:~# semanage fcontext -l
SELinux fcontext    type             Context

/                   directory        system_u:object_r:root_t:s0
/.*                 all files        system_u:object_r:default_t:s0
/[^/]+              regular file     system_u:object_r:etc_runtime_t:s0
/\.autofsck         regular file     system_u:object_r:etc_runtime_t:s0
...
```

You can temporarily change the file context with the command chcon if SELinux is in permissive mode:

```
root@server1:~# chcon -t httpd_t file1
```

But the context will be changed during context restoration. A better way is to set up the context with semanage, then restore it with restorecon.

The first way is to set the context as the context for some existing file or directory:

```
root@server1:~# semanage fcontext -a -e /etc /mydb
root@server1:~# restorecon -Rv /mydb/
Relabeled /mydb from unconfined_u:object_r:default_t:s0 to
unconfined_u:object_r:etc_t:s0
```

The second way to set up SELinux type directly:

```
root@server1:~# semanage fcontext -a -t etc_t /mydb2
root@server1:~# restorecon -Rv /mydb2/
Relabeled /mydb2 from unconfined_u:object_r:default_t:s0 to
unconfined_u:object_r:etc_t:s0
```

Similar to files, network ports are labeled too:

```
root@server1:~# semanage port -l | grep http_port
http_port_t                    tcp      80, 81, 443, 488, 8008,
8009, 8443, 9000
http_port_t                    udp      80, 443
pegasus_http_port_t            tcp      5988
root@server1:~# semanage port -a -t http_port_t -p tcp 10000
root@server1:~# semanage port -l | grep http_port
http_port_t                    tcp      10000, 80, 81, 443,
488, 8008, 8009, 8443, 9000
...
```

SELinux booleans are another way to tweak SELinux policy. Usually, it is the way to disable a specific part of SELinux policy.

To list all booleans with a description, you can use `semanage boolean`:

```
root@server1:~# semanage boolean -l
SELinux boolean                State  Default Description

abrt_anon_write                (off  ,  off)  Allow abrt to
anon write
abrt_handle_event              (on   ,   on)  Allow abrt to
handle event
abrt_upload_watch_anon_write   (on   ,   on)  Allow abrt to
upload watch anon write
auditadm_exec_content          (on   ,   on)  Allow auditadm to
exec content
authlogin_nsswitch_use_ldap    (off  ,  off)  Allow authlogin
to nsswitch use ldap
...
```

There are two values in this output: first, "State" is the current status; second, "Default" is the state after reboot. To change a boolean, you can use `setsebool`. With option `-P`, you are setting the default value without a runtime value:

```
root@server1:~# setsebool httpd_can_sendmail on
root@server1:~# setsebool -P httpd_can_sendmail off
```

Summary

In this chapter, we learned that SELinux (Security-Enhanced Linux) is a mandatory access control (MAC) system that works after the traditional Unix permissions (DAC). Its purpose is to enforce strict security policies and address DAC's weaknesses, such as the "superuser problem" and the lack of minimum necessary privileges. We discovered that SELinux relies on contexts (labels), primarily the Type field, to determine access. We learned how to troubleshoot denials using the AVC logs, manage operational modes with `setenforce`, permanently fix labels with `restorecon`, define custom rules using `semanage fcontext`, and fine-tune policies with Booleans and port labeling.

Exercises

1) Write the two commands necessary to check the SELinux context (label) for both the running `sshd` process and the `/etc/ssh/sshd_config` file.
2) You have created a new directory, `/srv/www/`, which needs to be served by Apache. Write the two commands required to permanently set the context for this directory and all its contents to `httpd_sys_content_t`.
3) The company wants to run a secondary HTTP server on port 8988. Write the command to permanently label TCP port 8988 as a valid `http_port_t` port.
4) Find and enable the SELinux boolean permanently that allows the Apache web server to use NFS.

CHAPTER 12

Manage Containers

The topic of managing containers was removed from the RHCSA 10 requirements compared to RHCSA 9. However, the author decided to keep the very basics of containers, even though they are not part of the exam, for parity with previous versions. You do not need to study this chapter as part of preparation, and it has no exercises at the end.

Introduction to Containers

Unlike the "vertical" abstraction of virtualization, containers provide "horizontal" partitioning of the operating system into separate, isolated environments. Unlike virtualization, each container doesn't require a separate operating system instance, resulting in significantly lower overhead. The downside is that you can't run different operating systems, such as Windows and GNU/Linux, on the same host within containers.

It's also worth noting that containers are often used on top of virtual machines, which can be located in either a private or public cloud.

Thus, containers provide some of the benefits of virtual machines while using fewer hardware resources. The advantages of using containers over virtual machines include

- Horizontal application isolation
- Reduced infrastructure overhead

A. Markelov, *Red Hat RHCSA 10 Study Companion*, Certification Study Companion Series,
https://doi.org/10.1007/979-8-8688-2226-1_12

- Isolation not at the operating system level, but at the application environment level (required libraries)
- Application deployment speed and application restart speed
- Concurrent operation of multiple environments of a single application
- "Application virtualization" - independence of the application from the operating system and libraries, which simplifies updates and testing
- The ability to reuse the same container for multiple applications on a single node

When using containers, keep the following in mind:

- Containers on a single machine can be the basis for a PaaS cloud, but not a PaaS cloud in itself. Examples of PaaS cloud platforms include Cloud Foundry and Red Hat OpenShift.
- Although containers technically only change the way applications are packaged, this can entail changes to the application architecture.
- Containers are not the opposite of virtualization. Containers can and often are run inside virtual machines.

All containers on a single node share the same operating system kernel. From the perspective of the GNU/Linux operating system kernel, there is no such thing as a "container." Containers are simply GNU/Linux processes that use standard Kernel isolation mechanisms.

GNU/Linux operating systems use standard Linux Kernel technologies to isolate containers and ensure security, including

- Namespaces (Linux Namespaces)
- Control groups (cgroups)
- Privilege management tools (Linux Capabilities)
- Additional, mandatory control security systems such as AppArmor (in Debian and Ubuntu) or SELinux (in RHEL)

Let's look at these technologies in more detail.

The control group mechanism (cgroups) provides a tool for fine-grained control over the allocation, prioritization, and management of system resources. Control groups are implemented in the Linux Kernel. In modern distributions, cgroup management is implemented through systemd. The main hierarchies of control groups (also called controllers) are listed below:

- **blkio** - Sets limits on I/O operations and access to block devices.
- **cpu** - Uses the process scheduler to distribute CPU time among tasks.
- **cpuacct** - Creates automatic reports on CPU resource usage. Works in conjunction with the cpu controller described above.
- **cpuset** - Assigns specific processors and memory nodes to tasks.
- **devices** - Regulates task access to specific devices.
- **freezer** - Pauses or resumes tasks.

- **memory** - Sets limits and generates reports on memory usage by tasks in a control group.
- **net_cls** - Tags network packets with a class identifier (classid). This allows to take these tags into account when processing traffic.
- **perf_event** - Enables monitoring of control groups using the perf utility.
- **hugetlb** - Enables the use of large virtual memory pages and applies limits to them.

Namespaces control access to kernel data structures rather than resource allocation. This effectively means isolating processes from each other and allowing for parallel, but distinct, hierarchies of processes, users, and network interfaces. If desired, different services can even have their own loopback interfaces.

Examples of namespaces used by containers:

- **PID, Process ID** - Process hierarchy isolation
- **User** - User ID (UID) and group ID (GID) isolation
- **NET, Networking** - Network interface isolation
- **IPC, Interprocess communication** - Interprocess communication management
- **MNT, Mount** - Mount point management
- **UTS, Unix timesharing system** - Isolation of hostname and NIS domain name

A mechanism called Capabilities allows root user privileges to be broken down into smaller groups and assigned individually. This functionality has been available in GNU/Linux since kernel version 2.2. By default, containers are launched with a limited set of privileges. Using CLI command options, you can allow or deny actions such as

- Mounting operations
- Socket access
- Performing certain file system operations, such as changing file attributes or ownership

For more information on privileges, see the GNU/Linux `CAPABILITIES(7)` man page.

The set of utilities that support container operations is called a container engine, and the portion of it responsible for launching and monitoring containers is called a container runtime.

In RHEL, the container engine is Podman, and container runtimes are runc and crun (optional). In general, Podman is compatible with Docker, which is available in other distributions. Docker can be installed on RHEL, but not supported by Red Hat. Other tools used in RHEL for working with containers:

- `buildah` – For operations related to building images.
- `scopeo` – For operations related to inspecting and copying containers.
- Podman Desktop – GUI tool for managing containers. This tool is also available for Mac and Windows machines (`https://podman-desktop.io/`).

While working with containers, you need to know some definitions:

- Containers are isolated user environments in which applications run, using operating system technologies. The simplest definition of a Docker container is an application running from an image.
- Images are read-only application templates. New image layers can be added on top of existing images, which collectively represent a file system, modifying

or supplementing the previous layer. Typically, a new image is created either by saving an already running container as a new image on top of an existing one or by using special instructions in the Dockerfile or Containerfile.

- Registries containing image repositories are network-based image storage. They can be either private or public. The most well-known registry is Docker Hub. The book also mentions repositories containing RPM packages. These can be accessed using the `dnf` commands. Don't confuse repositories used for installing operating system packages with container repositories.

Basic Operations

To install the container's CLI utilities, you can use a meta-package `container-tools`:

```
root@localhost:~# dnf install container-tools
```

By default, in RHEL 10, two Red Hat registries and Docker Hub are configured:

```
root@localhost:~# grep -v '^\s*#' /etc/containers/
registries.conf
unqualified-search-registries = ["registry.access.redhat.com",
"registry.redhat.io", "docker.io"]
short-name-mode = "enforcing"
```

To search the container's images in the configured registries, you can use `podman search`:

```
root@localhost:~# podman search httpd
NAME                                     DESCRIPTION
registry.redhat.io/rhscl/httpd-24-rhel7  Platform for running
                                         Apache httpd 2.4
                                         or bui...
registry.redhat.io/rhel8/httpd-24        Platform for running
                                         Apache httpd 2.4
                                         or bui...
...
docker.io/inventis/httpd                 apache container
                                         with support for
                                         https only
docker.io/buzzardev/httpd                 ...
```

Some of the container registries require a login before you can pull images. For example, if you want to access Red Hat registries, you have to use your Red Hat username and password, the same credentials that you use on the website:

```
root@localhost:~# podman login registry.redhat.io
Username: My_username
Password: My_password
Login Succeeded!
```

Now it will be possible to pull (download) the image:

```
# podman pull registry.redhat.io/rhel10/httpd-24
Trying to pull registry.redhat.io/rhel10/httpd-24:latest...
Getting image source signatures
Checking if image destination supports signatures
Copying blob 15664c6066c9 done   |
Copying blob 25ae5a651b7b done   |
Copying blob 1da72969c7bd done   |
```

```
Copying config acf5c37233 done   |
Writing manifest to image destination
Storing signatures
acf5c372333a00e53f72d57e099d6878b609256e1636c37c37a8779f1c
7cd92d
```

In addition to the image itself, the base image and all intermediate images that determine the download capability were downloaded.

As you can see, it was pulled `httpd-24:latest`. The image name comes from the registry, the name itself, and after the colon is the tag that represents the version. By default, if you do not specify a tag, as in our example, the "`latest`" tag will be used. It's recommended not to use the "`latest`" tag exclusively in production environments. Different images may appear under this tag at different times. It's possible that a new "`latest`" image will appear in a day or month that isn't backward compatible. Use tags that clearly indicate the version in addition to "`latest`."

You can list tags and check what you can pull:

```
root@localhost:~# podman search --list-tags registry.redhat.io/
rhel10/httpd-24
NAME                                TAG
registry.redhat.io/rhel10/httpd-24  10.0
registry.redhat.io/rhel10/httpd-24  10.0-1745527928
...
```

You can view the list of downloaded images using the `podman images` command:

```
root@localhost:~# podman images
REPOSITORY                          TAG         IMAGE
ID        CREATED        SIZE
```

```
registry.redhat.io/rhel10/httpd-24  latest      acf5c372333a
3 weeks ago  288 MB
```

You don't need to download an image to run a container. If one is available, it will be downloaded automatically. Let's try running an Ubuntu container. We won't specify a registry, and the official image supported by Canonical will be downloaded. Furthermore, if you don't specify a tag, the latest LTS release will be downloaded and run. The corresponding command is

```
root@localhost:~# podman run -it ubuntu
Resolved "ubuntu" as an alias (/etc/containers/registries.
conf.d/000-shortnames.conf)
Trying to pull docker.io/library/ubuntu:latest...
Getting image source signatures
Copying blob 20043066d3d5 done   |
Copying config c3a134f2ac done   |
Writing manifest to image destination
root@88a707d9b564:/#
```

In addition to the run command, we specified two options: `-i` (the container should start in interactive mode) and `-t` (a pseudo-terminal should be allocated). As you can see from the output, we have root privileges in the container, and the container ID is displayed as the hostname. This may not be true for all containers and depends on the container developer. Let's verify that this is indeed an Ubuntu environment:

```
root@88a707d9b564:/# cat /etc/*release
DISTRIB_ID=Ubuntu
DISTRIB_RELEASE=24.04
DISTRIB_CODENAME=noble
DISTRIB_DESCRIPTION="Ubuntu 24.04.3 LTS"
...
```

The uname -a command cannot be used to verify the distribution, since the container uses the host's Linux Kernel.

One option could be to specify a unique container name, which can be conveniently referenced in addition to the container ID. It is specified as --name <name>. If this option is omitted, the name is generated automatically.

The automatically generated container names are meaningless, but an interesting fact is that they are randomly generated from an adjective and the name of a famous scientist, inventor, or hacker. The generator code for each name contains a brief description of what the individual is known for.

You can view a list of running containers using the podman ps command. To do this, open a second terminal:

```
root@localhost:~# podman ps
CONTAINER ID  IMAGE                            COMMAND
CREATED          STATUS           PORTS        NAMES
88a707d9b564  docker.io/library/ubuntu:latest  /bin/bash   50
seconds ago  Up 50 seconds                  suspicious_kowalevski
```

Suppose you need to run a container with a process that doesn't require interactive behavior, such as a daemon, use the -d option. Let's do just that with the following container:

```
# podman run -d mysql
docker.io/library/mysql:latest
Trying to pull docker.io/library/mysql:latest...
```

However, if we run the podman ps command, we won't find the container created from the mysql image. Let's use the -a option, which shows all containers, not just running ones:

```
root@localhost:~# podman ps -a
CONTAINER ID  IMAGE                                 COMMAND
CREATED                STATUS
PORTS                   NAMES
```

```
1b17a69411aa  docker.io/library/mysql:latest
mysqld      About a minute ago  Exited (1) About a minute
ago  3306/tcp, 33060/tcp  agitated_darwin
...
```

The status is Exited. To figure out the cause, you can check the log:

```
root@localhost:~# podman logs agitated_darwin
2025-12-13 11:40:37+00:00 [Note] [Entrypoint]: Entrypoint
script for MySQL Server 9.5.0-1.el9 started.
2025-12-13 11:40:37+00:00 [Note] [Entrypoint]: Switching to
dedicated user 'mysql'
2025-12-13 11:40:37+00:00 [Note] [Entrypoint]: Entrypoint
script for MySQL Server 9.5.0-1.el9 started.
2025-12-13 11:40:37+00:00 [ERROR] [Entrypoint]: Database is
uninitialized and password option is not specified
    You need to specify one of the following as an environment
    variable:
    - MYSQL_ROOT_PASSWORD
    - MYSQL_ALLOW_EMPTY_PASSWORD
    - MYSQL_RANDOM_ROOT_PASSWORD
```

Apparently, the required parameters weren't specified when the container was launched. You can find a description of the environment variables required to launch the container by seeing the official MySQL image on Docker Hub. Let's try again using the -e option, which sets environment variables in the container:

```
root@localhost:~# podman run --name mysqltest -e MYSQL_ROOT_
PASSWORD=podman123 -d mysql
```

```
ae7f8c4c4f1c29536087d973e1db4674e43b4774f3166dc0adede5f08677008b
root@localhost:~# podman ps
CONTAINER ID  IMAGE                            COMMAND
CREATED            STATUS           PORTS                 NAMES
ae7f8c4c4f1c  docker.io/library/mysql:latest  mysqld
26 seconds ago  Up 26 seconds  3306/tcp, 33060/tcp  mysqltest
```

You can connect to a running container using the following command:

```
root@localhost:~# podman exec -it mysqltest bash
bash-5.1#
```

The last parameter is the command we want to execute within the container. In this case, it's the Bash command interpreter. The `-it` options serve the same purpose as those used earlier in the `podman run` command. `podman top` will show us `mysqld` and bash running in the `mysqltest` container:

```
root@localhost:~# podman top mysqltest
USER        PID         PPID        %CPU        ELAPSED
TTY         TIME        COMMAND
mysql       1           0           0.731       6m50.56793859s
?           3s          mysqld
root        217         0           0.000       4m55.568074633s
pts/0       0s          bash
```

Complete information about running a container can be obtained with `podman inspect`:

```
root@localhost:~# podman inspect mysqltest
[
     {
          "Id": "ae7f8c4c4f1c29536087d973e1db4674e43b4774f3166d
          c0adede5f08677008b",
```

```
        "Created": "2025-12-12T12:52:35.273989757+01:00",
        "Path": "docker-entrypoint.sh",
...
```

We have learned how to launch a container with a daemon running inside it. But such a container isn't handy. We also need to be able to connect to the service from the external network. One possible way is to use port forwarding from containers to the host. Let's experiment with a more visual example – the Apache web server. The official image page on Docker Hub is located at `https://hub.docker.com/_/httpd`. From the description, you can see that the web server's root directory is `/usr/local/apache2/htdocs/`.

Let's download the image and run it with the new `-p` option:

```
root@localhost:~# podman run -d -p 8888:80 --name
httpdtest httpd
docker.io/library/httpd:latest
Trying to pull docker.io/library/httpd:latest...
Getting image source signatures
...
```

This option connects the host's TCP port 8888 to the container's port 80. This port forwarding will also be visible in the `podman ps` command output:

```
root@localhost:~# podman ps
CONTAINER ID  IMAGE                           COMMAND
CREATED         STATUS          PORTS                   NAMES
64d4fa131ea2  docker.io/library/httpd:latest  httpd-
foreground  47 seconds ago  Up 47 seconds  0.0.0.0:8888->80/
tcp  httpdtest
```

Now we can test:

```
root@localhost:~# curl http://localhost:8888
<!DOCTYPE HTML PUBLIC "-//W3C//DTD HTML 4.01//EN" "http://www.
w3.org/TR/html4/strict.dtd">
<html>
<head>
<title>It works! Apache httpd</title>
...
```

You can stop the container with `podman stop`, then start it again with `podman start`. To delete a stopped container, use the `rm` verb; to delete an image, use the `rmi` verb:

```
root@localhost:~# podman stop httpdtest
httpdtest
root@localhost:~# podman rm httpdtest
httpdtest
root@localhost:~# podman rmi httpd
Untagged: docker.io/library/httpd:latest
Deleted: 627c383437d53d53f027b45edd5bf611313e47d619852f995fa81
d966ff543cc
```

We have learned how to run containers, but if you delete the container, your changes to, for example, index.html, will be lost. The httpd page on Docker Hub provides an example of container usage:

```
$ docker run -dit --name my-apache-app -p 8080:80 -v "$PWD":/
usr/local/apache2/htdocs/ httpd:2.4
```

For sure, you must replace Docker with Podman if you are working in RHEL or Fedora Linux. What's new here is the `-v` option. This option allows you to mount a host directory inside the container. The target directory in this example is `/usr/local/apache2/htdocs/`, and the directory being mounted is the current working directory, whose path is contained in the $PWD environment variable. Let's use the suggested syntax to create index.html in a dedicated directory:

```
root@localhost:~# mkdir wwwroot
root@localhost:~# echo "My WWW server" > wwwroot/index.html
root@localhost:~# podman run -d -p 8888:80 -v /root/wwwroot:/
usr/local/apache2/htdocs/ --name httpdtest2 httpd
root@localhost:~# curl http://localhost:8888
<!DOCTYPE HTML PUBLIC "-//W3C//DTD HTML 4.01//EN" "http://www.
w3.org/TR/html4/strict.dtd">
<html><head>
<title>403 Forbidden</title>
</head><body>
<h1>Forbidden</h1>
<p>You don't have permission to access this resource.</p>
</body></html>
```

This is not working because the directory's SELinux type is incorrect. The easiest way to fix this is to add the :z option; Podman will automatically relabel the mounted host directory so the container process can access it:

```
root@localhost:~# podman stop httpdtest2
httpdtest2
root@localhost:~# podman rm httpdtest2
httpdtest2
root@localhost:~# podman run -d -p 8888:80 -v /root/wwwroot:/
usr/local/apache2/htdocs/:z --name httpdtest2  httpd
21bba5d8816d8a60220a4911866f31ab273bec3554a545eb26f69f81513a
5282
root@localhost:~# curl http://localhost:8888
My WWW server
```

Summary

This chapter provided a foundational look at Linux containers, a highly efficient application deployment method, despite the topic's removal from current RHCSA exam requirements.

Containers achieve horizontal partitioning, isolating applications at the environment level while sharing the host's kernel. This makes them significantly more resource-efficient than traditional virtual machines.

APPENDIX A

RHEL 10 Installation with Graphical Installer

For most tasks, you need only one virtual or physical server with 2–4 vCPU, 1.5 GB of RAM, and 10 GB of disk space. For selected exercises, such as NFS file system mounting, it is beneficial to have two servers; however, you can install both the server and client on a single machine.

As you can see, with the minimal requirements for RHEL installation, you can even use the Free tier on major public cloud providers. You can use local desktop solutions, such as VirtualBox, VMware Workstation, or KVM (Kernel-based Virtual Machine) and QEMU (Quick Emulator), for native GNU/Linux virtualization.

If you choose to use RHEL 10 as a platform for virtual machines, you must follow the "Configuring and managing Linux virtual machines" book in the documentation to enable virtualization support. Basically, it is two commands: to install the required software and to enable services:

```
root@server1:~# dnf install qemu-kvm libvirt virt-install
virt-viewer
```


A. Markelov, *Red Hat RHCSA 10 Study Companion*, Certification Study Companion Series,
https://doi.org/10.1007/979-8-8688-2226-1

```
root@server1:~# for drv in qemu network nodedev nwfilter secret
storage interface; do systemctl start virt${drv}d{,-ro,-admin}.
socket; done
```

To verify your system is ready, you can use `virt-host-validate`:

```
root@server1:~# virt-host-validate
  QEMU: Checking for hardware virtualization                 : PASS
  QEMU: Checking if device '/dev/kvm' exists                 : PASS
  QEMU: Checking if device '/dev/kvm' is accessible          : PASS
...
```

The recommended tool for managing virtual machines in RHEL 10 is Cockpit. The traditional GUI tool `virt-manager` is now officially deprecated, but you can still use it. The only thing you need to do is enable the CodeReady Linux Builder (CRB) repository first:

```
root@server1:~#  subscription-manager repos --enable codeready-
builder-for-rhel-10-$(arch)-rpms
root@server1:~#  dnf install -y virt-manager
```

To download the RHEL 10 image, you need to register at `https://developers.redhat.com/` to obtain a Red Hat login and a one-year trial of different Red Hat products, including RHEL.

You will need to boot from the virtual CD-ROM where the RHEL 10 image (**rhel-10.0-x86_64-dvd.iso)** is attached. You have two main options after booting, as you can see: install right away or first check the installation media and then proceed with the installation. You can see this menu in Figure A-1.

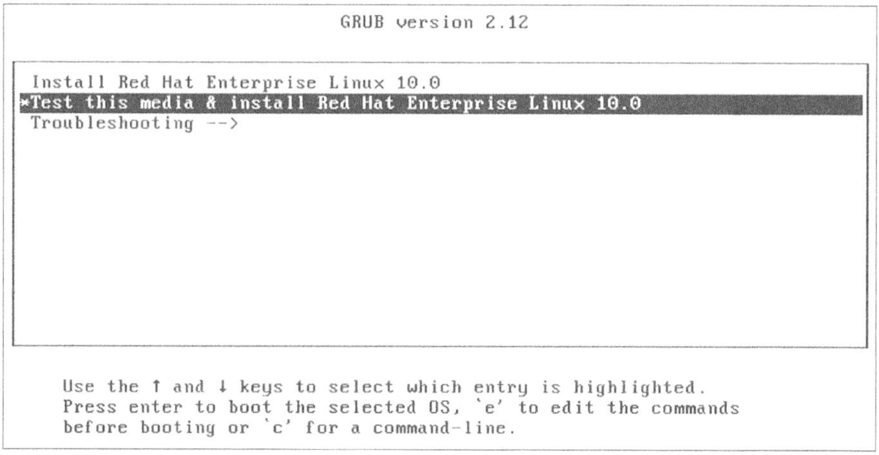

Figure A-1. *Opening the Terminal application in graphical mode*

The third option is troubleshooting, where you can boot into a live environment from the CD-ROM. It is helpful if you need to troubleshoot boot issues of installed RHEL.

Start from the second option if you just loaded the ISO from the Internet.

The first graphical screen will allow you to choose the language you will use during the installation process. It is shown in Figure A-2.

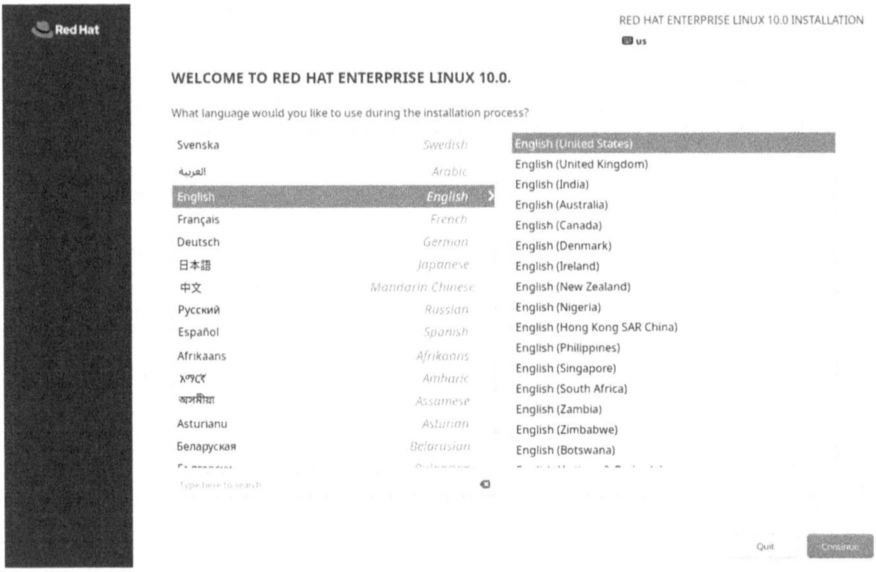

Figure A-2. *Choosing a language during the installation process*

The next screen, shown in Figure A-3, is the main installation screen. From this screen, you can access specific screens, such as Network Setup or Time and Data settings. You can see some of the settings are marked with red comments. Until you click on related menus and select some options or enter data, you will not be able to proceed, and the `Begin Installation` button will be inactive. As shown in Figure A-3, you must visit the `Root Account`, `User Creation`, and `Installation Destination`.

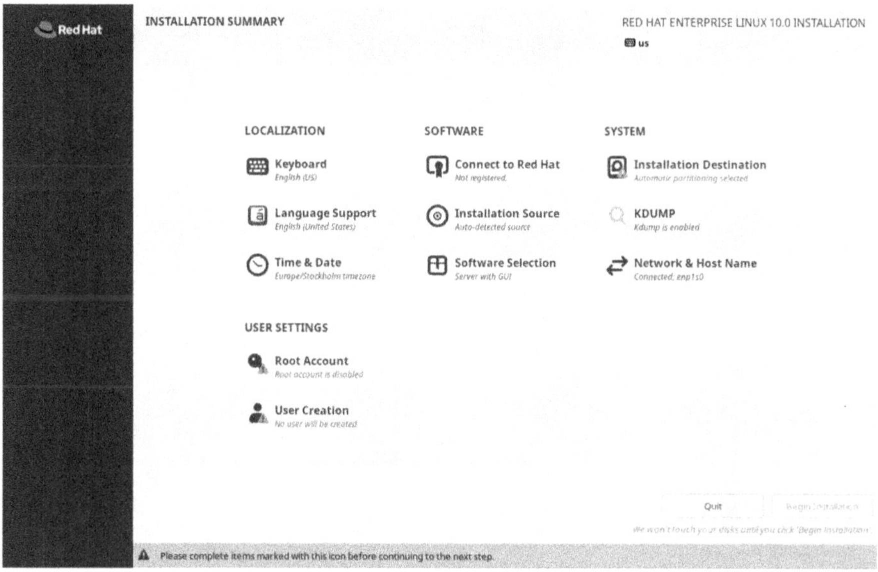

Figure A-3. *Main installation screen*

The first mandatory step is the installation destination screen shown in Figure A-4. You need to select the disk on which you want to install the operating system. For the rest of the settings in our lab, you can keep them as is or choose custom and change the default partition scheme. Click Done to return to the main screen.

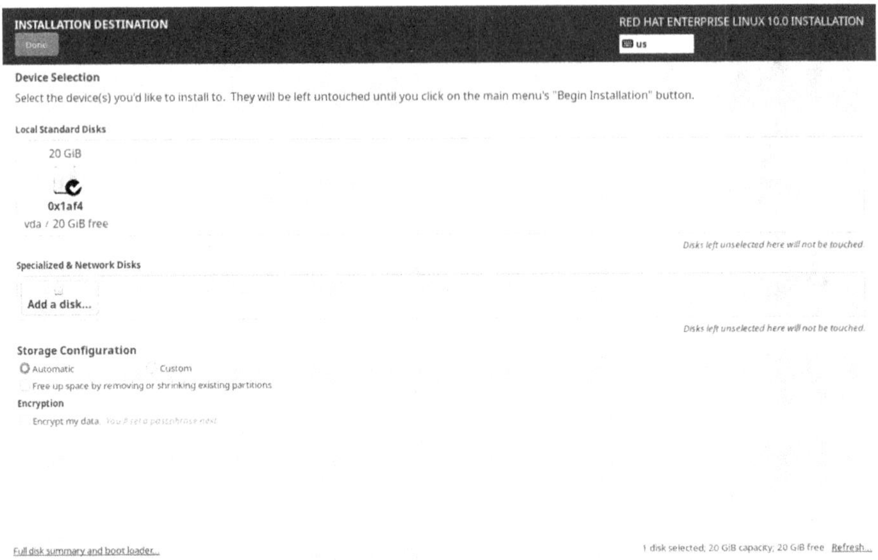

Figure A-4. *Installation destination*

Two additional mandatory screens are shown in Figures A-5 and A-6. It is the root account settings and the user account settings. By default, the root account is disabled. For lab simplicity, you can enable it and enter the password. At the bottom, you can see a warning in case you choose one of the dictionary words like "password" or "redhat". Do not use anything based on dictionary words in a real environment. On the Create User screen, ensure that the box with administrative privileges for the user is selected.

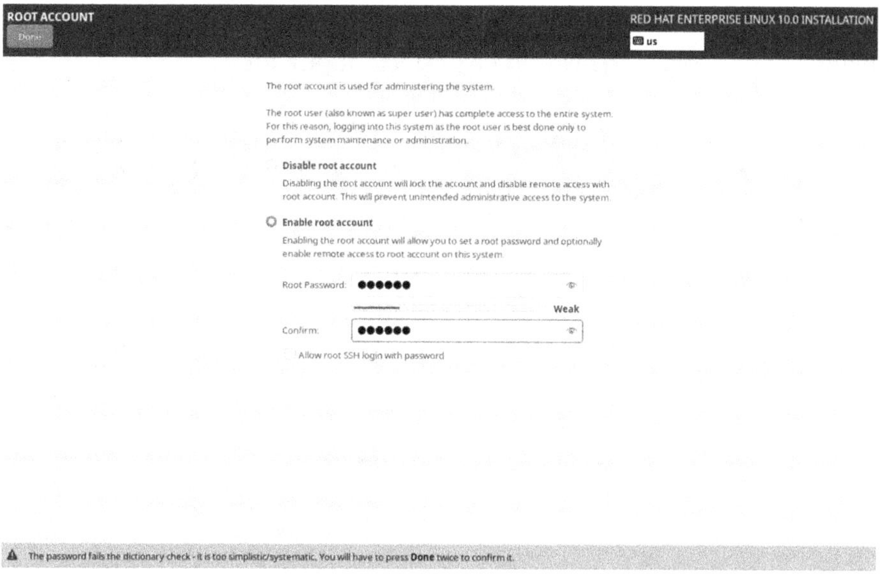

***Figure A-5.** Root account settings*

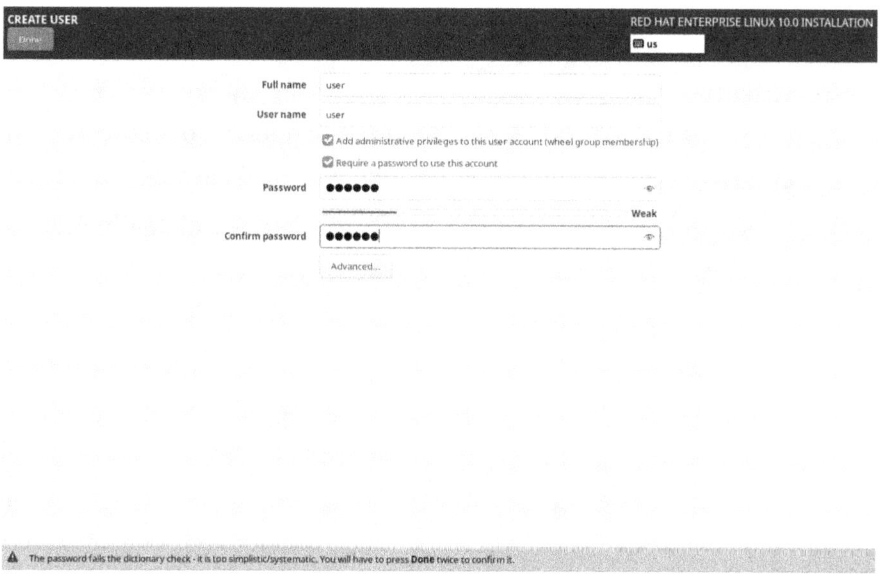

***Figure A-6.** Create User screen*

You can check the Software Selection screen shown in Figure A-7. The default `Server with GUI` would be perfect for our study.

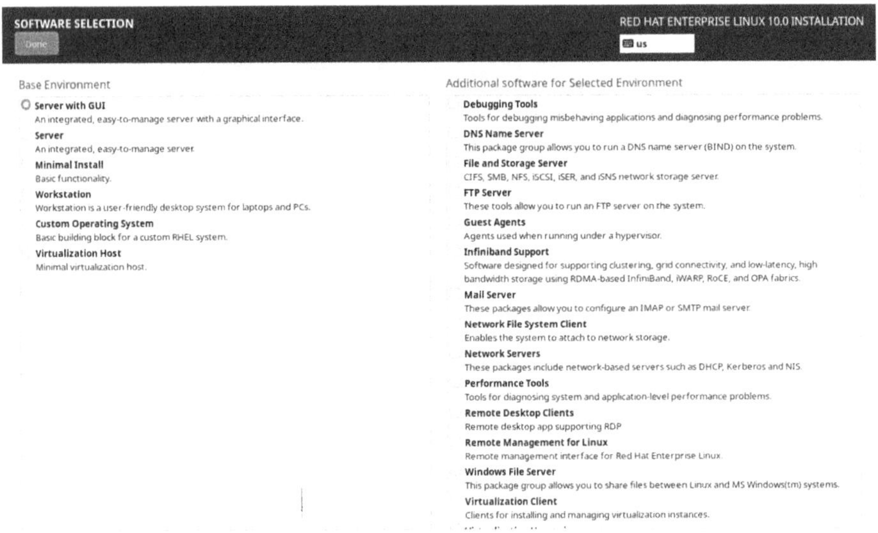

***Figure A-7.** Software Selection*

We will often install software, so it is necessary to register your virtual machines in Red Hat Network. At the `Connect to Red Hat` screen, enter your Red Hat login and password, and click `Register` as shown in Figure A-8. If successful, you will see a message similar to "`The system is registered`" (Figure A-9).

***Figure A-8.** Registering in Red Hat Network*

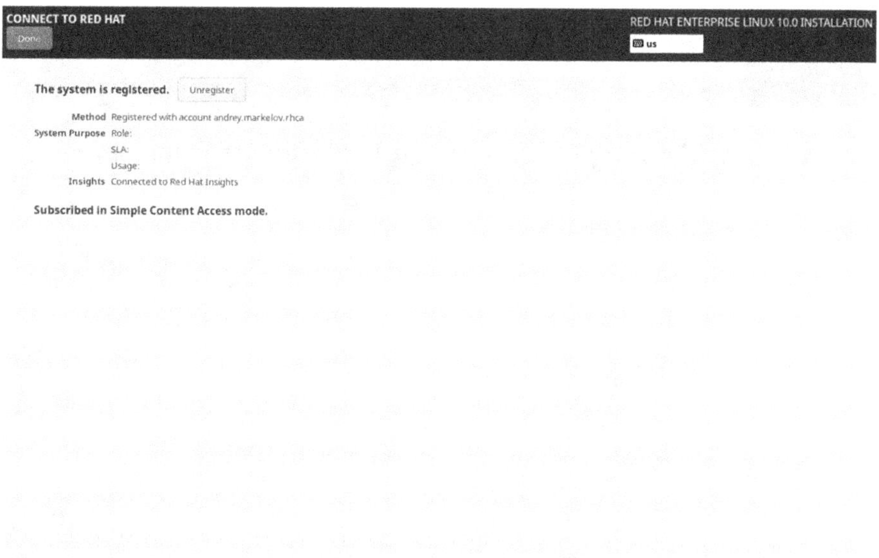

***Figure A-9.** The system is registered*

Finally, you can begin the installation. After installation is complete, you will see the same screen as shown in Figure A-10. You need to disconnect your CD-ROM drive and ensure that the virtual boot disk is selected. If you are using virt-manager, the process will be done automatically for you.

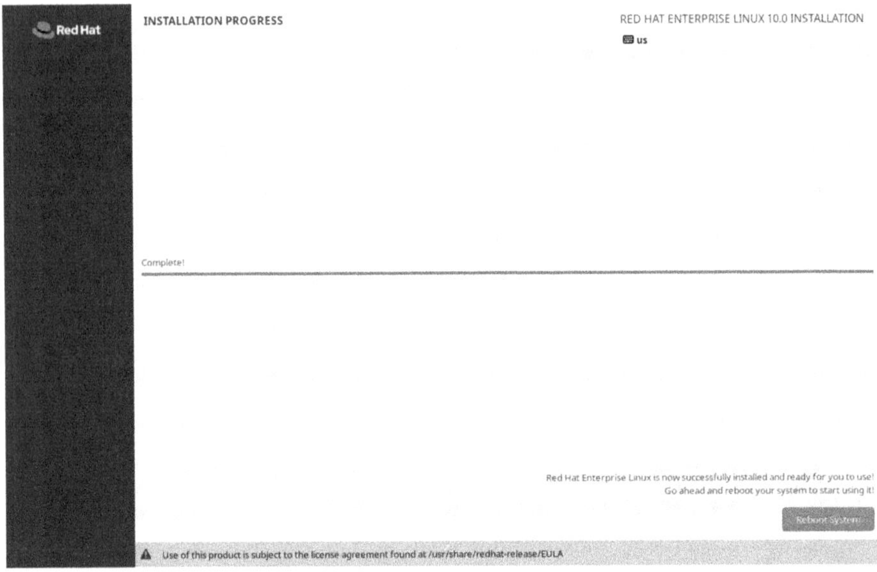

***Figure A-10.** Opening the Terminal application in graphical mode*

APPENDIX B

Answers to Exercises

Answers and other examples are available in the GitHub repository: `https://github.com/andreyamarkelov/adminbook`.

Chapter 2

1. Check the man page for the file passwd to find the name of the fifth field and why it has this name.

   ```
   $ man 5 passwd
   ```

2. Call `info info` and read the tutorial. If missed, install the `info` package.

   ```
   $ info info
   ```

3. Find in the bash manual page description of aliases and create an alias `lls` for `ls -lah`.

   ```
   $ man bash
   ```

   Type `/ALIASES` and press Enter to search.

   ```
   $ echo "alias lls='ls -lah'" >> ~/.bashrc
   $ source ~/.bashrc
   ```


A. Markelov, *Red Hat RHCSA 10 Study Companion*, Certification Study Companion Series,
https://doi.org/10.1007/979-8-8688-2226-1

4. By using a pipe and a find tool, make a command that will display the number of files in the /etc directory containing "an" in the name.

```
# find /etc -type f -name "*an*" 2>/dev/null | wc -l
```

5. Run the command vimtutor, and follow the exercises (it will take about 20 minutes).

```
$ vimtutor
```

Chapter 3

1. Create a script that takes two numbers as command-line arguments and prints their sum.

```
$ cat sum.sh
#!/bin/bash

if [ $# -ne 2 ]; then
    echo "Error: Two numbers required"
    echo "Usage: $0 number1 number2"
    exit 1
fi

if ! [[ "$1" =~ ^-?[0-9]+$ ]] || ! [[ "$2" =~ ^-?[0-9]+$
]]; then
    echo "Error: Both arguments must be numbers"
    exit 1
fi

sum=$(( $1 + $2 ))
echo "Sum of $1 and $2 is: $sum"
```

2. Write a script that checks if a file provided as a command-line argument exists.

```
$ cat check_file.sh
#!/bin/bash
# Script: check_file.sh

if [ $# -eq 0 ]; then
    echo "Error: No filename provided"
    echo "Usage: $0 filename"
    exit 1
fi

filename="$1"

if [ -f "$filename" ]; then
    echo "File '$filename' exists"
    ls -lh "$filename"
    exit 0
elif [ -d "$filename" ]; then
    echo "'$filename' is a directory, not a regular file"
    exit 2
else
    echo "File '$filename' does not exist"
    exit 1
fi
```

3. Create a script that creates a directory if it doesn't already exist.

```
$ cat create_dir.sh
#!/bin/bash
# Script: create_dir.sh

if [ $# -eq 0 ]; then
```

```
    echo "Error: No directory name provided"
    echo "Usage: $0 directory_name"
    exit 1
fi

dirname="$1"

if [ -d "$dirname" ]; then
    echo "Directory '$dirname' already exists"
    ls -ld "$dirname"
    exit 0
fi

if [ -e "$dirname" ]; then
    echo "Error: '$dirname' exists but is not a directory"
    exit 1
fi

if mkdir -p "$dirname"; then
    echo "Directory '$dirname' created successfully"
    ls -ld "$dirname"
    exit 0
else
    echo "Failed to create directory '$dirname'"
    exit 1
fi
```

4. Create a script that performs a numeric countdown from a given starting number to 1. If no argument is provided or the argument is not a positive integer, print an error message and exit.

```
$ cat countdown.sh
#!/bin/bash
# Script: countdown.sh
```

```
if [ $# -eq 0 ]; then
    echo "Error: No starting number provided"
    echo "Usage: $0 positive_integer"
    exit 1
fi

start="$1"

if ! [[ "$start" =~ ^[0-9]+$ ]]; then
    echo "Error: '$start' is not a valid positive integer"
    exit 1
fi

if [ "$start" -le 0 ]; then
    echo "Error: Number must be greater than 0"
    exit 1
fi

echo "Starting countdown from $start..."
for ((i=start; i>=1; i--)); do
    echo "$i"
done

echo "Countdown complete!"
```

5. Write a script that lists all executable regular files in the current directory.

```
#!/bin/bash
# Script: list_executables.sh

echo "Executable files in current directory:"

count=0

for file in *; do
```

```
    if [ -f "$file" ] && [ -x "$file" ]; then
        ls -lh "$file"
        ((count++))
    fi
done

echo "Total executable files found: $count"

if [ $count -eq 0 ]; then
    echo "No executable files found"
    exit 1
else
    exit 0
fi
```

Chapter 4

1. Create a new devusers group. Create new users named devuser1, devuser2, and devuser3, and add them to the devusers group. Add devuser1 to the wheel group.

```
$ sudo groupadd devusers
$ sudo useradd -G devusers devuser1
$ sudo useradd -G devusers devuser2
$ sudo useradd -G devusers devuser3
$ sudo usermod -aG wheel devuser1
$ sudo passwd devuser1
$ sudo passwd devuser2
$ sudo passwd devuser3
$ id devuser1
uid=1004(devuser1) gid=2002(devuser1) groups=2002(devuser1),
10(wheel),2001(devusers)
$ id devuser2
```

```
uid=1005(devuser2) gid=1005(devuser2) groups=1005(devuser2),
2001(devusers)
$ id devuser3
uid=1006(devuser3) gid=1006(devuser3) groups=1006(devuser3),
2001(devusers)
$ getent group wheel
wheel:x:10:devuser1
$ getent group devusers
devusers:x:2001:devuser1,devuser2,devuser3
```

2. Modify the devuser3 account. Change the comment field to "Senior Developer - devuser3", add him to an existing secondary group named sshd, and change their default shell to /usr/sbin/nologin. Ensure that existing secondary groups are preserved.

```
$ sudo usermod -c "Senior Developer - devuser3" -aG sshd -s
/usr/sbin/nologin devuser3
$ getent passwd devuser3
devuser3:x:1006:1006:Senior Developer - devuser3:/home/
devuser3:/usr/sbin/nologin
$ id devuser3
uid=1006(devuser3) gid=1006(devuser3) groups=1006(devuser3),
74(sshd),2001(devusers)
```

3. Lock the devuser2 account. Verify the change by checking the entry in /etc/shadow.

```
$ sudo usermod -L devuser2
$ sudo grep devuser2 /etc/shadow
devuser2:!...:20429:0:99999:7:::
```

4. Delete the devuser2 account, ensuring the home directory is also deleted. Verify that the entry is no longer in /etc/passwd.

```
$ sudo userdel -r devuser2
$ sudo grep devuser2 /etc/shadow
$ sudo ls /home
```

5. For devuser1, set the minimum number of days between password changes to 8 and the maximum number of days to 40. Set the warning period before devuser1's password expires to 14 days. Force devuser1 to change their password on the next login. Set the devuser1's account to expire on December 30, 2028.

```
$ sudo chage -m 8 -M 40 -W 14 -d 0 -E 2028-12-31 devuser1
$ sudo chage -l devuser1
Last password change                                : password
                                                      must be
                                                      changed
Password expires                                    : password
                                                      must be
                                                      changed
Password inactive                                   : password
                                                      must be
                                                      changed
Account expires                                     : Dec 30,
                                                      2028
Minimum number of days between password change     : 8
Maximum number of days between password change     : 40
Number of days of warning before password expires: 14
```

6. Create a new file `/etc/sudoers.d/devs` using `visudo` with option `-f`. In this new file, add a rule that allows the user `devuser2` to run all commands as `root` without needing a password. Add a rule that allows the group `devusers` to run all commands defined by alias `SERVICES` from `/etc/sudoers` as `root` that require a password. Make sure `SERVICES` is uncommented in /etc/sudoers. Will `devuser2` be required to use a password for `/usr/bin/systemctl` start?

```
$ sudo visudo -f /etc/sudoers.d/devs
devuser2 ALL=(ALL) NOPASSWD: ALL
%devusers ALL=(ALL) SERVICES
```

No, `devuser2` will not be required to use a password for `/usr/bin/systemctl start`.

Chapter 5

1. Assuming you have a new, unpartitioned 20Gb disk named `/dev/sdb`. Use `fdisk /dev/sdb` to enter the interactive mode. Create a new DOS (MBR) partition table for the disk. Create one primary partition of 2 Gb and one extended partition. Within the extended partition, create two logical partitions of 500 MiB each.

```
$ sudo fdisk /dev/sdb
```

```
Welcome to fdisk (util-linux 2.40.2).
Changes will remain in memory only, until you decide to
write them.
Be careful before using the write command.
```

```
Device does not contain a recognized partition table.
Created a new DOS (MBR) disklabel with disk identifier
0x0b090e8c.

Command (m for help): n
Partition type
   p   primary (0 primary, 0 extended, 4 free)
   e   extended (container for logical partitions)
Select (default p): p
Partition number (1-4, default 1):
First sector (2048-41943039, default 2048):
Last sector, +/-sectors or +/-size{K,M,G,T,P}
(2048-41943039, default 41943039): +2G

Created a new partition 1 of type 'Linux' and of size 2 GiB.

Command (m for help): n
Partition type
   p   primary (1 primary, 0 extended, 3 free)
   e   extended (container for logical partitions)
Select (default p): e
Partition number (2-4, default 2):
First sector (4196352-41943039, default 4196352):
Last sector, +/-sectors or +/-size{K,M,G,T,P}
(4196352-41943039, default 41943039):

Created a new partition 2 of type 'Extended' and of
size 18 GiB.

Command (m for help): n
All space for primary partitions is in use.
Adding logical partition 5
First sector (4198400-41943039, default 4198400):
Last sector, +/-sectors or +/-size{K,M,G,T,P}
(4198400-41943039, default 41943039): +500M
```

```
Created a new partition 5 of type 'Linux' and of size
500 MiB.

Command (m for help): n
All space for primary partitions is in use.
Adding logical partition 6
First sector (5224448-41943039, default 5224448):
Last sector, +/-sectors or +/-size{K,M,G,T,P}
(5224448-41943039, default 41943039): +500M

Created a new partition 6 of type 'Linux' and of size
500 MiB.

Command (m for help): p
Disk /dev/sdb: 20 GiB, 21474836480 bytes, 41943040 sectors
Disk model: QEMU HARDDISK
Units: sectors of 1 * 512 = 512 bytes
Sector size (logical/physical): 512 bytes / 512 bytes
I/O size (minimum/optimal): 512 bytes / 512 bytes
Disklabel type: dos
Disk identifier: 0x533f1b42

Device     Boot   Start      End  Sectors  Size Id Type
/dev/sdb1          2048  4196351  4194304    2G 83 Linux
/dev/sdb2       4196352 41943039 37746688   18G  5 Extended
/dev/sdb5       4198400  5222399  1024000  500M 83 Linux
/dev/sdb6       5224448  6248447  1024000  500M 83 Linux

Command (m for help): w
The partition table has been altered.
Calling ioctl() to re-read partition table.
Syncing disks.
```

2. Convert partitions to LVM type if you used any other.

   From the remaining space, create another one.

```
$ sudo fdisk /dev/sdb

Welcome to fdisk (util-linux 2.40.2).
Changes will remain in memory only, until you decide to
write them.
Be careful before using the write command.

Command (m for help): p
Disk /dev/sdb: 20 GiB, 21474836480 bytes, 41943040 sectors
Disk model: QEMU HARDDISK
Units: sectors of 1 * 512 = 512 bytes
Sector size (logical/physical): 512 bytes / 512 bytes
I/O size (minimum/optimal): 512 bytes / 512 bytes
Disklabel type: dos
Disk identifier: 0x533f1b42

Device     Boot   Start      End  Sectors  Size Id Type
/dev/sdb1          2048  4196351  4194304    2G 83 Linux
/dev/sdb2       4196352 41943039 37746688   18G  5 Extended
/dev/sdb5       4198400  5222399  1024000  500M 83 Linux
/dev/sdb6       5224448  6248447  1024000  500M 83 Linux

Command (m for help): t
Partition number (1,2,5,6, default 6): 1
Hex code or alias (type L to list all): 8e

Changed type of partition 'Linux' to 'Linux LVM'.

Command (m for help): t
Partition number (1,2,5,6, default 6): 5
Hex code or alias (type L to list all): 8e
```

```
Changed type of partition 'Linux LVM' to 'Linux LVM'.

Command (m for help): t
Partition number (1,2,5,6, default 6): 6
Hex code or alias (type L to list all): 8e

Changed type of partition 'Linux' to 'Linux LVM'.
Command (m for help): n
All space for primary partitions is in use.
Adding logical partition 7
First sector (6250496-41943039, default 6250496):
Last sector, +/-sectors or +/-size{K,M,G,T,P}
(6250496-41943039, default 41943039):

Created a new partition 7 of type 'Linux' and of
size 17 GiB.

Command (m for help): t
Partition number (1,2,5-7, default 7): 7
Hex code or alias (type L to list all): 8e

Changed type of partition 'Linux' to 'Linux LVM'.

Command (m for help): p
Disk /dev/sdb: 20 GiB, 21474836480 bytes, 41943040 sectors
Disk model: QEMU HARDDISK
Units: sectors of 1 * 512 = 512 bytes
Sector size (logical/physical): 512 bytes / 512 bytes
I/O size (minimum/optimal): 512 bytes / 512 bytes
Disklabel type: dos
Disk identifier: 0x533f1b42
```

```
Device     Boot   Start      End  Sectors  Size Id Type
/dev/sdb1          2048  4196351  4194304    2G 8e
Linux LVM
/dev/sdb2       4196352 41943039 37746688   18G  5 Extended
/dev/sdb5       4198400  5222399  1024000  500M 8e
Linux LVM
/dev/sdb6       5224448  6248447  1024000  500M 8e
Linux LVM
/dev/sdb7       6250496 41943039 35692544   17G 8e
Linux LVM

Command (m for help): w
The partition table has been altered.
Calling ioctl() to re-read partition table.
Syncing disks.
```

3. Using the LVM partitions you created in a previous exercise, create physical volumes, and include into the vg01 group.

```
$ sudo pvcreate /dev/sdb{1,5,6,7}
  Physical volume "/dev/sdb1" successfully created.
  Physical volume "/dev/sdb5" successfully created.
  Physical volume "/dev/sdb6" successfully created.
  Physical volume "/dev/sdb7" successfully created.
$ sudo vgcreate vg01 /dev/sdb{1,5,6,7}
  Volume group "vg01" successfully created
$ sudo vgdisplay vg01
  --- Volume group ---
  VG Name               vg01
  System ID
  Format                lvm2
  Metadata Areas        4
```

```
Metadata Sequence No  1
VG Access             read/write
VG Status             resizable
MAX LV                0
Cur LV                0
Open LV               0
Max PV                0
Cur PV                4
Act PV                4
VG Size               19.98 GiB
PE Size               4.00 MiB
Total PE              5115
Alloc PE / Size       0 / 0
Free  PE / Size       5115 / 19.98 GiB
VG UUID               xOx8XF-OhwX-UdOO-5qYI-89y8-
                      P51S-LvJQcG
```

4. From the vg01 volume group, create a new logical volume named lv01 with a size of 3 GiB. Create a second logical volume named lv02 that uses 40% of the remaining free space in the volume group.

```
$ sudo lvcreate -n lv01 -L 3G vg01
  Logical volume "lv01" created.
$ sudo lvcreate -n lv02 -l 40%FREE vg01
  Logical volume "lv02" created.
```

5. Delete all LVs and VG.

```
$ sudo lvremove /dev/vg01/lv0{1,2}
Do you really want to remove active logical volume vg01/
lv01? [y/n]: y
  Logical volume "lv01" successfully removed.
```

```
Do you really want to remove active logical volume vg01/
lv02? [y/n]: y
  Logical volume "lv02" successfully removed.
root@localhost:~# sudo vgremove vg01
  Volume group "vg01" successfully removed
$ sudo pvremove /dev/sdb{1,5,6,7}
  Labels on physical volume "/dev/sdb1" successfully wiped.
  Labels on physical volume "/dev/sdb5" successfully wiped.
  Labels on physical volume "/dev/sdb6" successfully wiped.
  Labels on physical volume "/dev/sdb7" successfully wiped.
```

Chapter 6

1. Use the parted command to create a new GPT partition table on a disk (e.g., /dev/sdb), and then create a new primary partition using 30% of the available space. Format this partition with the XFS file system.

```
$ sudo parted /dev/sdb
GNU Parted 3.6
Using /dev/sdb
Welcome to GNU Parted! Type 'help' to view a list of
commands.
(parted) mktable gpt
(parted) mkpart primary xfs 0% 30%
(parted) print
Model: QEMU QEMU HARDDISK (scsi)
Disk /dev/sda: 21.5GB
Sector size (logical/physical): 512B/512B
Partition Table: gpt
Disk Flags:
```

```
Number  Start   End     Size    File system  Name     Flags
 1      1049kB  6442MB  6441MB  xfs          primary

(parted) quit
Information: You may need to update /etc/fstab.
$ sudo mkfs.xfs /dev/sdb1
```

2. Modify the `/etc/fstab` file to ensure the new XFS partition mounts automatically to `/mnt/newxfs` every time the system boots. Use the partition's UUID for the entry.

```
$ mkdir -p /mnt/newxfs
$ blkid /dev/sdb1
/dev/sdb1: UUID="6161333e-921d-492e-ac44-5585fd806d61"
BLOCK_SIZE="512" TYPE="xfs" PARTLABEL="primary" PARTUUID="
bc63b027-0192-44c0-86fe-581754200e6f"
$ vi /etc/fstab
UUID=6161333e-921d-492e-ac44-5585fd806d61 /mnt/newxfs xfs
defaults 0 0
$ sudo findmnt --verify
   [W] your fstab has been modified, but systemd still uses
   the old version;
       use 'systemctl daemon-reload' to reload

0 parse errors, 0 errors, 1 warning
$ sudo 'systemctl daemon-reload
$ sudo mount -a
```

3. Use the `parted` command to create a new partition with LVM type using 50% of the available space. Add a partition to the existing LVM group and extend / file system.

```
sudo parted /dev/sdb
GNU Parted 3.6
```

```
Using /dev/sdb
Welcome to GNU Parted! Type 'help' to view a list of
commands.
(parted) mkpart primary 30% 80%
(parted) set 2 lvm on
(parted) print
Model: QEMU QEMU HARDDISK (scsi)
Disk /dev/sdb: 21.5GB
Sector size (logical/physical): 512B/512B
Partition Table: gpt
Disk Flags:

Number  Start   End     Size    File system  Name     Flags
 1      1049kB  6442MB  6441MB  xfs          primary
 2      6442MB  17.2GB  10.7GB               primary  lvm

(parted) quit
$ sudo vgdisplay
  --- Volume group ---
  VG Name               rhel
...
$ sudo vgextend rhel /dev/sdb2
  Physical volume "/dev/sdb2" successfully created.
  Volume group "rhel" successfully extended
```

4. Use the `lsblk --fs` or `blkid` commands to list all file systems on your system and their corresponding UUIDs.

```
$ sudo lsblk --fs
```

5. Create a directory `/tmp/shared_project` and a group named `devops`. Set the directory's group ownership to `devops`, and apply the SGID bit. Add your user to the `devops` group, and verify that any new files you create in that directory inherit the `devops` group ownership.

```
$ sudo mkdir /tmp/shared_project
$ sudo groupadd devops
$ sudo chgrp devops /tmp/shared_project
$ sudo chmod 2770 /tmp/shared_project
$ sudo usermod -aG devops $USER
$ ls -ld /tmp/shared_project/
drwxrws---. 2 root devops 6 Dec  7 16:41 /tmp/shared_
project/
$ newgrp devops
$ touch /tmp/shared_project/testfile
$ ls -l /tmp/shared_project/testfile
-rw-r--r--. 1 user devops 0 Dec  7 16:44 /tmp/shared_
project/testfile
```

6. Create a 1 Gb file at `/tmp/swapfile` using dd. Use the `mkswap` command to format the file as a swap area. Activate the swap file with the `swapon` command, and verify the new total swap size with `free -h`.

```
$ sudo dd if=/dev/zero of=/tmp/swapfile bs=1M count=1024
$ sudo chmod 600 /tmp/swapfile
$ sudo mkswap /tmp/swapfile
$ sudo swapon /tmp/swapfile
$ free -h
```

Chapter 7

1. Use `systemctl` to find the default `systemd` target on your system. Use `systemctl` to temporarily switch your system to `multi-user.target`.

```
$ systemctl get-default
graphical.target
$ sudo systemctl isolate multi-user.target
```

2. Examine the output of `journalctl -b` to review the messages from the most recent system boot.

```
$ sudo journalctl -b
```

3. Use the `ps` command to identify the top three processes consuming the most CPU and memory.

```
$ ps aux --sort=-%cpu | head -n 4
$ ps aux --sort=-%mem | head -n 4
```

4. Start a new process with a non-default nice value using the `nice` command, and then verify the change with `ps`.

```
$ nice -n 10 sleep 3600 &
[1] 1870
$ ps lax | grep sleep
0  1000    1870    1780  30  10 226820  1700 hrtime SN
pts/0      0:00 sleep 3600
0  1000    1872    1780  20   0 227688  2176 pipe_r S+
pts/0      0:00 grep --color=auto sleep
```

5. Use renice to change the niceness of a running process, and then confirm the change with ps.

```
$ renice -n 15 1870
1870 (process ID) old priority 10, new priority 15
$ ps lax | grep sleep
0  1000    1870    1780  35  15 226820  1700 hrtime SN
pts/0      0:00 sleep 3600
0  1000    1889    1780  35  15 227688  2176 pipe_r
SN+  pts/0      0:00 grep --color=auto sleep
```

6. Use tuned-adm active to determine which performance profile is currently active on your system. Switch the active TuneD profile to throughput-performance using the tuned-adm profile command.

```
$ tuned-adm active
Current active profile: balanced
$ sudo tuned-adm profile throughput-performance
$ tuned-adm active
Current active profile: throughput-performance
```

Chapter 8

1. Execute the sleep 1200 command in the background. Immediately verify it is running, and then note its job number.

```
$ sleep 1200 &
[1] 1810
$ jobs -l
[1]+  1810 Running                 sleep 1200 &
```

2. Start a `ping 127.0.0.1` process in the foreground. Stop it using the appropriate key sequence, and then send the stopped process to the background so it resumes running.

```
user@localhost:~$ ping 127.0.0.1
PING 127.0.0.1 (127.0.0.1) 56(84) bytes of data.
64 bytes from 127.0.0.1: icmp_seq=1 ttl=64 time=0.086 ms
^Z
[2]+  Stopped                 ping 127.0.0.1
user@localhost:~$ jobs
[1]-  Running                 sleep 1200 &
[2]+  Stopped                 ping 127.0.0.1
user@localhost:~$ bg 2
[2]+ ping 127.0.0.1 &
64 bytes from 127.0.0.1: icmp_seq=5 ttl=64 time=0.054 ms
```

3. Schedule a command using at to execute 5 minutes from now. The command should redirect the output of date to a file named `~/test_output.txt`.

```
$ at now + 5 minutes
warning: commands will be executed using /bin/sh
at Sun Dec  7 18:42:00 2025
at> date > ~/test_output.txt
at> <EOT>
job 1 at Sun Dec  7 18:42:00 2025
```

4. Immediately after scheduling the job, use the command to view the job queue.

```
$ atq
1     Sun Dec  7 18:42:00 2025 a user
```

5. Edit your user's crontab file to run the command `/bin/echo "Cron!" > ~/cron.log` every day at 9:00.

```
$ crontab -e
no crontab for user - using an empty one
crontab: installing new crontab
user@localhost:~$ crontab -l
0 9 * * * /bin/echo "Cron!" > ~/cron.log
```

6. Use the Systemd utility to display the current system time, time zone, and the status of the NTP service.

```
$ timedatectl
               Local time: Sun 2025-12-07 18:40:53 CET
           Universal time: Sun 2025-12-07 17:40:53 UTC
                 RTC time: Sun 2025-12-07 17:40:53
                Time zone: Europe/Stockholm (CET, +0100)
System clock synchronized: yes
              NTP service: active
          RTC in local TZ: no
```

7. Generate a new key pair. Use a strong passphrase for security. What are the names of the two files created in your `~/.ssh/` directory?

```
$ ssh-keygen
...
user@localhost:~$ ls .ssh
id_ed25519  id_ed25519.pub
```

8. You need to enable key-based authentication for the user root on the local server 127.0.0.1. Use the specialized utility to securely copy your users' public key to the server.

```
$ ssh-copy-id -i .ssh/id_ed25519.pub root@127.0.0.1
```

As an additional exercise, think if this will work for a separate VM. (Hint: PermitRootLogin)

9. Which two lines would you modify in the main OpenSSH server configuration file (`/etc/ssh/sshd_config`) to disable password authentication and prevent the `root` user from logging in directly?

```
PasswordAuthentication no
PermitRootLogin no
```

Chapter 9

1. Use DNF to search for packages related to the "network" term, listing only packages that are not yet installed.

```
$ sudo dnf list available *network*
```

2. Install the `zsh` package using DNF, ensuring the installation proceeds without any interactive prompts.

```
$ sudo dnf install -y zsh
```

3. Remove the `zsh` package and any dependencies that are no longer needed, using a single DNF command.

```
$ sudo dnf remove -y zsh
```

4. Display a detailed description and list of packages (mandatory, default, and optional) included in the `"Legacy UNIX Compatibility"` package group.

```
$ sudo dnf group info "Legacy UNIX Compatibility"
```

5. Determine which installed RPM package owns the /etc/filesystems file.

```
$ rpm -qf /etc/filesystems
setup-2.14.5-4.el10.noarch
```

6. Use the rpm command to list all files included in the installed bash package.

```
$ sudo rpm -ql bash
/etc/skel/.bash_logout
/etc/skel/.bash_profile
...
```

7. Use the dnf config-manager utility to enable the codeready-builder-for-rhel-10-x86_64-rpms repository.

```
$ sudo dnf config-manager --enable codeready-builder-for-
rhel-10-x86_64-rpms
Updating Subscription Management repositories.
```

8. Install the virt-manager package.

```
$ sudo dnf install -y virt-manager
```

9. Write the flatpak command to add the Flathub remote repository only for the current user, without system-wide privileges, and only if the remote doesn't already exist.

```
$ flatpak remote-add --user --if-not-exists flathub
https://dl.flathub.org/repo/flathub.flatpakrepo
```

10. Install Gimp from Flathub.

```
$ flatpak install flathub org.gimp.GIMP
```

Chapter 10

1. Use the ip a command to list all network interfaces. Identify the IP address, netmask (in CIDR format), and MAC address for your primary Ethernet interface.

```
$ ip addr show
```

2. Use the `ip route show` command to display the system's current routing table. Identify the default gateway and its associated metric.

```
$ ip route show
default via 192.168.122.1 dev enp1s0 proto dhcp src
192.168.122.60 metric 100
10.88.0.0/16 dev podman0 proto kernel scope link src 10.88.0.1
192.168.122.0/24 dev enp1s0 proto kernel scope link src
192.168.122.60 metric 100
```

3. Use nmcli con show to list all available NetworkManager connection profiles. Identify which connections are currently active and on which devices.

```
$ nmcli connection show
NAME     UUID                                  TYPE      DEVICE
enp1s0   9bf1af1b-9f39-3815-b996-0f11e2460d45  ethernet  enp1s0
lo       9f6447e9-616c-4fc0-9ffd-32c98a7986bd  loopback  lo
podman0  7dcf551c-9d89-433e-931f-4cf3bedc8f8d  bridge    podman0
```

4. Use nmcli to display all properties for your primary active connection. Note the `ipv4.method` value.

```
$ nmcli con show enp1s0
```

5. Add a new, persistent NetworkManager connection named `lab-dhcp` for your *second* (likely disconnected) Ethernet interface. Ensure it is configured to get an IP address automatically via DHCP and to `autoconnect`.

```
$ nmcli connection show
NAME    UUID                                  TYPE      DEVICE
enp1s0  9bf1af1b-9f39-3815-b996-0f11e2460d45  ethernet  enp1s0
lo      02bce9ef-815d-4a00-9988-3b5e23f68ba1  loopback  lo
$ sudo nmcli con add con-name lab-dhcp type ethernet ifname
enp8s0 ipv4.method auto connection.autoconnect yes
Connection 'lab-dhcp' (a550b3b5-0714-4b23-888b-3a4150aab89b)
successfully added.
user@localhost:~$ nmcli connection show
NAME      UUID                                  TYPE      DEVICE
enp1s0    9bf1af1b-9f39-3815-b996-0f11e2460d45  ethernet  enp1s0
lab-dhcp  a550b3b5-0714-4b23-888b-3a4150aab89b  ethernet  enp8s0
lo        02bce9ef-815d-4a00-9988-3b5e23f68ba1  loopback  lo
$ ip a
...
3: enp8s0: <BROADCAST,MULTICAST,UP,LOWER_UP> mtu 1500 qdisc fq_
codel state UP group default qlen 1000
    link/ether 52:54:00:33:9d:7c brd ff:ff:ff:ff:ff:ff
    altname enx525400339d7c
    inet 192.168.122.238/24 brd 192.168.122.255 scope global
dynamic noprefixroute enp8s0
       valid_lft 3596sec preferred_lft 3596sec
    inet6 fe80::4d94:3ccf:dc22:df9e/64 scope link noprefixroute
       valid_lft forever preferred_lft forever
```

6. Create a new, persistent connection named `static1` for your primary interface. Configure it with the following manual settings:

    - **IP address** - 192.168.122.55/24
    - **Gateway** - 192.168.122.1
    - **DNS server** - 8.8.8.8
    - **Autoconnect** - No

```
$ sudo nmcli con add con-name static1 type ethernet ifname
enp1s0 \
  ipv4.method manual \
  ipv4.addresses 192.168.122.55/24 \
  ipv4.gateway 192.168.122.1 \
  ipv4.dns 8.8.8.8 \
  connection.autoconnect no
Connection 'static1' (7a4aead2-887b-45d9-b392-a75facc72b61)
successfully added.
```

7. Bring the `static1` connection up. Use `ip a` and `ip route` to verify that the static IP and new default gateway are active.

```
$ sudo nmcli con up static1
$ ip a
$ ip route
```

8. Add a *second* IP address, `10.10.10.55/24`, to your active `static1` connection. Do *not* remove the original `192.168.122.55/24` address. Verify with `ip a` that the interface now has both IP addresses.

```
$ sudo nmcli con mod static1 +ipv4.addresses 10.10.10.55/24
```

```
$ sudo nmcli con up static1
$ ip a show enp1s0
2: enp1s0: <BROADCAST,MULTICAST,UP,LOWER_UP> mtu 1500 qdisc
fq_codel state UP group default qlen 1000
    link/ether 52:54:00:22:7d:c6 brd ff:ff:ff:ff:ff:ff
    altname enx525400227dc6
    inet 192.168.122.55/24 brd 192.168.122.255 scope global
    noprefixroute enp1s0
       valid_lft forever preferred_lft forever
    inet 10.10.10.55/24 brd 10.10.10.255 scope global
    noprefixroute enp1s0
       valid_lft forever preferred_lft forever
    inet6 fe80::c2d5:4b0a:28a3:28f/64 scope link
    noprefixroute
       valid_lft forever preferred_lft forever
```

9. Change your system's persistent hostname to server15.test.local.

```
$ sudo hostnamectl set-hostname server15.test.local
```

(Re-open the shell session)

10. Edit the /etc/hosts file to add a new entry. The entry should map the IP address 192.168.122.55 to the hostnames web55.test.local and web55.

```
$ sudo vi /etc/hosts
192.168.122.55  web55.test.local web55
```

11. Modify your active connection profile to use the static DNS servers 8.8.8.8 and 8.8.4.4.

```
$ sudo nmcli con mod enp1s0 ipv4.dns "8.8.8.8 8.8.4.4"
$ sudo nmcli con up enp1s0
$ cat /etc/resolv.conf
```

```
# Generated by NetworkManager
search test.local
nameserver 192.168.122.1
nameserver 8.8.8.8
nameserver 8.8.4.4
```

12. Modify the same connection profile to set `ipv4.ignore-auto-dns` to yes. Reactivate the connection, and then inspect the `/etc/resolv.conf` file to ensure *only* your manually set DNS servers are present.

```
$ sudo nmcli con mod enp1s0 ipv4.ignore-auto-dns yes
$ sudo nmcli con up enp1s0
$ sudo nmcli con mod lab-dhcp ipv4.ignore-auto-dns yes
$ sudo nmcli con up lab-dhcp
$ cat /etc/resolv.conf
# Generated by NetworkManager
search test.local
nameserver 8.8.8.8
nameserver 8.8.4.4
```

13. Add the `http` service to the default zone's runtime configuration. Verify it is listed. Then, reload the firewall using `firewall-cmd --reload`, and verify that the http service is now gone (because it was not permanent).

```
$ sudo firewall-cmd --add-service=http
success
$ sudo firewall-cmd --list-services
cockpit dhcpv6-client http ssh
$ sudo firewall-cmd --reload
success
$ sudo firewall-cmd --list-services
cockpit dhcpv6-client ssh
```

14. Permanently add TCP port 8080 to the public zone. Reload the firewall, and verify that the port is now active in the runtime configuration.

```
$ sudo firewall-cmd --zone=public --add-port=8080/
tcp --permanent
success
$ sudo firewall-cmd --reload
success
$ sudo firewall-cmd --zone=public --list-ports
8080/tcp
```

Chapter 11

1. Write the two commands necessary to check the SELinux context (label) for both the running `sshd` process and the `/etc/ssh/sshd_config` file.

```
$ ps -eZ | grep sshd
system_u:system_r:sshd_t:s0-s0:c0.c1023 1010
?   00:00:00 sshd
system_u:system_r:sshd_t:s0-s0:c0.c1023 1805 ?   00:00:00
sshd-session
unconfined_u:unconfined_r:unconfined_t:s0-s0:c0.c1023 1828
? 00:00:00 sshd-session
user@server15:~$ ls -Z /etc/ssh/sshd_config
system_u:object_r:etc_t:s0 /etc/ssh/sshd_config
```

2. You have created a new directory, /srv/www/, which needs to be served by Apache. Write the two commands required to permanently set the context for this directory and all its contents to httpd_sys_content_t.

```
$ sudo semanage fcontext -a -t httpd_sys_content_t "/srv/
www(/.*)?"
$ sudo restorecon -Rv /srv/www
Relabeled /srv/www from unconfined_u:object_r:var_t:s0 to
unconfined_u:object_r:httpd_sys_content_t:s0
```

3. The company wants to run a secondary HTTP server on port 8988. Write the command to permanently label TCP port 8988 as a valid http_port_t port.

```
$ sudo semanage port -a -t http_port_t -p tcp 8988
$ sudo semanage port -l | grep http_port_t
http_port_t                    tcp      8988, 80, 81, 443,
488, 8008, 8009, 8443, 9000
pegasus_http_port_t            tcp      5988
```

4. Find and enable the SELinux boolean permanently that allows the Apache web server to use NFS.

```
$ sudo semanage boolean -l | grep nfs | grep http
httpd_use_nfs                  (off  ,  off)  Allow httpd
to use nfs
$ sudo setsebool -P httpd_use_nfs on
```

//

Index

A

B

C

A. Markelov, *Red Hat RHCSA 10 Study Companion*, Certification Study Companion Series,
https://doi.org/10.1007/979-8-8688-2226-1

M

N

O

P

Q

R

S

T

U

V

W

X

Y

Z

www.ingramcontent.com/pod-product-compliance
Lightning Source LLC
LaVergne TN
LVHW052246200926
84848ILV00002B/285
9798868822254